Walk!
La Gomera

with

Jan Kostura
&
Charles Davis

DISCOVERY WALKING GUIDES LTD

Walk! La Gomera
ISBN 9781782750352

First published August 2000
Second Edition January 2004 **Reprinted** January 2008
Third Edition March 2013
Fourth Edition February 2017
Copyright © 2004, 2008, 2013, 2017

Published by
Discovery Walking Guides Ltd
10 Tennyson Close, Northampton NN5 7HJ, England

Maps are adapted from **La Gomera Tour & Trail Super-Durable Map** published by **Discovery Walking Guides Ltd.**

Photographs*
Photographs in this book were provided by the author/researchers.

Front Cover Photographs

Walk 4, El Palmar hamlet

Barranco de Arure (Walk 24)

Views to Playa del Cabrito (Walk 8)

Walk 19, Tackling the summit

Text and photographs* © Jan Kostura & Charles Davis 2017

All rights reserved. No part of this publication may be reproduced, stored in a retrieval system or transmitted in any form or by any means, electronic, mechanical, photocopying, recording or otherwise, without the prior written permission of the publishers.

The authors and publishers have tried to ensure that the information and maps in this publication are as accurate as possible. However, we accept no responsibility for any loss, injury or inconvenience sustained by anyone using this book.

Walk! La Gomera

CONTENTS

Contents	3
The Authors	6
Introduction — The Island	7
Aim & Scope, Climate, When To Go	8
Getting There, Getting About, Getting A Bed	8
The Walks	9
Long Distance Paths and Other Waymarked routes	10
Risks, Vertigo Flora and Fauna	10
Eating & Drinking	12
Tourist Stuff	12
Symbols Rating Guide	13
Map Information — Location Maps	14
Map Notes & Legend	16
Using GPS on La Gomera	17

WALKS IN THE EAST
The East - Commerce and Abandonment & Locator Maps 18

1 Degollada de Peraza - San Sebastián 20
4 walker, 2½ hours, 9 kilometres, ascents 100 metres, descents 1000 metres, 4 refreshments (linear)

2 Roque Sombrero & Playa de la Guancha 23
5 walker, 4 hours 40 mins, 16 kilometres, ascents 300 metres, descents 1300 metres, 4 refreshments (linear)

3 Los Roques 27
4 walker, 2 hours 40 minutes, 10.5 kilometres, ascents & descents 700 metres, 4 refreshments (circular)

4 Los Roques II - The Ultimate Garajonay Adventure 30
5 walker, 3¼ hours, 8.5 kilometres, ascents & descents 730 metres, vertigo risk, 0 refreshment (circular)

5 Pista Forestal de Majona & Playa de la Caleta 35
4 walker, 5¼-6 hours, 23 kilometres, ascents 500 metres, descents 950 metres, vertigo risk, 4 refreshments (linear)

WALKS IN THE SOUTH
The Sundrenched South & Locator Maps 39

6 Barranco & Lomo de Azadoe 42
3 walker, 1½ hours, 4 kilometres, ascents & descents 250 metres, vertigo risk, 2 refreshments (circular)

7 Jerduñe - Jardín Tecina 44
5 walker, 3½ hours, 14 kilometres, ascents 250 metres, descents 1150 metres, vertigo risk, 3 refreshments (linear)

8 Playa Santiago - San Sebastián 48
5 walker, 6¼ hours, 20 kilometres, ascents & descents 1060 metres, 4 refreshments (linear)

9	**Las Toscas - Degollada de Peraza** 4 walker, 2¾ hours, 10 kilometres, ascents 600 metres, descents 300 metres, 2 refreshments (linear)	**53**
10	**Playa Santiago - Targa** 4 walker, 4 hours, 15 kilometres, ascents & descents 670 metres, 3 refreshments (circular)	**56**
11	**Barranco de Benchijigua** 5 walker, 4 hours, 10.5 kilometres, ascents & descents 600 metres, vertigo risk, 0 refreshments (circular)	**60**
12	**Barranco de Guarimiar** 5 walker, 3 hours 25 mins, 12.5 kilometres, ascents & descents 850 metres, vertigo risk, 2 refreshments (circular)	**64**
13	**Imada - Garajonay** 4 walker, 3 hours 10 mins, 10 kilometres, ascents & descents 600 metres, vertigo risk, 2 refreshments (circular)	**68**

WALKS IN THE WEST
The West - Regal Grandeur & Locator Maps — **71**

14	**Arure - Las Hayas** 3 walker, 3¼ hours, 13 kilometres, ascents & descents 300 metres, 4 refreshments (circular)	**74**
15	**El Cercado - Valle Gran Rey** 4 walker, 2 hours 10 mins, 7.5 kilometres, ascents 0 metres, descents 1000 metres, vertigo risk, 4 refreshments (linear)	**77**
16	**La Mérica** 3 walker, 2¼ hours, 7.5 kilometres, ascents 100 metres, descents 800 metres, vertigo risk, 4 refreshments (linear)	**81**
17	**Valle Gran Rey - Las Hayas** 5 walker, 3 hours, 7.5 kilometres, ascents & descents 650 metres, vertigo risk, 4 refreshments (circular)	**84**
18	**Chipude - Garajonay** 4 walker, 3 hours 20 mins, 14.5 kilometres, ascents & descents 500 metres, 2 refreshments (circular)	**88**
19	**Fortaleza** 4 walker, 1 hour 40 mins, 4.7 kilometres, ascents & descents 250 metres, vertigo, 2 refreshments (circular)	**91**
20	**Barranco de Erque** 5 walker, 5½ hours, 13 kilometres, ascents & descents 750 metres, vertigo risk, 0 refreshments (circular)	**94**
21	**Ermita de Nuestra Señora de Guadalupe** 3 walker, 2 hours 45 mins - 3 hours, 10 kilometres, ascents & descents 350 metres, 4 refreshments (circular)	**99**
22	**Tequergenche** 4 walker, 3¼ hours, 12 kilometres, ascents & descents 350 metres, 0 refreshments (linear)	**102**

23	**Barranco de Argaga**	105

5 walker, 5¼ hours, 11 kilometres, ascents & descents 850 metres, vertigo risk, 2 refreshments (circular)

24	**Barranco de Arure**	109

2 walker, 1½ hours, 3.5 kilometres, ascents & descents 200 metres, 0 refreshments (linear)

25	**Lomo del Carretón**	111

4 walker, 2½ - 3 hours, 4.5 kilometres, ascents & descents 500 metres, vertigo risk, 3 refreshments (circular)

WALKS IN THE NORTH
The North - Traditional Values & Locator Maps — 114

26	**Las Mimbreras**	117

3 walker, 1 hour 20 mins, 4.5 kilometres, ascents & descents 200 metres, 4 refreshments (circular)

27	**Las Creces - Vallehermoso**	119

3 walker, 2 hours, 6.3 kilometres, ascents 50 metres, descents 900 metres, 3 refreshments (linear)

28	**Roque Cano**	122

4 walker, 3 hours, 10.5 kilometres, ascents & descents 600 metres, 5 refreshments (circular)

29	**Ermita de Santa Clara**	125

5 walker, 4 hours, 14 kilometres, ascents & descents 650 metres, 3 refreshments (circular)

30	**Las Rosas - Hermigua**	129

2 walker, 2¼ hours, 8.5 kilometres, ascents 200 metres, descents 600 metres, 3 refreshments (linear)

31	**Pared de Agulo**	132

5 walker, 3 hours, 10 kilometres, ascents & descents 600 metres, vertigo risk, 4 refreshments (circular)

32	**The Head of the Table and The Fat Back**	135

5 walker, 4½-5 hours, 14 kilometres, ascents & descents 750 metres, vertigo risk, 3 refreshments (circular)

33	**El Cedro Tunnel**	140

3 walker, 1½ hours, 5.5 kilometres, ascents & descents 340 metres, 4 refreshments (circular)

34	**Classic Garajonay**	143

4 walker, 3 hours 40 mins, 11 kilometres, ascents 180 metres, descents 1030 metres, vertigo risk, 4 refreshments (linear)

Glossary		147
Appendices	A Useful Information	149
	B Bus, Ferry & Inter-island Flight Timetables	150
	C Cycle Hire, Publications, Museums	154
Place Names Index		156

THE AUTHORS

After university, **Jan Kostura** set off on his travels, living and working in various far-flung places inspired by his passion for stimulating multicultural environments. However, being a stressed out desk-jockey in a hectic consulting business turned out not to be his thing, so after two years slouching in a chair he swapped the office for the more liberating environment of the great outdoors.

He found his second home in the Canary Islands, where he fell in love with the ambiance, the warm-hearted people, the constant sun, the stunning mountains and flamboyant nature.

Jan is also co-author (with Charles Davis) of **Walk! La Palma** (3rd edition), published by Discovery Walking Guides Ltd.

Nowadays Jan works as a mountain guide, organizing hiking expeditions and adventure holidays, and writes articles on travelling.

After twenty years travelling the world pretending to be a teacher, **Charles Davis** concluded that wandering about mountain tops was a more productive way of spending his time than standing in front of a classroom, a decision that has lead to over a dozen books for Discovery Walking Guides.

He is also the author of several novels, published by The Permanent Press. He is accompanied in his peregrinations by Jeannette (a refugee from the French education system) and assorted dogs that other people saw fit to dump in the local Rescue Centre, often for very good reasons. For more information, see:-

http://charlesdavis2.wix.com/charlesdavis

ACKNOWLEDGEMENTS

Many people contribute to a walking guide, but our greatest and overriding acknowledgment must go to the Gomerans for giving the lie to common definitions of 'insularity'. Thank you for sharing your home with us. And what a home it is!

As they say in Spain, "Mi casa es su casa". Go forth and enjoy.

INTRODUCTION

In 1981, a group of Canadians, anxious to escape the hectic racket of a world made small by noisy machines and modern media, retreated to a remote farm on the isolated and little known islands of…the Falklands. In 1986, in the aftermath of a breathtakingly incompetent experiment at the Chernobyl nuclear power station, the population of La Gomera doubled as ageing German hippies hurried 'home', anxious not to be imbibing radioactive milk and eating day-glo lambs. Guess who made the right choice? La Gomera is the ultimate get-away-from-it-all island, easy-going, unspoilt, friendly, isolated from the hustle and bustle of modern living, and so laid back it's virtually supine - even the volcanoes have been dormant for millions of years. The walks, however, are a bit more energetic.

For the new edition of our guide to this small island paradise, Jan has once again been busy deploying his wide experience and passion for the Canaries, as well as an invaluable eye for detail (not to mention a pair of very eager legs), checking, re-walking and revising existing routes, and adding a couple more of his own, including one adventure that qualifies as a new 'Top Three' Gomeran walk.

Two itineraries have been dropped, having become too dangerous since they were first researched, but the good news is that many of the more harum-scarum walks have been improved through path clearing and the addition of railings to the vertiginous stretches. The other good news is that the devastating forest fires of 2012 have proved not nearly as devastating as we feared, leaving most of our itineraries unscathed. So there's every reason to take off and explore this lovely island, or to return with the new edition of the book to revive old acquaintance and make a few new discoveries at the same time.

THE ISLAND

Like a large fluted meringue capped with a crown of green icing, La Gomera or The Round Island, would have reduced Roman road-builders to tearful incoherence. There isn't a straight line on the island and the only way to make a road that doesn't wind about like a snake in a pinball machine is to bore a hole through solid rock. The bane of road-builders and blessing for ramblers, are the myriad ravines (*barrancos*) radiating like spokes from the island's central peak, the **Garajonay**, which have militated against attempts to create an elaborate modern infrastructure and obliged generations of shepherds and peasants to trailblaze a network of paths climbing, crossing and circumnavigating a baffling complex of natural obstacles.

There was a theory, long discredited but beguiling nonetheless, that the Canary Islands were the westernmost tip of the Atlas mountains, or even the remains of a broken African peninsula. Certainly, La Gomera looks like some giant scooped up a handful of North Africa and dolloped it down in the middle of the Atlantic. Arriving by boat, the island can seem unforgivingly brown and barren. And yet its ravines cluster round the celebrated *laurisilva* forest of **Garajonay**, arguably the finest remaining example of the woods that covered southern Europe until the last Ice Age.

Though the laurel family predominates, the *laurisilva* is composed of many different species of tree, notably willow and holly, and more plant life than can be catalogued in a chapter, let alone a paragraph. Often compared to a sponge, **Garajonay** epitomises the importance of trees to a living environment, mopping up moisture from the mists brought by the trade winds, and providing as much as half of the island's water supply. Its name comes from a pre-hispanic legend concerning the young lovers, Gara, a Gomeran girl, and Jonay, a boy from Tenerife. Confronted by the customary troubles with elders legendary young lovers generally face, Gara and Jonay took to the mountain and died in one another's arms, speared on a thorn tree. As for the island itself, biblical scholars once claimed it was named for one of Noah's grandsons, Gomer, but a more likely hypothesis is that it's an eponym for early settlers from Mauritania.

AIM AND SCOPE

This book is aimed at the independent traveller intending to structure a trip round daily walks. There are walks to suit all tastes and capacities, covering classic itineraries, plus several obscure but no less attractive 'original' routes.

CLIMATE, WHEN TO GO

In summer and early autumn, the heat will probably be too much for most people (particularly at lower altitudes and in the south), though the ocean currents and trade winds mean some hiking is still possible, and Jan enjoys walking on la Gomera into early summer. However, to get the best of the island at all altitudes, late autumn, winter and spring are probably best the times to go, especially lower down where rocks and shrubs that look shabby and flat under intense sunlight reveal themselves in an extraordinary complexity of form and colour.

GETTING THERE, GETTING ABOUT, GETTING A BED

There's an **airport** in La Gomera. And there are white elephants in Burma. Since the runway is too short to take any but the most modest modern planes, the principal consequence has been the widening of the road down to **Playa Santiago** and an extension of bus services. Most travellers arrive from Tenerife, on the regular **ferry** services run by Naviera Armas and Fred Olsen.

Hire-car or **motorbike** is the simplest way of getting about, though a handicap for one-way linear walks. Many routes are accessible by **bus**. There are three main lines with buses five times a day that serve the principal walking areas with four twice-daily lines linking these routes and more marginal areas. Timetables rarely change (see the Appendices at the back of this book) but call at the Tourist Office for up-to-date information. **Taxi** drivers are used to dropping people off at the start of more popular routes. **Hitching** is also a practical option on this friendliest of islands.

Accommodation in hotels, pensions, apartments and *casas rurales* is plentiful and geared to independent travellers rather than block-booking packages. The walks are evenly spread and, since the island is small, accessible wherever you maybe staying, so **choosing a base** is a question of taste rather than practicality. **San Sebastián** is best for bus routes, with **Valle Gran Rey** a close second. The facilities in each are comparable, though **Valle**

Gran Rey has a slight edge in terms of tourist-centred services. **Playa Santiago** and **Valle Gran Rey** are as 'touristy' as it gets on **La Gomera**, though food shops in the former are poor. Both are good if you want a bathe at the end of a day's walking. **Hermigua** and **Vallehermoso** perhaps boast the best balance between facilities, affordability and an authentically Gomeran atmosphere. Tranquility seekers should check out the *Casas Rurales*. If time allows, it's worth spending three or four days in each area, in which case contact one of the agencies dealing with *casas rurales, viviendas,* and *apartamentos*.

THE WALKS

One unfortunate consequence of having so many ravines is that Canarians have a regrettable tendency to build roads right over the top of their highest mountains, which is all very well for conventional tourists, but a bit dispiriting for walkers. Getting somewhere one can't otherwise go is, after all, one of the great pleasures of walking and it's a bit galling to get to the top only to find yourself on a main road with a regular bus service. Hence the linear descents. Nonetheless, exceptional circuits demand exceptional efforts, so we make our excuses in advance, first for the logistical hassles of those walks involving public transport at both ends, second for itineraries that have you toiling up a mountain only to be met by a coach load of baffled tourists wondering why you didn't take the package.

All the walks are walks and require no special equipment or expertise, with the exception of Walk 33, on which a torch is all but essential. Otherwise, all you need are walking boots or tough walking sandals, and protection appropriate to the weather and altitude. In the Garajonay it's advisable always to have a waterproof and/or light sweater. At lower altitudes, a sun hat and sun cream are essential. Within each section, the first walk is suitable as a test walk for the first day. The remaining walks are arranged according to a vaguely geographical logic, not by difficulty or length.

Timings are all 'pure' timings excluding snacking, snapping and simply standing still staring. It's highly unlikely you will complete these walks in exactly the time specified. Try a shorter walk first to see how your times compare to ours. As a rule of thumb, add fifteen minutes to every timed hour. But above all, take 'your' time. There's nothing more frustrating than trying to walk at somebody else's pace, be it slower or faster than yours. Similarly, all assessments of exertion are subjective and are bound to vary according to personal prejudice, general temperament and the mood of the day.

We have tried to give enough detail in the descriptions for those who need confirmation they're on the right path, but not so much as to irritate more confidant pathfinders with superfluity. *Italics* are used for discrete Spanish words, most of which are found in the glossary, and single quotes indicate a place name written on a signpost. **Bold Text** is used for place names, including named geographic features, and also for street names and the names of bars and businesses encountered on the walks. Consistency rather than deficient vocabulary accounts for all ascents and descents being 'gentle', 'steady', or 'steep'.

As a general guide a dirt track or *pista forestal* indicates something that could be driven, albeit sometimes at a pinch, a trail refers to something reasonably broad but better suited to feet, hooves or two wheels rather than four, a path is a path, and a way either aspires to being a path or was once a path and has long since given up an unequal battle with erosion and/or vegetation. To link more interesting paths, road walking is sometimes inevitable. No road on the island is really big or busy, so don't be alarmed by references to main roads, most of which would be considered bucolically peaceful in Britain. As for what we call lanes, they are frequently little more than tracks with a barrow load of tarmac tipped on top and smeared about a bit.

LONG DISTANCE PATHS AND OTHER WAYMARKED ROUTES

There are two long distance paths on La Gomera, the **GR131 Camino Natural Cumbres de La Gomera**, a 37 kilometre trail between **San Sebastián** and **Vallehermoso**, and the **GR132**, a 114 kilometre circuit of the entire island linking the main villages as well as some of the more obscure hamlets. Naturally, many of our itineraries coincide with stretches of these LDPs, however, we have been wary of using the GR signposts in describing our own walks. For one thing, the GR kilometre markers rarely coincide with key decision points. Moreover, despite being recently installed, some of the markers have already been vandalized or are unreadable as a result of sun blistering, which is also a problem with the mapboards. Finally, the island has recently been deprived of its European Ramblers' Association waymarking standard, meaning the authorities had to drop the yellow PRs and green SLs. Admittedly, a lot of effort has gone into the GR signposting, but until the durability of these has been proven by time, we prefer to support our walk descriptions with more permanent waymarkers, such as landscape features, buildings, and junctions. That said, nothing is immutable. In revising the present guidebook, we were momentarily baffled by the absence of a large bottling plant at the start of an itinerary. It had been demolished! So use your discretion. If the GR waymarks seem dependable, by all means take advantage of them, notably for pacing progress. Just bear in mind that we have some reservations about their utility and reliability.

Though the PR and SL waymarking system has been abandoned, there are numerous green waymarked 'Rutas', the signposts for which are generally reliable.

RISKS

Aggressive dogs, disagreeable **landowners**, and theft are not a problem. **Forest fires** are a danger in summer and early autumn. **Dehydration** is the most prevalent risk, especially at lower altitudes. Take half a litre of water per person per hour and bear in mind that dehydration affects the entire body, including joints and tendons. If you suspect your knees might come in handy in thirty years' time, drink plenty before descending. **Swimming** can be dangerous, especially in the north and west. As a general rule, don't swim unless you see other people getting in and, more importantly, getting out.

VERTIGO

On an island like La Gomera, it is inevitable that some paths are going to be vertiginous. When we were preparing the new edition, we did try to settle upon some sort of vertigo 'rating' to match the exertion and refreshment ratings, but vertigo is such a subjective thing that we eventually decided a numerical rating was futile at best, counterproductive at worst. The basic advice is that, if it's got a vertigo warning and you suffer from vertigo, don't do it. That said, many of us manage to master our vertigo to a lesser or greater degree and, if you're staying on the island for a long time or coming back on repeat visits, you will probably find yourself wanting to do one of the vertiginous walks. If so, we suggest experimenting with an itinerary where the risk is relatively mild (for example Walk 7 or Walk 13) before tackling more dramatic adventures. For what it's worth, most of the vertigo assessments in the book come from Charles, who has hitherto ended up on his hands and knees with the GPS receiver between his teeth, but who has now mastered his vertigo enough to deal with most precipitous paths so long as the vertiginous bits are not too long and too narrow.

FLORA & FAUNA

The **Garajonay Park Visitors' Guide** claims 980 plant species and subspecies exist on La Gomera (there's 27 species of ferns alone!), which makes one short paragraph look a little silly, but to give you a rough idea of what to expect, the following observations (and they are observations, what we noticed, not what a professional eye might discern) may serve as a rough introduction. Bear in mind that anything liable to be a shrub in continental Europe will be a bush here, while familiar bushes take on the dimension of trees, the obvious example being the heath-tree or *brezo.*

The first thing you'll notice are palm trees, which are so prevalent the fronds assume the same function broom used to in Britain. In drier areas you will see plenty of prickly pear (often spotted with the flaky white parasite from which cochineal was extracted), agave, wax-plants, fennel, St. John's wort, spurge, house-leeks, sow-thistle, tajinaste, bugloss, cistus, tansy, several types of daisy and more varieties of broom than you can shake a palm frond at. The real glory of the island's flora though, is to be found in the green crown of **Garajonay**. In the text, we use *laurisilva* loosely as shorthand for the **Garajonay** woods, though inevitably the flora, even of superficially similar woodland, is more complex than this suggests. In drier areas the correct term is *fayal-brezal*, a composite of the Spanish words for wax-myrtle and tree-heath. To get an idea of how rich this forest is, go to the **Centro de Visitantes** near **Las Rosas** and ask for the park's free pamphlet of Self-Guider Paths.

By comparison, La Gomera seems relatively poor in fauna. The odd hoopoe may brighten your day and there are numerous varieties of finches and tits, otherwise the most common birds are turtle doves, kestrels and hawks. There are said to be 2000 species of insect on the island, the most eye-catching being the remarkably varied dragonflies, not just electric blue but pale blue and, most startlingly, scarlet. Apart from rabbits and partridge, there is no game on La Gomera. The most common reptile is the Gomeran lizard, a dark-skinned, antediluvian looking creature usually seen belting about in the crevices of rocks. You may also see the coppery backed *lisa*, which resembles a slow-worm with legs. It's worth noting that there are no poisonous reptiles in the Canaries. We've met people who avoided walking through *laurisilva*, because they were put off by all the rustling. On La Gomera, rustling things are not biting things.

EATING AND DRINKING

Possibly the most distinctive dish on La Gomera is cress soup (*sopa de berros*). More of a broth than a soup, it's an ideal walkers' meal, filling but not sleep inducing. The other characteristic ingredient of local cuisine is maize meal or *gofio*, a beige flour that you're expected to sprinkle on your soup. Otherwise, standard Canary cuisine prevails; meat (*carne*) and potatoes (*patatas* or *papas*) with lashings of *mojo*, a sauce variously made of red (*mojo rojo*) or green peppers and coriander (*mojo verde*). Various it is, too, everybody boasting that their own recipe is better than everyone else's.

Meat is *asado* (which on the mainland means roast but here sometimes means braised), *a la plancha* (griddled), *a la brasa* (barbecued), *frita* (fried), or *con salsa* (stewed). *Cabra* is goat, *cerdo* pork, *buey, ternera* or *res* beef, and *cordero* lamb. Notable specialities are *cabra con salsa* and *carne fiesta*, fried marinated pork. Potatoes are 'wrinkled' (*papas arrugadas*), boiled in their jackets with salt and little water, resulting in a taste and texture that suggests parboiling and baking. They tend to be cooked early and left to stand, so don't be surprised if they're lukewarm. Pulses are not as common as elsewhere in Spain, though chick peas (*garbanzos*) are ubiquitous, often as a labourer's mid-morning 'snack', and you may see beans (*judías*) or lentils (*lentejas*).

Fish (*pescado*) is not so widespread as one would expect either, though tuna (*atún*) is on most menus. Salad is nearly always the standard mix (*ensalada mixta*). As for cheese (*queso*); there's a choice of white (local goat's cheese - *blanco*) or yellow (*amarillo*), a limp sheet of plastic imported from the mainland. *Almogrote* is a piquant pâté of grated cheese, garlic and peppers – only worthwhile if freshly prepared; avoid the potted gunge sold in supermarkets and tourist shops.

Local beers (*cerveza*), *Dorada*, *Reina*, and *Tropical*, are additive free and good. Most of the island's viniculture is destined for private rather than commercial use, but Gomeran red and white wines are available. They're not great, but good enough. Finally, you may notice locals being served coffee with a sludge of condensed milk lurking about at the bottom of the glass (a *barraquito*). Occasionally the condensed milk is diluted with ordinary milk and sometimes, a shaving of lemon rind is added for flavour.

TOURIST STUFF

La Gomera is refreshingly free of the compulsion to be constantly grabbing your attention and extracting wads of money from your wallet, which means there is little to excite the conventional tourist apart from the views. If you have a chance to see and hear something of **silbo**, the island's ancient whistling language, it's worth taking the opportunity. Declared a Masterpiece of the Oral and Intangible Heritage of Humanity by UNESCO, silbo developed in response to the geographical constraints, enabling messages to be conveyed across ravines for distances up to five kilometres. The language declined dramatically during the last century, but has been revived through various government and community initiatives. If you want a day off walking but don't want to be stuck indoors, the *ermitas* make good **picnic spots**, notably **San Juan** at **Benchijigua**, **Nuestra Señora de Guadalupe** above **Gerián**, **San Salvador** in **Taguluche**, **San Isidro** at the **Chorros de Epina**, **Santa Clara**, **Lourdes** and **Las Nieves** on the GM2.

Best **beaches** for an afternoon lazing around in the sun and swimming are **Las Salinas**, south of **Valle Gran Rey**, **Playa del Medio** and **Playa Chinguarime** east of **Playa Santiago**, and **Playa Alojera** north of **Valle Gran Rey**, **Chinguarime** and **Alojera** being the beauty spots favoured by the transient hippie community. If you want a swim and don't fancy the waves and murky water of the northern beaches, the pool at **Playa de Vallehermoso** is highly recommended. At the time of going to press it was under reconstruction, but should have reopened by the time you read this.

Scuba **diving** is possible from **Playa Santiago** and **Valle Gran Rey**. The one undisputed non-pedestrian tourist attraction on the island is a **boat trip** from **Valle Gran Rey** to the cliffs of **Los Órganos**, an excursion that may also include whale-watching.

SYMBOLS RATING GUIDE

DWG's Symbols Rating Bar shows key information about a walking route in a quick glance. Remember that effort/exertion and refreshment ratings are the authors' opinions and the time shown is walking time without stops.

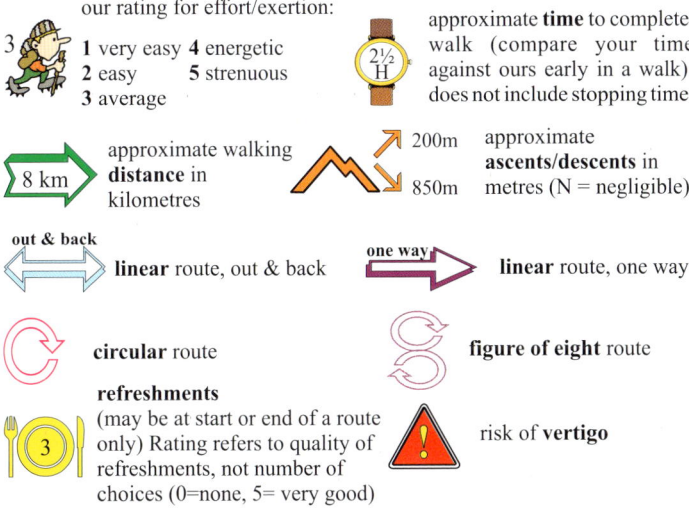

our rating for effort/exertion:
1 very easy 4 energetic
2 easy   5 strenuous
3 average

approximate **time** to complete a walk (compare your times against ours early in a walk) - does not include stopping time

approximate walking **distance** in kilometres

approximate **ascents/descents** in metres (N = negligible)

linear route, out & back

linear route, one way

circular route

figure of eight route

refreshments (may be at start or end of a route only) Rating refers to quality of refreshments, not number of choices (0=none, 5= very good)

risk of **vertigo**

Walk descriptions include: timing in minutes, shown as (40M), compass directions, shown as (NW), heights in metres, shown as (1355m) GPS waypoints, shown as (Wp.3).

A Note About Walking Times
Walking times create more discussion than any other aspect of walking guide books. Our walking times are for ***continuous walking*** at an easy pace without stops, representing the quickest time you are likely to complete a route. Most of us walk at a similar pace; approx 4-6kmh. As our routes are planned as fun adventures you are unlikely to simply march along the route from start to finish. We all take stops to enjoy the views, marvel at the flora, or simply to take a break. As a result, we suggest you add 25-50% to those continuous walking times, to allow for the stops you'll make along the route.

LOCATION MAPS

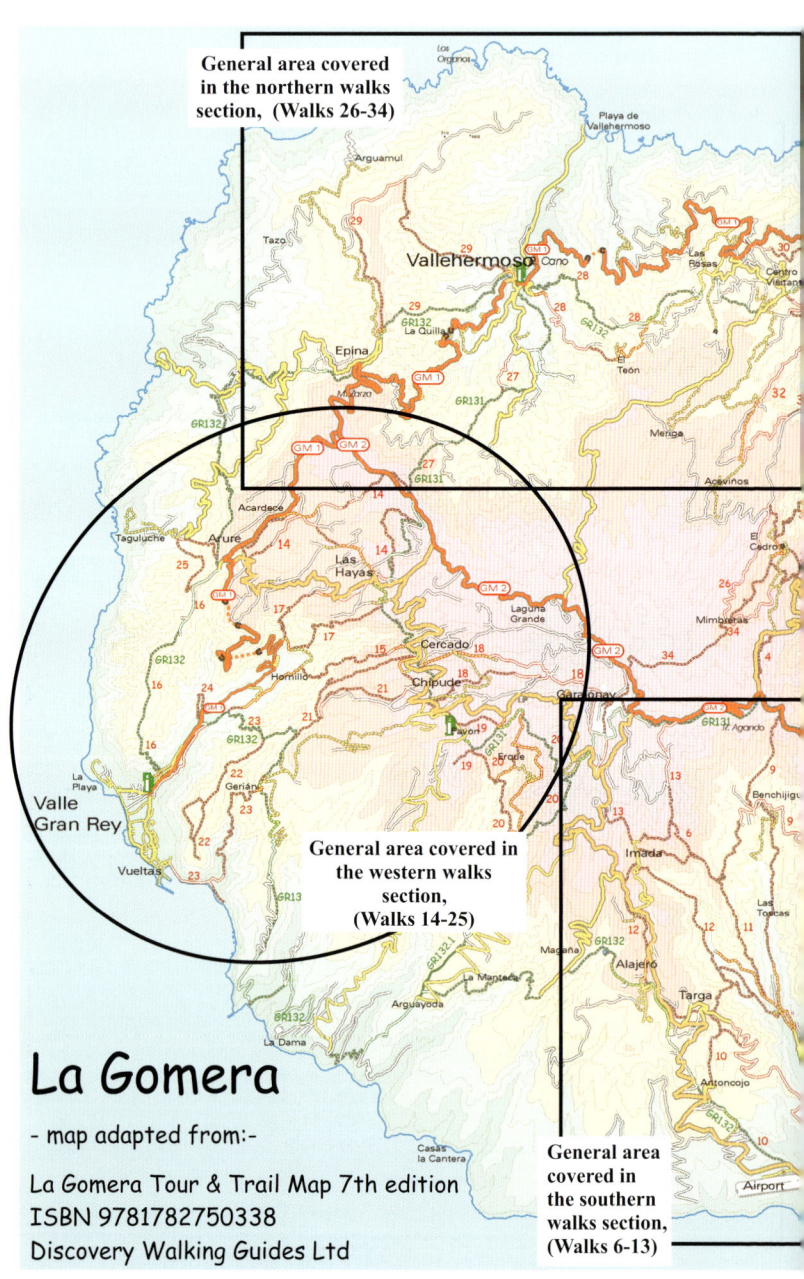

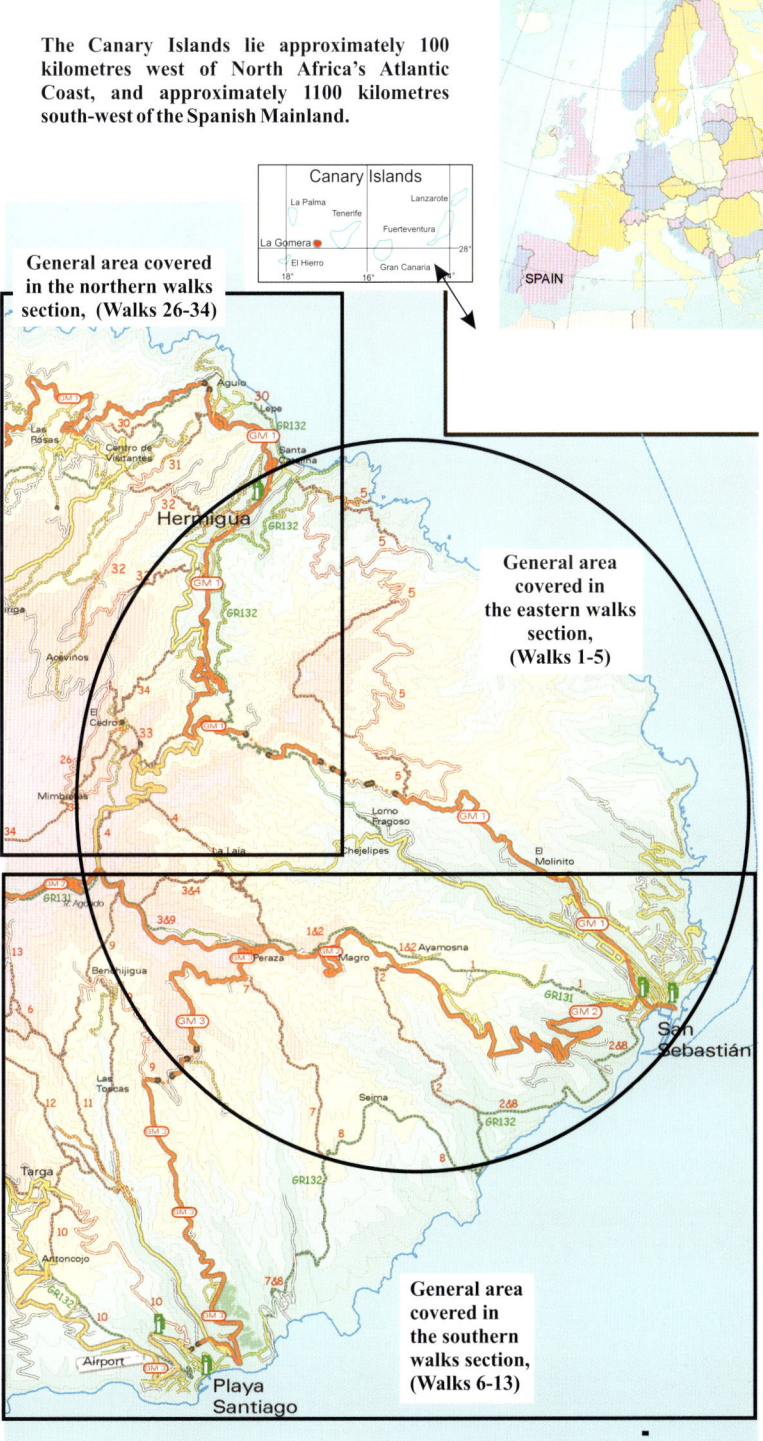

MAP NOTES & LEGEND

The map sections used in this book have been adapted from **La Gomera Tour & Trail Super-Durable Map** (7th edition 2016, ISBN 9781782750338) published by Discovery Walking Guides Ltd.

La Gomera Tour & Trail Super-Durable Map is a 1:35,000 full colour map. For more information on DWG publications, visit:
www.dwgwalking.co.uk

Altitude

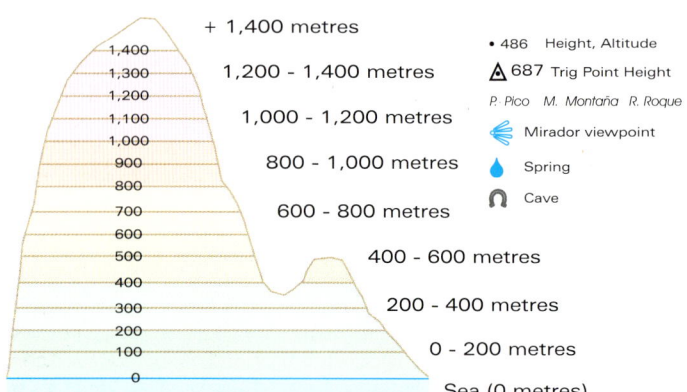

Roads

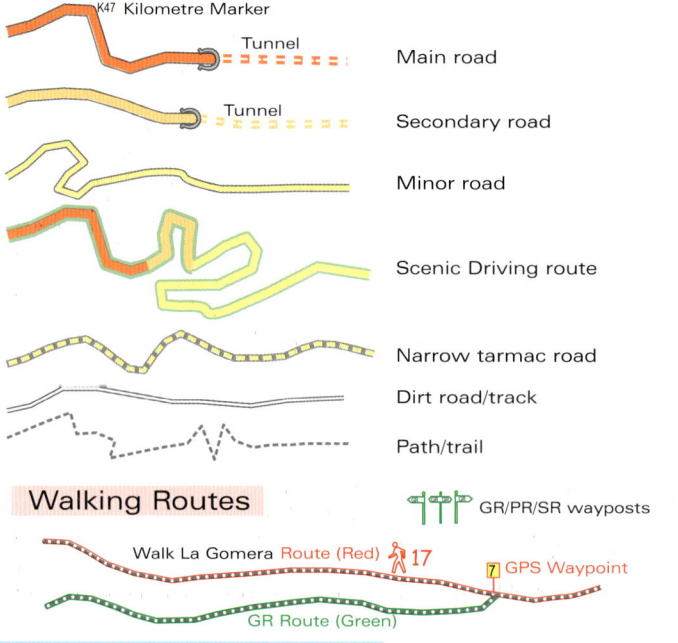

16 Walk! La Gomera

Major Hotel   Important House   Hotel   Petrol

Forestry House, Casa Forestal   House   Ruin/Barn

Lighthouse   Bar/Restaurant (with parking)

Tower   Information Office   P Parking   Sports Ground

Church   Chapel/Ermita   Cemetery

Picnic area   Wind Turbine   Camping

USING GPS ON LA GOMERA

Every walking route in a Walk! guidebook can be easily and reliably navigated simply by following the detailed walk description. All of our routes are researched using a GPS so that we have an accurate record of where we have been. Even if you do not use a GPS yourself, you can be reassured that all Walk! routes have been accurately recorded.

Using a GPS with our waypoints will enable you to navigate the route with pin-point accuracy. Your GPS will show you where you are on the route in relation to the waypoints. Waypoints are provided for the key decision points on each walking route e.g. at trail junctions. Our GPS waypoints are most reassuring when you are adventuring in a new destination, as you know exactly where you are. Finding the start of a walk is simplicity itself as Waypoint 1 is at the start of each walking route.

GPS accuracy depends upon the local conditions affecting the reception of GPS signals. In the Laurel Forest (eg Walk 34), in steep *barrancos* and on cliff faces, you will get a lower standard of accuracy but in these situations you will find there is only one obvious trail to follow.

Waypoint Lists for Walk! La Gomera are available as a free download zip file from www.dwgwalking.co.uk/gpxDownloads.htm; simply download the zip file and unzip it into its separate waypoint files in a choice of gpx, wpt or text waypoint files.

Garmin GPS users can purchase and download the **La Gomera Tour & Trail Custom Map** on DWG's website www.dwgwalking.co.uk which will enable you to use the map as your basemap on your GPS. The **La Gomera Tour & Trail Super-Durable Map** includes details of how to download the digital Custom Map version for free.

If you are interested to know more about GPS, we have made **GPS The Easy Way** available as a free download at www.dwgwalking.co.uk/gps.htm.

Remember:
A Compass points North
But a GPS shows you where you are,
Shows you where you have been,
And can show you where you want to go.

THE EAST - COMMERCE AND ABANDONMENT

Arriving by ferry from **Los Cristianos**, San Sebastián's small port seems dwarfed by the boat, and in many ways the island's capital has also been diminished by the development of an organized tourist industry. Frequent ferry departures mean that business travellers no longer have to stay overnight, while vastly improved roads hasten tourists away to the resorts of **Valle Gran Rey** and **Playa Santiago**, as a result of which, many visitors miss the town altogether.

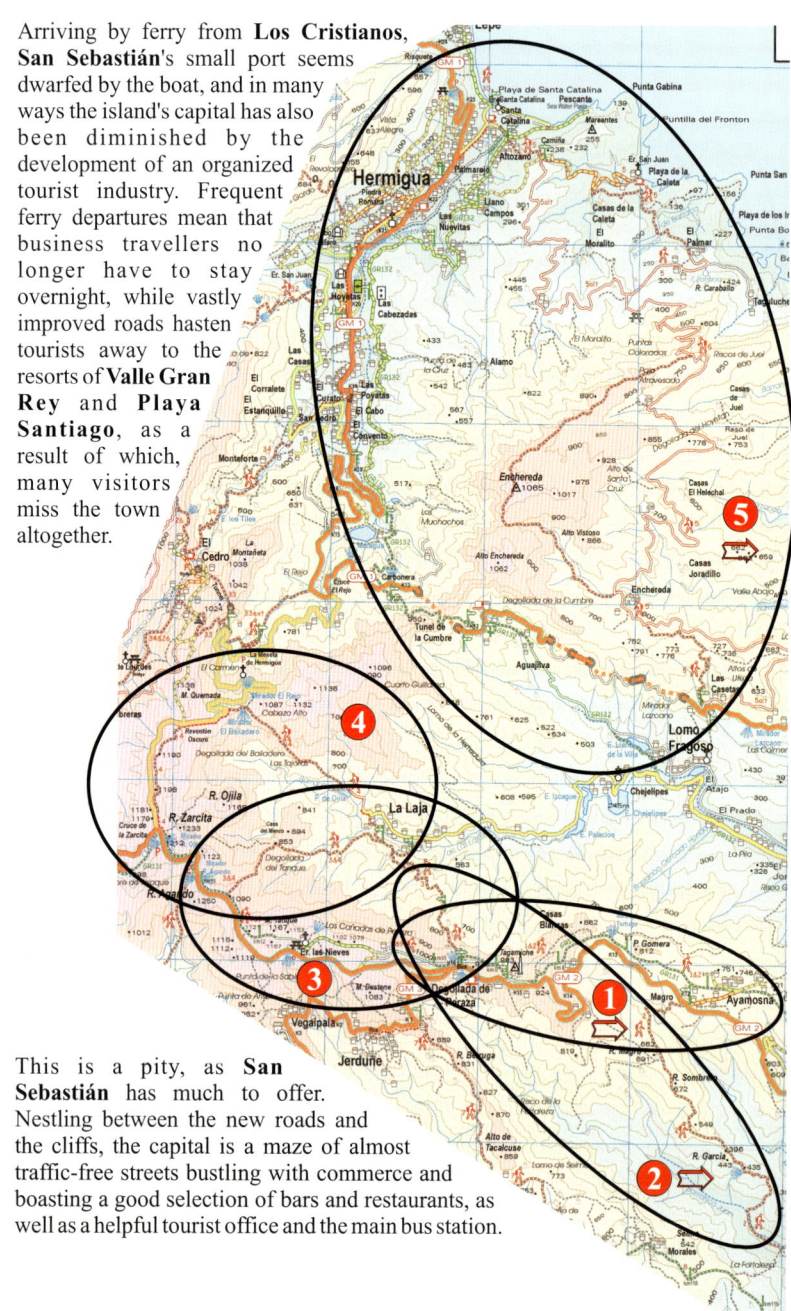

This is a pity, as **San Sebastián** has much to offer. Nestling between the new roads and the cliffs, the capital is a maze of almost traffic-free streets bustling with commerce and boasting a good selection of bars and restaurants, as well as a helpful tourist office and the main bus station.

18 Walk! La Gomera

EASTERN WALKS LOCATOR MAP

Accommodation remains plentiful and varied, too, ranging from the impressive **Parador** down to hostels and guest houses, making **San Sebastián** a good base for drivers who want to enjoy the sedate grandeur of the **Parador**, and for non-drivers who want good bus connections plus a bit of nightlife.

San Sebastián still trades on its Christopher Columbus connection, but the town's main tourist attraction is the bustling yacht marina which has drawn sailors from Tenerife and further afield, the combination of a maritime town with a good harbour making this one of the best yachting bases in the Canary Islands. Beyond the city limits, the barren ridges above the **Barranco de la Villa** and **Barranco Hondo** valleys have a brooding, enigmatic air which we experience on Walks 1 & 2, while **Playa de la Guancha** is just a short walk away (following Walk 2 in reverse) for a more relaxing day off.

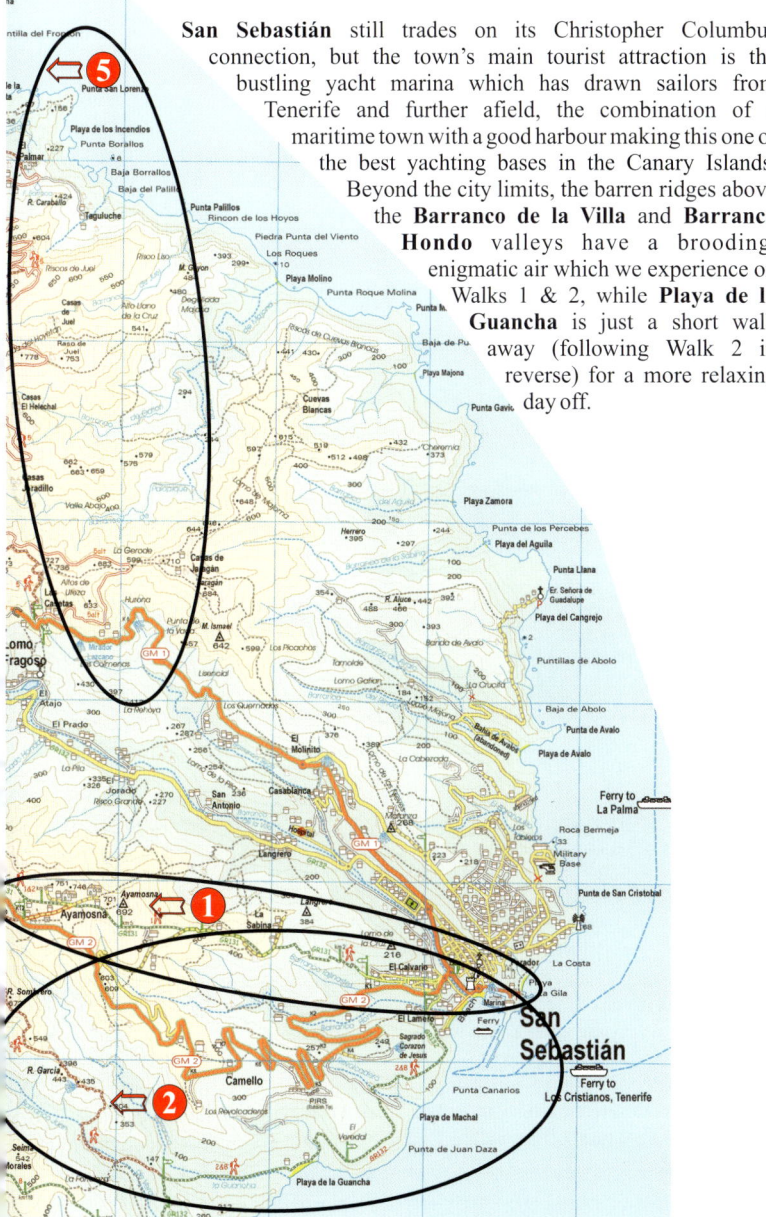

Walk! La Gomera 19

1 DEGOLLADA DE PERAZA - SAN SEBASTIÁN

Following the remains of a traditional donkey trail, our first itinerary is a good introduction to La Gomera's gateway landscape, offering great views over the rocky countryside behind the capital, **San Sebastián**. A fine excursion in its own right, it is also a useful 'commuting' route for those piecing together a long distance walking tour. The walk is recommended on a blustery winter's day, but not when it's hot or wet.

The route is part of the **GR131** and is clearly waymarked, featuring path defining lines of stones, GR kilometre posts, and signposts at every crucial junction, so once on trail, stow the book and just enjoy the views. If you stop at the **Peraza Bar** before setting off, it makes sense to follow the main road east for 300 metres to connect directly with Wp.3. It's worth noting that between Wps.2&3 there is a stretch protected by a handrail where there is a sign warning of a landslide. At the time of writing this poses no problems, but if conditions should deteriorate, you can use the road to skip this stretch. The first part of the itinerary is the same as for Walk 2. If time is limited, check out Walk 2 first to decide which of the two itineraries is most suitable for you.

| 4 | 2½H | 9 km | 100m / 1000m | one way | 4* |

Looking in the direction of the walk from Wp.1

*in San Sebastián

Access (by bus)
From **San Sebastián** bus station, take Línea 1 or Línea 3 to **Degollada de Peraza**. If arriving in **San Sebastián** by car, park along the seafront road then walk to the bus station.

The walk ends near this parking area.

From the **Degollada de Peraza** bus-stop (Wp.1 0M), which is about 200 metres north-west of the restaurant, we follow the joint **GR131** and **La Laja** trail zigzagging down to the north for 200 metres, where our GR trail forks off

20 Walk! La Gomera

The junction at Wp.2

to the right at a 'La Laja/San Sebastián' signposted junction (Wp.2 3M). Bearing east, we pass a small rock cellar and a tiny water reservoir, then climb past a pylon to a GR signpost (Wp.3 16M), in sight of the main road and two white bungalows.

Passing in front of the bungalows, we ignore the concrete track leading to the antenna-topped peak of **Tagamiche**, and bear right on a track marked with a wooden waypost. 120 metres later, we turn left onto the old, intermittently cobbled *camino real* trail, which begins with a few stone steps, then curves to the east of **Tagamiche** before descending through a series of switchbacks.

Approaching the 'sea-monster'

Descending gently, we cross an abandoned dirt track (Wp.4 25M), then pass several stone ruins before approaching a rocky outcrop resembling a sea-monster's head rising out of the earth. The trail swings right just before the head to climb onto its neck, where the **Mirador de La Tortuga** mapboard gives a different reading of the sea monster (Wp.5 46M).

Our trail then skirts the southern side of the diminutive, table-top **Pico Gomera**, with fine views of the conical **Roque Sombrero** (see Walk 2). Below **Pico Gomera**, a telephone line runs into the trail (Wp.6 53M), after which we traverse long-abandoned terraces. Large flat rocks replace the cobbles as we approach the first of the **Ayamosna** farms, where our trail runs alongside then joins a tarmac lane in front of two farmhouses.

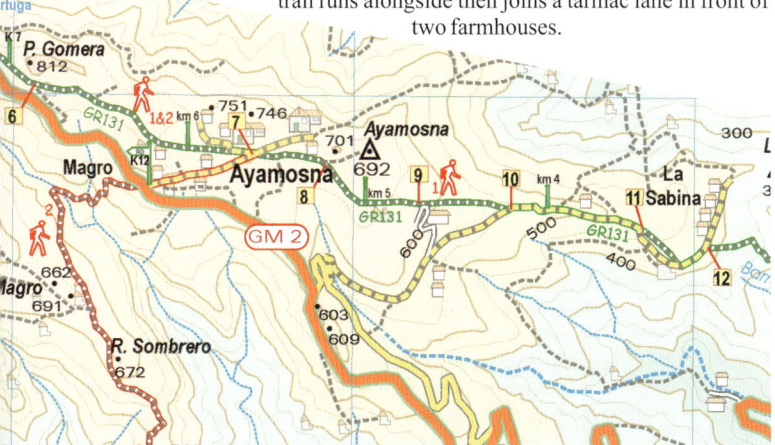

Walk! La Gomera 21

Wp.7 - Walks 1 and 2 diverge here

A little over 50 metres later, Walks 1 & 2 diverge at a tarmac junction (Wp.7 72M). Ten metres to the left of the junction, we pass a mapboard and leave the tarmac to recover the donkey trail. After a transformer hut, we pass below the third **Ayamosna** farm, and the quay at **San Sebastián** comes into view.

At the next signposted junction, we ignore the branch on the right for 'Lomada del Camello/San Sebastián' (Wp.8 78M) and stay on the main GR trail, which descends behind two partially interred bunkers, bunkers of sufficient ugliness to suggest total burial might have been preferable. Following the fence to the left of the bunkers (Wp.9 85M), we pass to the left of the next electricity pylon, after which we join a tarmac lane (Wp.10 98M).

Recovering the donkey trail at Wp.12

When the lane swings right for the second time, we continue straight ahead (E) on a shortcut path (Wp.11 106M), rejoining the lane 20 metres below a byre.

Bearing left and following the lane for a little over 100 metres, we turn right in front of **Casa Laguau**, recovering the donkey trail (Wp.12 112M).

Zigzagging down a long *lomo* amid a sea of house-leeks, we pass under a telephone cable next to a 'finger rock', eventually descending below a water hut to the end of a tarmac lane (where there is GR-signpost and a mapboard) on the fringes of **San Sebastián** (Wp.13 145M). Turning left, we follow **Avenida de las Galanas** down past **Plaza Las Galanas**. Just before the pedestrian zone, we bear left into **Calle Fuerteventura**, then right at a playground into **Calle Cañada del Herrero** to descend to a roundabout (Wp.14 160M) next to the bridge into town.

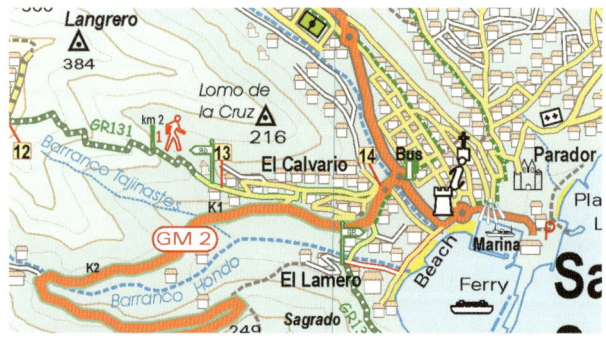

2 ROQUE SOMBRERO & PLAYA DE LA GUANCHA

If you only have time to do one walk in the east, this is the one to do. Following a long ridge studded with *roques*, notably the distinctively conical **Sombrero**, it's every bit as wild and exciting as it looks from the road, possibly a little more. A word of warning, though. The main descent is little frequented and, though never difficult, requires considerable confidence, not to mention stamina, as we follow negligible paths in very isolated countryside. If you don't fancy the full version of this very full-on itinerary, see the end of the text for a shorter option doing the walk in reverse directly to **Playa de la Guancha**.

5 | 4H 40M | 16 km | 300m / 1300m | one way | 4*

Short Version
San Sebastián - Playa de la Guancha (description at the end of the main walk)

*in San Sebastián

Access (by bus):
From **San Sebastián** bus station, take Línea 1 or Línea 3 to **Degollada de Peraza**. If arriving in **San Sebastián** by car, park along the seafront road then walk to the bus station. The walk ends near this parking area.

We start as per Walk 1, but turn right (W) for 'Magro' at Wp.7 (67M) where Walks 1 and 2 diverge. When the **Ayamosna** access lane joins the main road, we cross the road and slip between the concrete and metal crash barriers directly ahead of us (Wp.8 72M), as indicated by a

Wp.8, between concrete and metal barriers

Walk! La Gomera 23

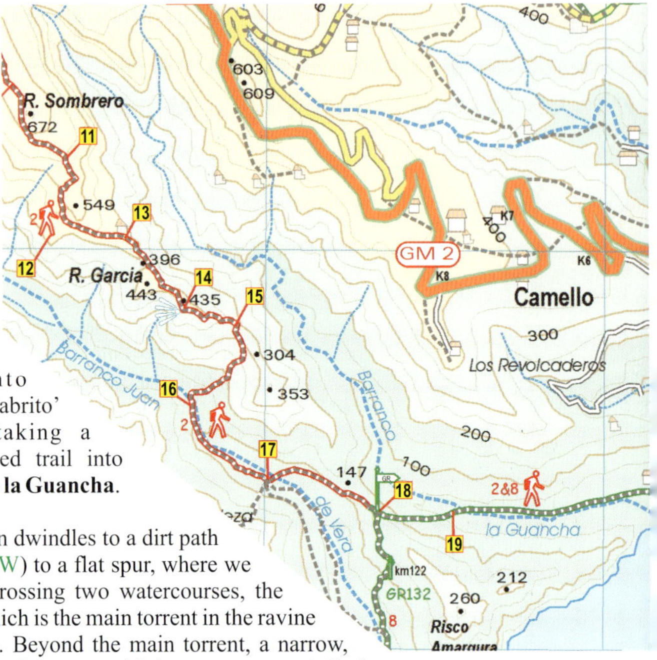

'Monumento natural El Cabrito' signpost, taking a roughly paved trail into **Barranco de la Guancha**.

The trail soon dwindles to a dirt path descending (W) to a flat spur, where we bear right, crossing two watercourses, the second of which is the main torrent in the ravine (Wp.9 87M). Beyond the main torrent, a narrow, waymarked path crosses a third watercourse and climbs to a wall, intended to restrict cattle rather than ramblers. Stepping round the wall, we climb steadily across terraces on a battered but obvious path toward a line of tall palms below **Roque Magro**. The path gets fainter toward the top and the main route to the **Roque Magro** hamlet, though evident from the road, is less apparent on the ground.

Approaching Roque Sombrero

We can either maintain direction to pick our way along the path or (as mapped) bear left on a cairn-marked terrace and pass below the palms, where a faint trodden way leads to a corner post in a wire mesh fence. Squeezing between the fence and the terrace wall, we follow the terrace until we see the first of the **Roque Magro** ruins.

Bearing right, we climb directly across the terraces to the lower ruin, where another terrace curves round to a faint dirt path (Wp.10 107M) crossing the saddle behind **Roque Sombrero**.

Skirting to the right of **Roque Sombrero**, with fine views over **Barranco Juan de Vera**, we cross another wall, then follow a raised path toward the nameless, 549 metre *roque* (hereafter referred to as '549'), getting our first glimpse of the coastal oasis of **El Cabrito**. After a small windbreak (Wp.11 122M), the path loses definition in rough yellow rocks. Staying on top of the ridge, we pick our way through the rocks toward **549**, passing to the right of a long outcrop of grey rock.

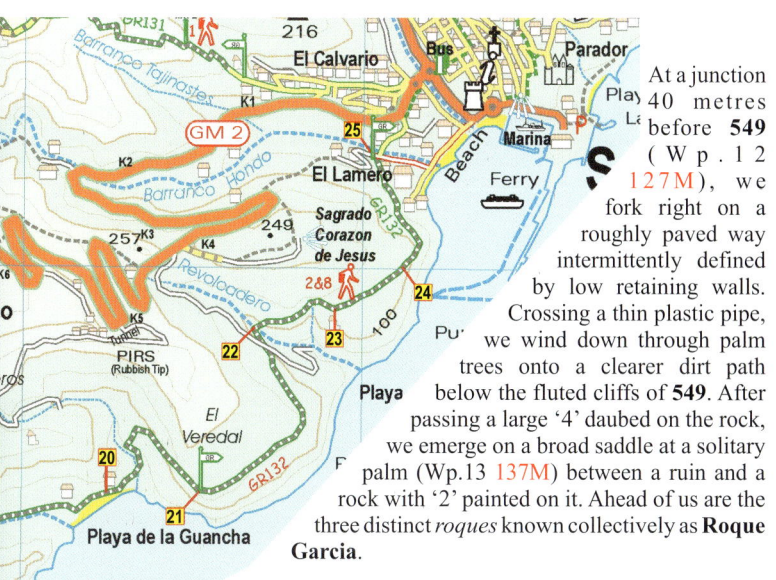

At a junction 40 metres before **549** (Wp.12 127M), we fork right on a roughly paved way intermittently defined by low retaining walls. Crossing a thin plastic pipe, we wind down through palm trees onto a clearer dirt path below the fluted cliffs of **549**. After passing a large '4' daubed on the rock, we emerge on a broad saddle at a solitary palm (Wp.13 137M) between a ruin and a rock with '2' painted on it. Ahead of us are the three distinct *roques* known collectively as **Roque Garcia**.

Crossing the saddle, we climb to the right of the smaller, central *roque*, after which we bear right then immediately left (ESE) on a broad ledge running between the easternmost *roque* and a precipitous slope. At the end of the ledge, we climb past a partially walled cave onto a spur, from where **El Cabrito** is visible again (Wp.14 147M). Continuing alongside the ridge, we descend to a narrow spine distinguished by a 3-metre rock 'hand' (Wp.15 152M) - admittedly a somewhat freakish and mutilated hand, but a hand nonetheless - just after which, we see a green-and-white waymark.

From here a direct descent into **Barranco de la Guancha** would be possible and even describable, but it would also be pathless and perhaps undesirable. Instead, we follow the green-and-white waymarked route, winding down into **Barranco Juan de Vera**, where we cross the riverbed and join the end of a dirt track (Wp.16 171M). To return to **Barranco de la Guancha**, we will re-cross the ridge at its lowest point, just before the pylon we can see to the east.

The track drops down into a wide bend of the riverbed, where you may see cairns and a solitary green-and-white waymark to the left. These indicate an alternative way up to Wp.17, but after 15 minutes fruitless boulder-hopping, we failed to find it! Far simpler to follow the dirt track till you come to a cross-roads with a path, a metal sign indicating 'Seima' to the right and a flurry of cairns and red-and-white waymarks tracing our route across the riverbed to the left (Wp.17 176M).

Turning left, we follow the abundant waymarks and cairns across the river to a rough dirt and rock path climbing gently (ESE) before zigzagging steeply up to a signposted junction (Wp.18 190M) (where the present itinerary is joined by Walk 8 from **El Cabrito**) overlooking the welcome sight of **Playa de la Guancha**. Don't get too excited, though. The descent takes longer than it looks. Winding steeply down the far side of the ridge, we pass a rough bar-gate and metal posts that once carried a chain handrail, after which we descend steadily to the stream bed (Wp.19 200M).

Crossing the stream bed, we follow a clear path along its left bank before rejoining the watercourse and eventually passing between a couple of stone beach huts, emerging on the beach between a white cabin and rubber life buoy (Wp.20 215M). By this time, a swim will probably seem imperative, but remember, all Gomeran beaches are potentially dangerous and this particular beach shelves very steeply – you are very much on your own here.

Looking back at Playa de la Guancha

Continuing along the pebble-lined path in front of the white cabin, we pass animal pens and chicken coops before bearing left up a minor *barranco*. The *barranco* path runs into a roughly paved trail climbing steadily (NE) up the **Costado de la Guancha** before bearing right on a gentler gradient for a long ESE traverse (visible from the beach).

San Sebastián harbour

A final steep climb leads to a 'Monumento Natural' signpost (Wp.21 235M), after which a broad, clear trail running along a contour line gradually brings **San Sebastián** into sight. After dipping down (NW) to cross the **Revolcadero** watercourse (Wp.22 250M), we climb (NE) past a small ruin (Wp.23).

The trail then levels out before descending gently to pass a threshing circle (Wp.24 270M), after which it crosses bare rock for its final steady descent (NW) to the town's power plant (Wp.25 280M), where we either turn right on the riverbed-track to the sea-front promenade, or carry straight on to go directly to the bus station.

Short Version
If you don't fancy the full walk and don't intend doing Walk 8, it's worth visiting **Playa de la Guancha**, doing the end of the present itinerary in reverse. To find Wp.18, turn inland 75 metres from the southern end of **San Sebastián** promenade, at the playground and green kiosk above the penultimate, double-staircase to the beach, and take the riverbed-track past the UNELCO power plant. The path, identified by a GR signpost ('El Cabrito 6.7km'), starts a little over 250 metres from the beach, immediately after the UNELCO gates, on a dirt way running alongside a green fence. Once on the path, it's easy to follow, except on the rise above the port. When you see a rough wooden cross to your left, veer right as indicated by a waymark and traverse bare rock, after which the way is obvious.

3 LOS ROQUES

In terms of volcanic history, La Gomera has been a peaceable place for several million years, but the *roques*, bulky little peaks fashioned by erosion round lava fills, are a reminder of less tranquil times. Exploring the most celebrated cluster of *roques* (**Agando**, **Carmona**, **Zarcita** and **Ojila**), this circuit combines perfectly contrasting trails, descending across classic Gomeran hillside, all light and expansive views with tiny terraces tucked between converging watercourses, then climbing through narrow ravines flanked by dark pine forest. Better still, the route is so simple, description is virtually, though not quite, superfluous. Once on trail, the only places you really need to consult the book are at Wps.3&8.

Note, our original version of this itinerary started at **La Laja**. However, the narrow approach road, very limited parking (just a few spaces west of the transformer tower midway through the settlement), the lack of bus access, and the fact that most people would probably be passing the top of the route in their cars en route to the start, persuaded us to change the starting point to the **Ermita de las Nieves** (for those with cars), and to **Degollada de Peraza** for those approaching by bus. However, if you're staying in **San Sebastián** and have a car, the **La Laja** start is still preferable (always bearing in mind the proviso about limited parking), doing the climb first.

* depending on the option taken. If starting from **La Laja**, add 20-30 minutes

Access (by bus and car): Línea 1 or 3 to **Degollada de Peraza** (Wp.3). If arriving by car, take the lane to the **Ermita Las Nieves** recreation area where there is plenty of parking space (Wp.1).

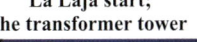

La Laja start;
the transformer tower

Alternative start from La Laja:
From the transformer tower 1km after the village limit sign, take the path to the south, signposted 'Agando 3.6km'. (Wp.18 0M). Turn sharp right after 15 metres at **Casa El Lomito**, then cross a concrete footbridge 50 metres upstream. Climbing steeply, we pass behind house **No.26** and in front of **No.29**, following a stone-and-concrete path. Bearing left away from **No.32** and right below the next, unnumbered house, we come to a pillar signpost indicating 'Degollada de Peraza' to the left and 'Roque Agando' to the right (Wp.17 10M).

Turning right, we pass the last houses of **La Laja** and the junction with the shortcut path (Wp.9 see main text), after which we come to another pillar signpost (Wp.10 15M) where we fork left and resume our steady climb.

For the main featured start, we set off from the **Ermita de las Nieves** *área recreativa* (Wp.1 0M), walking back along the *área recreativa* access road (E) and, shortly before it swings sharp right to descend to the main road, bear left on a stony GR-signposted track (Wp.2 10M).

Ermita de las Nieves at Wp.1

Ignoring two branches on the left, we follow this track across a barren *lomo* with fine views of Tenerife and the south-eastern *barrancos*. The track heads toward a distinct red-and-white transmitter, eventually running into a roughly cobbled path that ends in a mildly vertiginous descent (mitigated by a sturdy handrail) to the road, west of the **Playa de Santiago** turn-off. Just east of the junction is the **Degollada de Peraza** bus-stop, adjacent to **Mirador de la Laja** (Wp.3 25M), the starting point for those without a car.

Our descent to **La Laja** starts immediately next to the bus-stop and **Mirador de la Laja**. Once you're on this path, there's no going wrong. All you have to do is stick to the main cobbled trail and ignore all branch paths including, shortly after starting the descent, the GR for **San Sebastián**, which branches off to our right.

Winding down along the cobbled donkey trail, we pass a small ruin (Wp.4 40M) and a pillar signpost (Wp.5 45M).

The pillar signpost at Wp.5

28 Walk! La Gomera

After several glimpses of individual clusters of houses in **La Laja**, we round a corner onto a level stretch of trail (Wp.6 55M) from where we have clear views of the entire settlement and, up the valley, of the *roques*.

At the end of the level stretch, a series of tight zigzags descend to cross the watercourse of a narrow *barranco* (Wp.7 65M). 100 metres later, we climb over a small rise where we have two options.

Doing the itinerary top-down, we can save 40 metres climbing, by forking left on the rise just before a sharp left bend, taking an unmarked yet distinct path (Wp.8 71M) that serves as a shortcut, traversing the hillside to join the main route up from **La Laja** (Wp.9 78M). If you started from **La Laja**, carry straight on to rejoin the outward route at the first **Roque Agando** pillar signpost (Wp.17).

Turning left at the junction at Wp.9 (N then NW), we come to a pillar signpost after 150 metres (Wp.10). Forking left, we climb steadily, entering one of the many affluents feeding the **Barranco de las Lajas**, the flanks of which are studded with a splendid display of houseleeks. Crossing the watercourse (Wp.11 96M), we climb through mixed pine and eucalyptus, traversing a stubby rise into the next *barranco*, which is itself split into two affluents, crossed via wooden bridges (Wps.12 101M & 13 106M). After a third bridge a few minutes later, we climb steadily to a semi-ruinous but superbly situated forestry worker's hut, the **Casa del Manco** (Wp.14 121M), from where we have fine views of all four *roques*. The path continues up the spur behind the hut (SW), views opening out towards Tenerife and the tall mast marking **Tagamiche**. After a steady climb, we emerge on the road (Wp.15 136M) just east of **Roque Agando**.

Turning left for **Degollada de Peraza**, we follow the GR trail alongside the road for 200 metres. At the end of a stretch of metal-grid walkway, the path becomes a cobbled way, climbing away from the road to a narrow cutting, beyond which we join the end of an old dirt track (Wp.16 151M) leading to the barbecue sheds and picnic tables at the **Ermita de las Nieves**.

4 LOS ROQUES II - THE ULTIMATE GARAJONAY ADVENTURE

As long as you've got a good head for heights, this fabulous walk is not to be missed. Picturesque, adventurous, and varied, it explores one of La Gomera's most unspoiled and peaceful valleys, a verdant haven tucked below the island's most spectacular crags and full of fascinatingly diverse plant life, including (in early Spring) the rare dwarf bugloss (*tajinaste gomero*), a highly endangered plant in the borage family that can grow up to three metres tall and which offers a spectacular display of blue flowers.

Wonderful views (Wps. 11-12)

There is, however, a catch, as there often is with any walk prefaced by such effusive adjectives, and it is to be found in that little phrase 'a good head for heights'. Though most of the itinerary is on clear, signposted paths traversing stable ground, this is a real adventure walk, involving some modest scrambling (though not on the vertiginous stretches) and some pathfinding challenges for those not using GPS (see Wp.12). The pathfinding problems and the vertiginous stretches are on the ascent from **La Laja** to **El Bailadero**. There are several narrow, exposed passages to be negotiated and, though brief and secure underfoot, these will not be to everybody's taste. For details, see Wps.10-14. If in doubt, best opt for the tamer option of Walk 3 for exploring this area, but if you've got the necessary head for heights, this is one of the island's top walks. It's a grand adventure, albeit best not done alone, and certainly not recommended when it's wet.

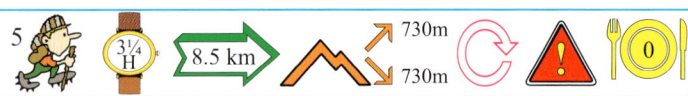

Access by bus and car: the walk starts from the **Cruce de la Zarcita** car-park at the junction of the GM-1 with the **El Cedro/Hermigua** road, which can be reached by the Línea 1 bus between **San Sebastián** and **Valle Gran Rey**.

Cruce de la Zarcita carpark (Wp.1)

From the **Cruce de la Zarcita** car-park (Wp.1 0M), we take the woodland path (SE) signed for 'Los Roques 0.5km, Alto de Garajonay 3.9km'. After about a minute, the long distance **GR131** joins our path from the other side of the road, while we maintain our direction. 30 metres later we bear right at a Y-junction of rocky paths. Log steps take us down to a small *mirador* with fine views over **Roque Agando**, before the path aligns with the main road.

The now cobbled trail comes out of the forest, from where stunning views of **Los Roques** open up in front of us. 100 metres later, we cross the main road to **Mirador de los Roques** (Wp.2 13M).

Stunning views shortly after the start

From the concrete-and-stone platform of the *mirador*, we descend away from the road toward **Roque de Agando**, following a path (occasionally slightly overgrown) down to the roadside **Mirador Roque de Agando** (Wp.3 19M), where there is a memorial to the Gomerans, who died in a forest fire in the nineteen eighties.

We cross the road toward the GR signpost and continue on a path running alongside the crash barrier, shadowing the road, until we reach a signposted junction for 'La Laja' (Wp.4 27M). Turning left, we take a broad trail (initially paved with concrete-and-stones), descending over set of steps (NE).

Wp.4 - our junction to La Laja

The well-maintained trail is very clear all the way to Wp.6; there's no chance of getting lost. After slightly over a kilometre, we pass the abandoned forestry worker's cabin **Casa del Manco** (Wp.5 53M), where there is a 'Limite Parque Nacional' sign.

Our first views of La Laja (Wps. 5-6)

It's worth pausing here to enjoy the splendid views of **Los Roques** that open up 20 metres to the north of the cabin's ruins. After taking in the views, we return to the main trail, passing a reinforced stone dyke across the stream bed. Descending along the streambed, we cross three wooden bridges (views opening up over **La Laja**

shortly after the second) and another dyke before reaching a junction marked by waveposts and a fingerpost (Wp.6 88M).

Bearing left for 'La Laja / El Bailadero', we descend below the hamlet'sfirst houses, where we ignore a fork to the left. Carrying straight on along a concrete walkway between a scattering of houses toward lamp posts, we come to a T-junction (Wp.7 92M), where we bear left to descend to a reservoir.

After crossing a bridge and climbing stone-and-concrete steps, we continue along a terrace, bearing right in front of **Casa del Leon y Graciana**, following the green-and-white waymarks. 30 metres after passing a green house (No.24), we carry straight on at a pedestrian crossroads, passing below house No.26 **Casa Jasmin**, before climbing concrete stairs to emerge on a signposted tarmac lane at the end of **La Laja** (Wp.8 100M).

Turning left, we climb towards 'Presa de Ojila / El Bailadero', the tarmac immediately giving way to concrete. Shortly after passing the top end of a small cargo cable-car, the concrete ends and we continue on a dirt track, ascending gently towards the **Presa de Ojila** dam.

The rough path (Wps.10-11)

The track crosses a watercourse twice before coming to a signpost at the dam (Wp.9 109M).

We stay on the dirt track which narrows then, after crossing a stream feeding the dam, dwindles to a trail. The trail circles above the dam, climbing alongside a pine forest. 40 metres after crossing the stream we reach a T-junction (Wp.10 111M), where we bear right, heading toward a double-headed rock formation, passing it on its left hand side, still following a clear dirt path carpeted with pine needles and neatly lined by lava stones.

32 Walk! La Gomera

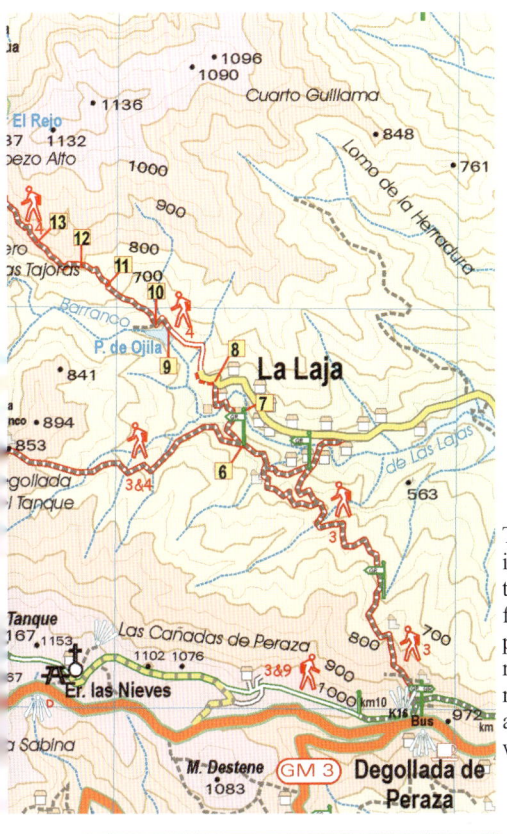

The path becomes increasingly rough as it climbs to another distinct rock formation, which we again pass to its left. Climbing roughly tailored steps, we reach our first exposed stretch, a ledge less than a metre wide, which we negotiate carefully.

Climbing along a ridge line on a trail lined by lava stones, we enjoy amazing views of **Roque de Ojila**.

.. a trail lined by lava stones ..

After crossing a silver water pipe (Wp.11 125M), the path swings onto the right side of the spur line, skirting a pine forest. 120 metres after the pipe, we climb in tight switchbacks back onto the spur, at which point we may briefly need to use our hands.

Back on the ridge line, we pass through a funnel of eroded rock, 50 metres after which (or 200 metres after the water pipe), we need to take care, as we are approaching the trickiest navigation point, a junction of two paths (Wp.12

129M). The more distinct path branches slightly right here and eventually climbs onto the spur. Ignore it. ***This is the wrong path!*** Our itinerary takes the less distinct path to the left, following cairns indicating a way passing to the left of the head of the spur.

Traversing the slope, we reach the corner of a plateau, where the trail swings right, taking us into sparse pine forest below **Mirador del Bailadero**, in which we pass a National Park limits sign (Wp.13 136M). Dipping in and out of the woods, we pass a narrower ledge, then climb steadily on a distinct, boulder-laid path zigzagging up a shrub covered slope. A hundred metres after the National Park limits sign, we come to a red-and-brown rock shelf, to the right of which there is (rare at this altitude) a solitary 'stray' palm.

Tackling another slightly exposed stretch, we climb steadily on a path carved into the rock, after which dirt steps take us back into the forest. Crossing a watercourse, we come to a shelf-plateau viewpoint (Wp.14 144M), from where a fenced antenna is visible above us.

Mirador de Bailadero handrail is visible above

Less than five minutes later, the path runs alongside a small metal fence on our left (look for blue *tajinastes* if you are here in late winter or early spring), at which point we can see the wooden railing of the **Mirador del Bailadero** above us. After a few minutes, we reach the **Mirador del Bailadero** (Wp.15 155M), where there are several notice boards.

Bearing west, we come to the main road (Wp.16 159M). Turning left, we follow the road for sixty metres until a path signposted 'Reventón Oscuro' ducks into the forest and continues slightly below the road. We follow this path (W), ignoring a forest track (blocked by logs and branches) that branches off to the left. After passing below a long retaining wall of the road above us, we reach **Reventón Oscuro** (Wp.17 171M), a junction with the road leading to **El Cedro**.

After a few metres on tarmac, we recover the woodland path and enjoy one of the most beautiful parts of the forest. Twenty minutes later, we come to a splendid natural *mirador* (Wp.18 192M) with great (yet again, but for the last time!) views of **Roque de Ojila** and **Tenerife**, before passing a group of tree stumps in the forest, three minutes from our starting point.

5 PISTA FORESTAL DE MAJONA & PLAYA DE LA CALETA

This lengthy but easy traverse is ideal for inexperienced walkers wanting to try a long distance hike through remote terrain without any pathfinding problems. Which is not to say more experienced walkers won't enjoy it. The views are great and it's a good introduction to the *barranco* architecture of La Gomera, but since most of the itinerary (all if preferred) is on well-stabilised dirt track, the walking itself is not particularly challenging - just a matter of one step after another and considerable stamina!

STOP PRESS! Shortly before going to print, we were alerted to an exciting development on this itinerary. The local authorities have cleared a new path climbing above the main dirt track, opening up the possibility of an alternative circular excursion or a more challenging linear route.

The new path, which is just under five kilometres long and appears to involve an extra 400 metres climbing, branches off to the left 850 metres after Wp.6, rejoining the track between Wps.10 & 11.

It should be stressed that we have not walked this route ourselves, but felt it was such an exciting development that it was worth including it on the new map despite the last minute revisions involved. We look forward to your feedback on the local authorities' work.

*includes La Caleta

If doing the walk in reverse the path at Wp.20 starts next to a mapboard and a series of signposts for 'Playa de la Caleta' and 'Pescante de Hermigua'. Leave the concrete path before it reaches the first house, bearing left on a dirt path marked with a cairn.

Access by bus or car:
The start of the walk is accessible by Línea 2 from **San Sebastián**. Ask for the **Pista** or **Camino Forestal de Majona**. Return from **Hermigua** on Línea 2. Alternatively, you could take a taxi from **San Sebastián**.

From the junction of the dirt track with the GM1 road (Wp.1 0M), we set off on the **Majona** *pista forestal* and, 30 metres after the start of the patterned concrete surfacing, branch left on a cobbled, wayposted path for 'Enchereda', entering the protected area of **Majona**; alternatively, for a longer but less steep start, stay on the

Our start at km7.2 (Wp.1)

Walk! La Gomera 35

track, rejoining the described itinerary at Wp.6.

The path climbs alongside a dry watercourse before veering right (E), curving round a large outcrop of rock on a spur, bringing into view a rock 'bridge' high above us on the **Altos de Utera** ridge.

After climbing along the eastern side of the spur, we zigzag onto its back behind the outcrop of rock (Wp.2 15M). Still favouring the eastern flank of the spur, the path levels out for 100 metres, after which zigzags lead us across a watercourse before returning to the spur, bringing **Roque Agando** into view (Wp.3 30M).

Going left onto the cobbled path

We then wind up onto a narrow pine fringed pass (Wp.4 35M), 150 metres west of the 'bridge', at which point we can see Tenerife, the *pista forestal*, and the first of the three ravines crossed on this itinerary, **Barranco de Palopique**.

Turning left, we follow a good dirt path along the northern side of the **Utera** ridge, passing the first of the red-and-white waymarks that accompany us for the remainder of our route. The path runs parallel to the *pista forestal*, cutting through a rock pass on a spur (Wp.5 45M) from where we see **Enchereda** farm, famed for its goat cheese, though the only livestock we saw were a handful of disconsolate looking pigs!

A gentle, slightly overgrown descent brings us back to the dirt track (Wp.6 55M), where we again bear left. We follow this track for nearly two hours until the junction at Wp.13. There is no risk of straying off trail, so the following notes are merely for timekeeping.

Strolling through finely sculpted, immensely peaceful countryside, we pass a white forestry house or *casa forestal* (first seen from Wp.4) (Wp.7 85M) and climb gently across the rise into the second ravine, **Barranco de Gallon**.

36 Walk! La Gomera

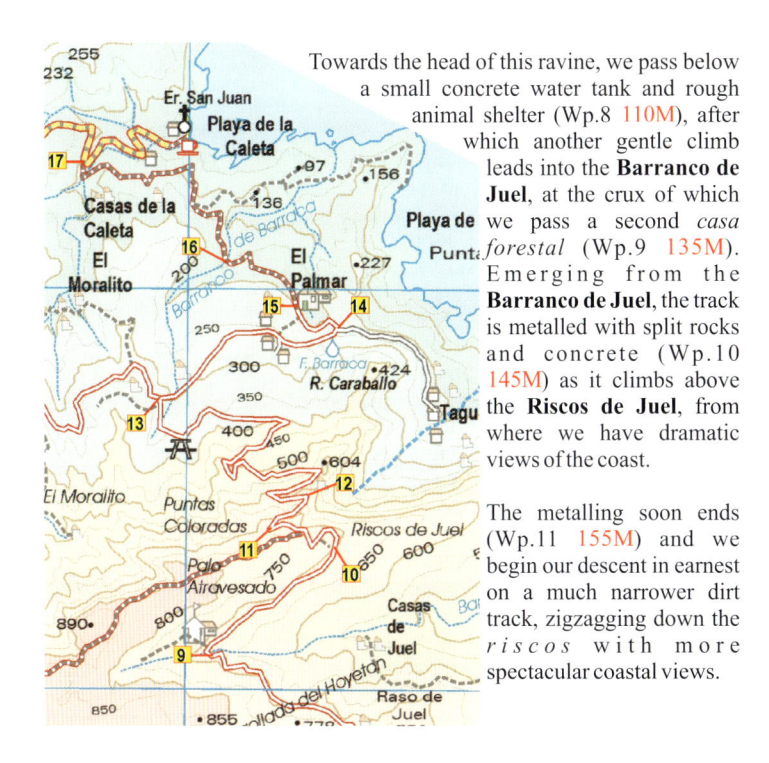

Towards the head of this ravine, we pass below a small concrete water tank and rough animal shelter (Wp.8 110M), after which another gentle climb leads into the **Barranco de Juel**, at the crux of which we pass a second *casa forestal* (Wp.9 135M). Emerging from the **Barranco de Juel**, the track is metalled with split rocks and concrete (Wp.10 145M) as it climbs above the **Riscos de Juel**, from where we have dramatic views of the coast.

The metalling soon ends (Wp.11 155M) and we begin our descent in earnest on a much narrower dirt track, zigzagging down the *riscos* with more spectacular coastal views.

After passing a concrete bend (Wp.12 160M), the zigzags become so tight they almost touch save for the 50 metre drops in between.

We then pass a small abandoned cabin, the only shelter on this route, after which longer, gentler descents, first west, then north-east, then west, bring us down past a small spring/picnic area to the junction with the main **Hermigua-Taguluche** dirt track (Wp.13 190M). If you're feeling weary, turn left here and follow the dirt track to the tarmac lane at Wp.19. If motivated by powerful thirst, keen hunger, a strong wish to swim, or simply an invincible desire always to do more, turn right for **Playa de la Caleta** – an extra 200-metre descent and ascent. The track passes between the rusting remains of a Morris Minor and a rapidly declining farmhouse, after which we pass three more houses of varying size and health.

El Palmar

150 metres after **Fuente de la Berraca**, we turn sharp left between red posts (Wp.14 210M) and descend to the scruffy, but tremendously friendly **El Palmar** farm, where the dirt track ends (Wp.15 215M) at a rock with 'La Caleta' painted on it. From the farm, a faint path, initially running alongside a green fence and dotted with

Walk! La Gomera 37

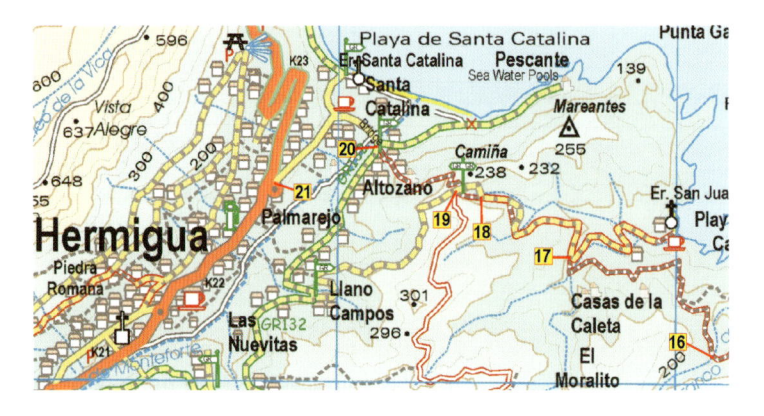

cairns throughout, winds down through rocks to cross a footbridge in the **Barranco de la Barraca** (Wp.16 225M). A clear, slightly vertiginous path, then crosses two 'horns' at the tip of a ridge, from the second of which we can see the beach.

La Caleta beach

Steps descend from the second horn onto a broad but still intermittently vertiginous path up the **Caleta** valley, which we eventually cross behind cultivated terraces before climbing onto a tarmac lane (Wp.17 245M) ten minutes from the beach. En route to the beach, we pass the first of two shortcut paths, this one following a narrow eroded ridge.

Swimming is safe at **La Caleta** WHEN THE SEA IS CALM and the eating is good at the little bar, which serves the usual Canarian specialties plus deliciously refreshing fresh juices. The only drawback to this diversion is that we now have a long slog up the new tarmac lane.

Toiling up the lane, the first shortcut serves no great purpose, but the second (Wp.18 280M) is useful, rejoining the lane (Wp.19 285M) just below the junction with the **Taguluche** track. Crossing the lane, we take a clear, cairn-marked path winding down an exposed spur. After passing a small empty house and an older ruin, we descend behind the northernmost inhabited houses of **Altozano** onto a concrete path leading to the road (Wp.20 300M).

Crossing the bridge over the **Monteforte** watercourse, we pass the **Apartamentos Playa**, which overlook banana plantations. After a left bend, we pass the **Bar/Restaurante El Piloto** and **El Faro** before climbing to the main road (Wp.21 315M). The nearest bus stop is 200 metres to the southwest of the roundabout at Wp.21 on the main road toward **Hermigua**. If you're going into the town centre for refreshments, you'll find several other bus-stops, but bear in mind there is a one-way system in operation.

THE SUNDRENCHED SOUTH

The abandoned hamlet of Contreras in the south

After zig-zagging up from **San Sebastián**, our first view of the south leaves an indelible impression. Massive ravines (*barrancos*) divided by broad backed ridges (*lomos*) sweep down to the ocean, providing a breathtaking spectacle for seekers of the sublime, one that is only marginally more impressive than the network of abandoned terraces left over from the distant days when the region was intensively farmed. After stopping off at the bar at the **Degollada de Peraza** or the nearby **Mirador de La Laja** to take in the scale of the '*barranco* architecture', we head down toward **Playa Santiago**, following a modern road that makes for a marked contrast with the area's small settlements and sun bleached landscapes. Only when we reach the villas and golf courses of the **Don Thomas** development and the impressive **Jardín Tecina Hotel** (worth trying the lift if you get a chance) do we begin to understand quite how dramatically the local economy has changed in the last fifty years.

Modern tourism, in the form of the **Jardín Tecina Hotel** and the **Balcón de Santa Ana**, brackets the traditional *hostals* and the apartment accommodation of **Playa Santiago** and **Laguna de Santiago,** but the traffic system and the decline of the once busy fishing port mean that these resorts remain relatively tranquil, while the mighty **Benchijigua** and **Guarimiar** *barrancos* inland are home to some of La Gomera's most impressive walking routes, the picturesque settlements a direct contrast to the coastal development.

Climbing past **La Trinchera**, we pass under the shadow of the little-used airport to zig-zag up to the regional capital of **Alajeró**. Once suffering near terminal decline the town has been regenerated by returning emigrés building new villas and nowadays three good bar/restaurants attest to its new found affluence. A stroll south to the **Ermita de San Isidor** on **Calvario** is a must to gaze out over the dramatic landscape that was once back-breakingly farmed. Sleepy, or fast asleep, most of the year, the town is transformed by the annual Fiesta de Buen Paso, renowned as La Gomera's noisiest fiesta.

Almost opposite the turning to the cliff-side village of **Imada** is the Drago, La Gomera's only wild 'Dragon' tree, an easy stroll from the road. Once left to its own devices, the Drago is now fenced off to protect it from souvenir hunters, and has its own manicured path and parking area. The sleepy hamlet of **Igualero**, nestling below the **Garajonay** peak, completes the southern landscapes with a spectacular view from its *ermita*.

SOUTHERN WALKS LOCATOR MAPS

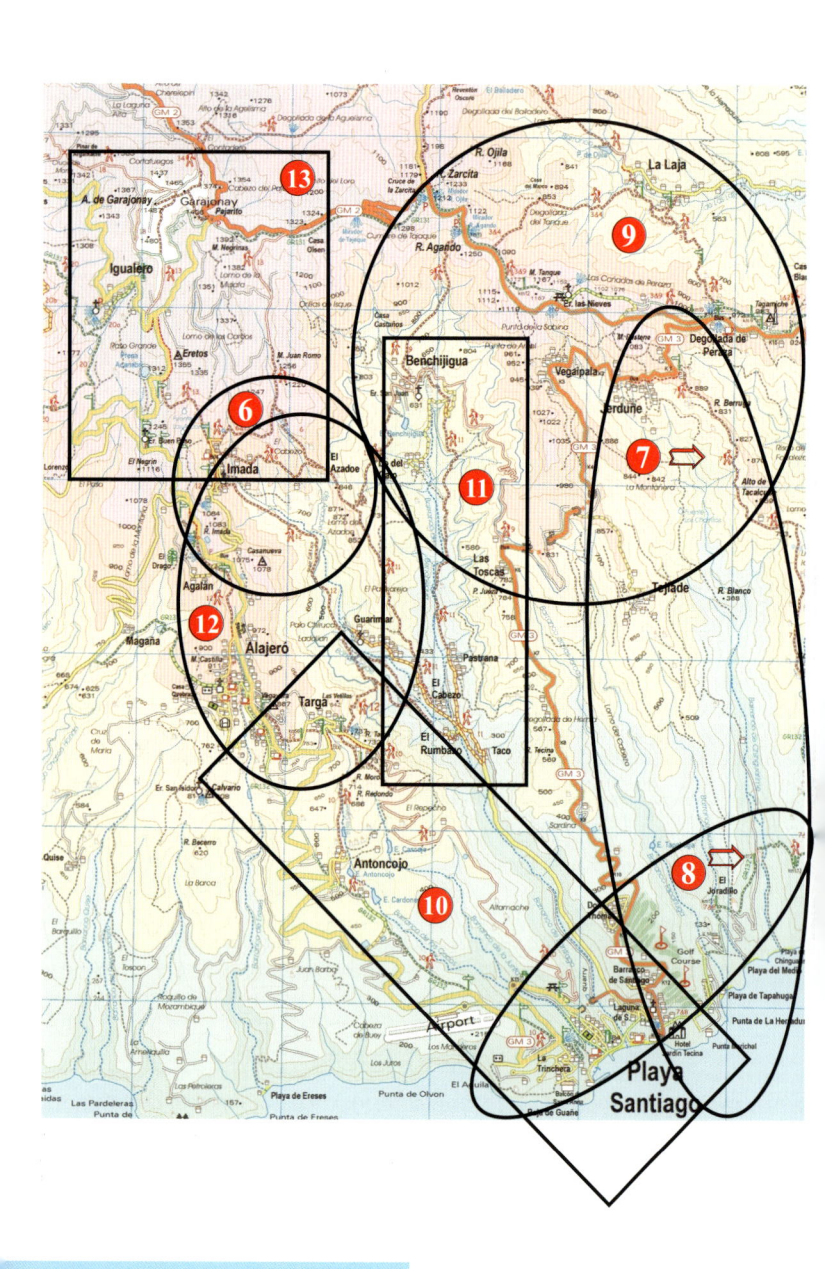

40 Walk! La Gomera

SOUTHERN WALKS LOCATOR MAPS

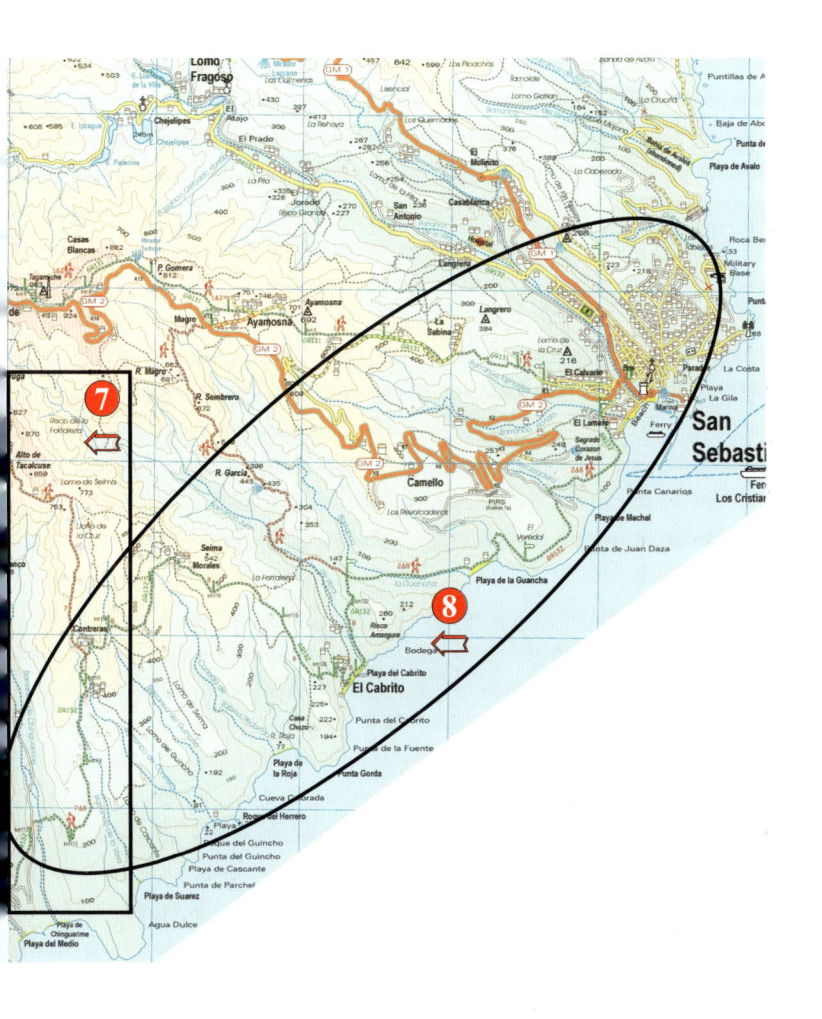

Walk! La Gomera 41

6 BARRANCO & LOMO DE AZADOE

A short walk for those who want to explore this wild corner of the island without any huge climbs or alarming cliff face paths. The **Lomo de Azadoe** pass is also included as a link to walks in the **Barranco de Benchijigua**.

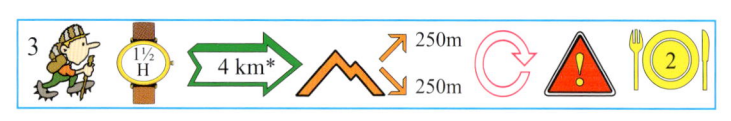

3 | 1½ H | 4 km* | 250m / 250m | ↻ | ⚠ | 2

Access by bus:
Línea 3 to **Imada** junction.

Access by car:
Parking in **Imada** is limited so it's better to start early if arriving by car. Parking spaces are available 50m south-east of the **Bar-Cafetería Arcilia**.

Starting from the bus stop in front of the **Bar-Cafetería Arcilia** (Wp.1 0M), we take the concrete path to the right of the bus-stop (currently marked by an old signpost for 'Benchijigua / Roque Agando'), which runs alongside a painted adobe garage with decorative stones embedded in its walls. Turning left at a T-junction after 40 metres, we join a cobbled path leading out of the village. Descending towards palms and ignoring a branch to the right (heading towards a distant transformer tower), we stay on the main paved path, crossing the reddish rocks of an affluent to the **Azadoe**.

Fine views of the *barrancos*

The paved way forks right towards houses, while we continue straight on, following a natural path over steps, some carved directly into the rock, climbing behind a small house to pass in front of a flat-roofed bungalow (Wp.2 10M), from where we have our first excellent views

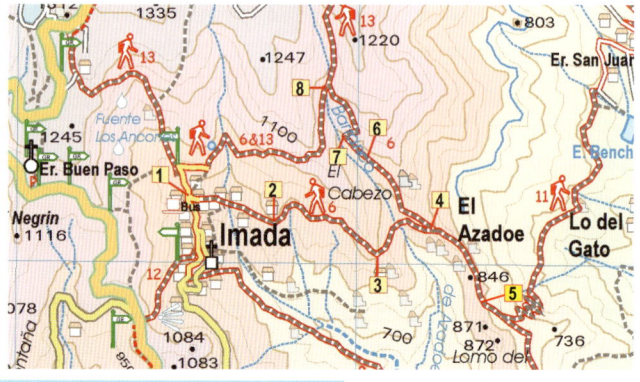

42 Walk! La Gomera

down the **Barrancos de Guarimiar** and **Santiago** to **Jardín Tecina**.

Sticking to the broader, higher traces, we follow the path round the nose of a spur, passing above an abandoned house and older ruins, onto a small platform from where we see both the **Barranco and Lomo de Azadoe** (Wp.3 20M). We then wind downwards, crossing the *barranco* onto an initially level path that soon climbs above a terrace to a Y-junction (Wp.4 30M).

To link up with Walk 11
We stay on the main right hand branch, passing several ruins before crossing the **Lomo de Azadoe** pass (Wp.5 35M), 100 metres above Wp.8 of Walk 11.

For a short circular walk
We bear left at the Y-junction, climbing to two ruins, where the path swings left on a broader, rockier way. The climb, steady at first, gradually becomes gentler then levels off altogether, as we go deeper into the palm fringed ravine, soon glimpsing a small stand of pine; way above us but only a little way above the point we're climbing to! Climbing again, we pass through a riotous mix of prickly pear, agave, wax-plants, house-leeks, bracken, almonds, palms and figs, with the odd vine threaded in between them.

The path levels off again briefly, running below a high retaining wall, before climbing gently and veering right (Wp.6 45M not counting Wp.5) in front of a fig tree, bearing away from the watercourse briefly before coming back to run alongside it for a steadier, partially paved climb. We then veer right again, passing a 'Paisaje Protegido Orone' signpost (Wp.7 50M). Climbing southeast, we have more good views of the *barrancos* below us, before resuming our north-westerly ascent. Climbing between terraces, we return to the watercourse above a dry waterfall (Wp.8 65M), joining the route of Walk 13 at Wp.4.

Walk 13 continues up the watercourse, but we turn left, crossing the watercourse to follow the start of Walk 13 back to the village. Heading south-south west (SSW) and passing one very slightly vertiginous stretch above the falls, we round a small spur and see **Imada**. A straightforward descent on an intermittently paved and stepped trail brings us back across the affluent crossed at the start of the walk, this time below an attractive waterfall. We then join the end of the village access road, which we follow back to our starting point.

7 JERDUÑE - JARDÍN TECINA

A dramatic ravine, remote countryside accessible only on foot, and a pristine pebble beach, make this essential walking for anyone wanting to get to know La Gomera. Not recommended in hot weather. There is one brief stretch of ledge path that is slightly vertiginous, though broad enough to be manageable for most walkers.

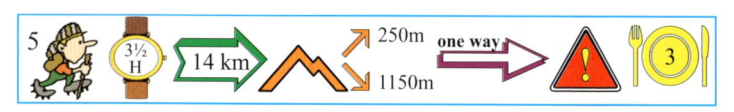

5 | 3½H | 14 km | 250m / 1150m | one way | ⚠ | 3

Access by bus:
Línea 3 for **Jerduñe**, return from **Hotel Jardín Tecina** in **Playa de Santiago**. Alternatively, take bus Línea 1 to the bar at **Degollada de Peraza** then walk along the main road west for 100 metres to the major junction and descend along the GM-3 road for 1 km to the start of the itinerary.

Access by car:
Park near **Hotel Jardín Tecina**, then bus to **Jerduñe**.

A few metres from the Km1 marker of the GM-3 road, 400 metres (direction **San Sebastián**) east of **Jerduñe** bus-stop, our itinerary starts on a dirt track (Wp.1 4M), signposted 'Ruta 25: Tecina 11.4km'.

Wp.1 at the signpost

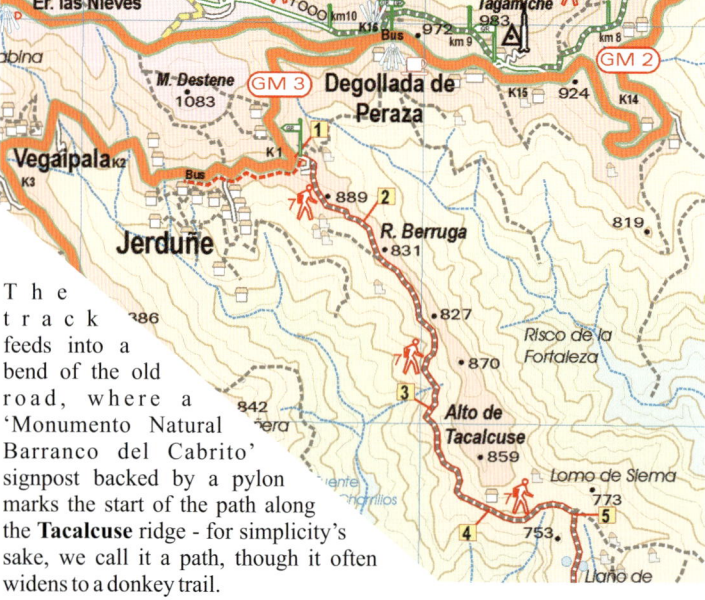

The track feeds into a bend of the old road, where a 'Monumento Natural Barranco del Cabrito' signpost backed by a pylon marks the start of the path along the **Tacalcuse** ridge - for simplicity's sake, we call it a path, though it often widens to a donkey trail.

44 Walk! La Gomera

The ruined hamlet visible from Wp.2

Descending along the western flank of the ridge with fine views over the **Barranco de Chinguarime**, we cross a grassy pass (Wp.2 20M) above a ruined hamlet, after which tiny terraces and cabins perched in improbable crevices on the far side of the ravine attest to the historical poverty of La Gomera - you really had to be desperate to shore up land in some of these places.

Staying west of the ridge and ignoring a very faint path branching right, we descend along the main trail below the cliffs of **Alto de Tacalcuse**.

Approaching the **Alto de Tacalcuse**, the path seems to disappear above crags riddled with half caves. In fact, it narrows to enter the first of three brief but steep climbs (Wp.3 40M) linked by a broad slightly vertiginous ledge below cliffs so roughly fragmented they resemble dry-stone walling. After the third climb, we see the golf-course/hotel complex above **Playa Santiago** and the cliffs behind **Llano de la Cruz**. Continuing in an easterly direction, we cross a broad sloping sheet of rock with steps carved into its lower end, after which we wind between boulders, passing a cabin built into the overhanging cliffs (Wp.4 55M). We then climb across terraces to a Y-junction (Wp.5 65M). The broader trail continues (SE) to **El Cabrito**, but we turn right (S) to cross **Llano de la Cruz** on a minor but clear and level path flanked by terrace walls.

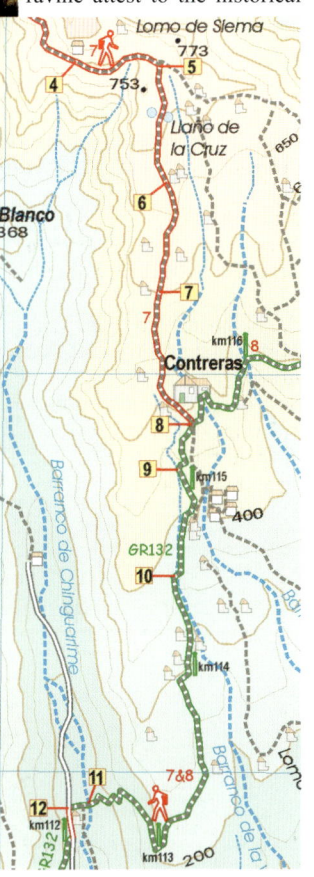

After passing between a buried reservoir and two natural watering holes, we descend across a wide, open sweep of terraces. Ignoring minor dirt paths along the terraces, we stick to the main rocky trail defined by crumbling walls, passing to the right of two ruins (Wp.6 75M), invisible from above but the first of many on this route. The path gets clearer, descending between two more ruins and approaching another solitary ruin, bringing into view the roofs and two palm trees of **Contreras**, until recently a working farm. Going to the left of the solitary ruin (Wp.7 85M) and the right of crags immediately behind the

Walk! La Gomera   45

abandoned farmstead of **Contreras**, we pass between the main house, an impressive two-storey building, and the lowest ruined outbuilding, where we join the red-and-white GR waymarked route between **San Sebastián** and **Playa Santiago** (Wp.8 95M).

Turning right, we descend a narrow, winding path, crossing (Wp.9 100M) then re-crossing one of the watercourses that subsequently carve out the **Barranco de la Vasa**. After following the watercourse for a while, we climb a small rise, where we ignore a branch path to a cluster of houses on the eastern side of the main watercourse. Sticking to the main path, we descend past two small abandoned farm buildings. After re-crossing the watercourse (Wp.10 110M) we follow its right bank as it broadens and deepens into **Barranco de la Vasa**. Maintaining direction (S) across a slab of bare rock, we pass two more ruins before running alongside (and briefly in) a shallow watershed.

Wp.11 - approaching the banana plantation

Passing one more ruin, we bear south-west, traversing the brow of a hill, after which we have a gentle then steady descent into the **Barranco de Chinguarime** (Wp.11 145M). Here we cross the riverbed and join a dirt track that defines the boundaries of a banana plantation.

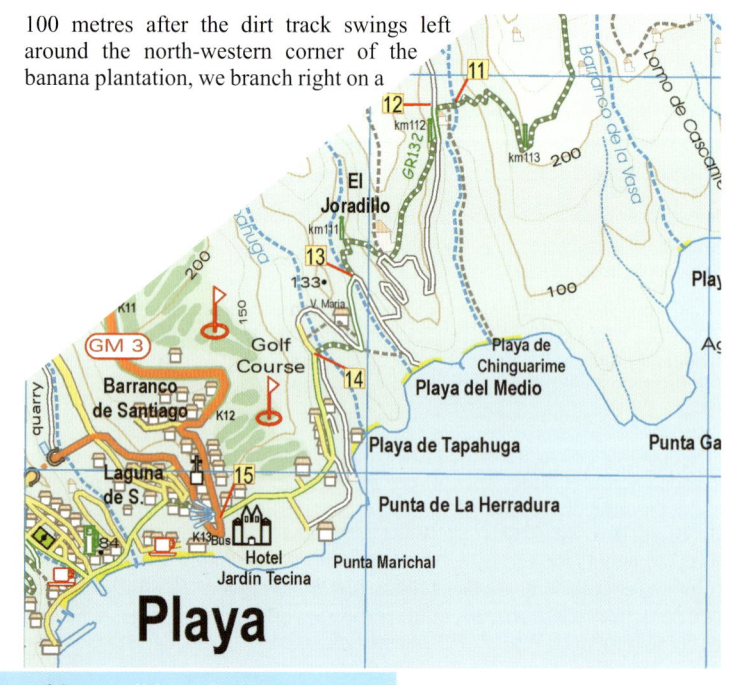

100 metres after the dirt track swings left around the north-western corner of the banana plantation, we branch right on a

46 Walk! La Gomera

waymarked path (Wp.12 150M), every bit as strenuous as it looks from the far side, climbing to pass in front of the lowest **Joradillo** farm-building, now abandoned, to a trail junction. We ignore the first path to the right for 'Tejiade/Las Nieves' and bear right immediately after this one on a clear path (marked 'Tecina/Playa Santiago') descending into the **Barranco Biquillo**.

Joining a tarmac lane (Wp.13 170M) in the *barranco*, it's a question of different strokes for different folks: those who will do anything for a dip, bear left for **Playa del Medio**; those for whom the very thought of swimming at this stage of a walk is enough to have them swooning into their rucksacks, bear right.

If you descend to the beach (safe swimming when calm), return to Wp.13 by the same route to resume the full walk.

Covered canal on the ridge line

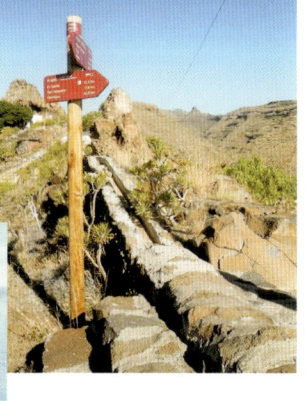

From Wp.13, we bear right on the tarmac lane then right again 250 metres later on a path traversing a ridge. The path crosses a covered canal on top of the ridgeline and swings left, crossing the tarmac lane and descending to the reinforced riverbed of **Barranco de Tapahuga**. Crossing the broad riverbed, we rejoin the tarmac at a Y-junction of lanes (Wp.14 190M).

There is another bathing option here at **Playa de Tapahuga**, descending sharp left towards a dull yellow bungalow on the beach.

Playa de Tapahuga

Otherwise, we take the sidewalk up the second lane to the left, which we follow for half a kilometre until it swings right and levels out to pass below a wooden bridge connecting two parts of the **Hotel Jardín Tecina** golf course. Following the lane between lush gardens and the golf course, we eventually stroll past the hotel entrance gate/booth to the main road (Wp.15 205M), where there's a phone booth, mailbox, taxi stand, bus-stop and the **Restaurante Tagoror**.

If you want to descend to the seafront and downtown **Playa Santiago**, take the stepped shortcut starting 100 metres down the road below the bus stop. Bear left at the La Laguna minimarket and follow the road that leads into town.

Walk! La Gomera 47

8 PLAYA SANTIAGO - SAN SEBASTIÁN

This splendid yet demanding coastal walk is a roller-coaster outing, its constant ups and downs dipping in and out of the enchanting beaches dotting the sun-drenched southern slopes of the island and visiting some of the region's long abandoned but sublimely picturesque hamlets, many of which resemble stage sets from the Wild West.

The highlight of a walk not short of highlights is the delightful hotel hamlet of **El Cabrito**, a tranquil oasis nestling in a ravine accessible only by boat and on foot, making it a favourite with discerning holidaymakers determined to really get away from it all.

If you don't fancy the full itinerary, the walk to **Playa del Medio** (see Wp.5) is a pleasant alternative.

| 5 | 6¼ H | 20 km | 1060m / 1060m | one way | 4* |

* Meals are only available at the start and end of the route. En route, we can get juices, ice-cream and free water at **El Cabrito**, but meals there are only for hotel guests.

Playa Santiago square on the seafront

Access by bus:
Línea 3 from **San Sebastián** to **Playa Santiago**. To save yourself a few hundred metres, you can also get off at **Hotel Jardín Tecina**. If arriving in **Playa Santiago** by car, parking is possible near the T-junction above the bus stop (Wp.3) or pretty much anywhere in town, notably along the seafront.

Starting beside the small podium in **Playa Santiago**'s seafront square (Wp.1 0M), we follow **Avenida Marítima** east, passing in front of the Tourism Office. At a mapboard for the 'Camino Natural Costas de la Gomera', the road leaves the seafront and heads out of town. We stay on the orchard lined road until the La Laguna mini-market (Wp.2 14M), in front of which we bear right on broad stairs between white and crimson houses. A swift climb along a cobbled walkway brings us back onto a road, on which we bear right to stroll along the sidewalk.

After passing a bus stop in a bend of the road (the alternative starting point), from where we can already see the lush garden of **Hotel Jardín Tecina**, we reach a T-junction (Wp.3 22M) opposite a yellow mailbox (the end of Walk 7).

Bearing right, following signs for 'Playa Tapahuga/En Medio/Chinguarime', we pass the hotel car park then skirt the tennis courts and golf course, bringing into view a dull yellow bungalow behind **Playa Tapahuga**. Brace yourselves! We are about to embark on the roller-coaster. The lane we have been following

Looking back, shortly before Wp.3

swings left (N) and drops into the bed of a *barranco*. Immediately after a branch lane forking off to the left in a sharp right U-bend, we leave the tarmac and take a broad, wayposted trail that begins with a couple of shallow steps (Wp.4 42M).

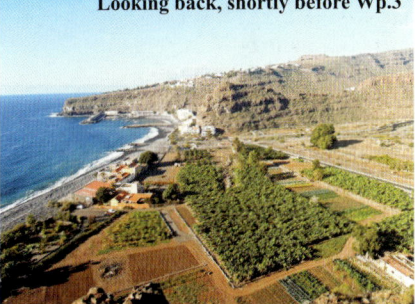

The trail crosses a reinforced river bed and starts to climb, soon crossing the tarmac lane, then a covered canal on a crest, before rejoining the lane. Heading inland (N), we follow the lane for 250 metres, until it swings right to descend to **Playa del Medio**, at which point we take the neatly cobbled trail to the left (Wp.5 55M). Climbing again, we emerge at a wayposted junction on a broad spur of **El Joradillo** (Wp.6 66M) in sight of some ruins. The lane feeds in from our right and a trail to the left climbs to **Tejiade**, but we continue along the right hand side of the ruins, soon bringing into view what will rapidly become the defining experience of this itinerary - our next ravine!

Descending onto a dirt track next to a banana plantation, we bear left and then right in front of a fenced compound.

On this walk, what goes down, must go up, and at the north-eastern corner of the plantation (Wp.7 83M) we carry straight on, taking a trail up a steep escarpment for another stiff climb.

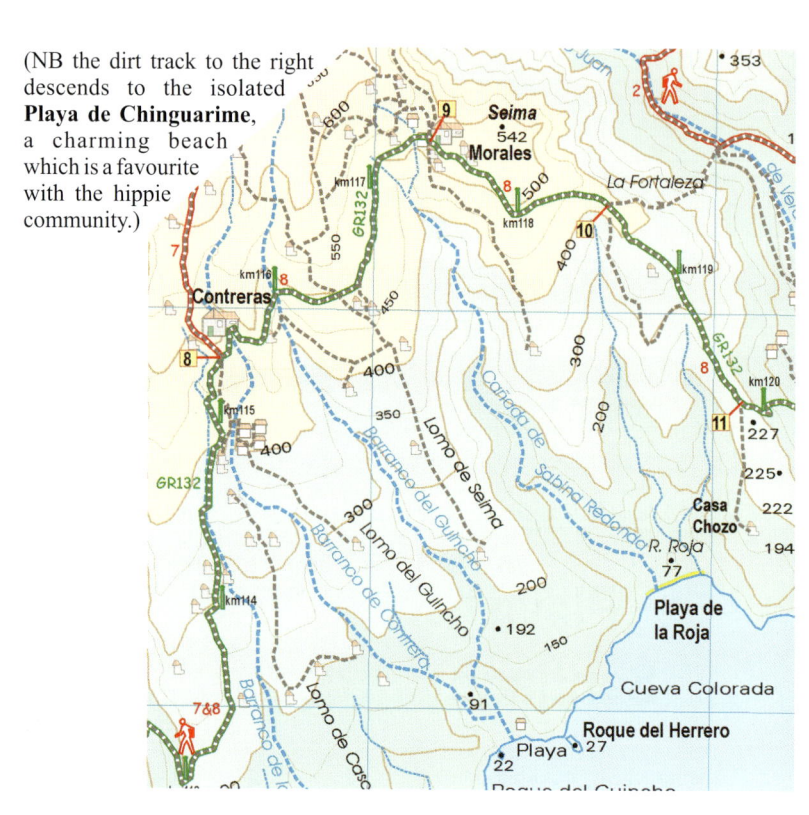

(NB the dirt track to the right descends to the isolated **Playa de Chinguarime**, a charming beach which is a favourite with the hippie community.)

A steady to steep climb brings us to a plateau and the km.113 marker of the **GR132**. Continuing along abandoned terraces now dominated by *tabaiba* groves, we pass a few ruins, our general direction being defined by two electricity pylons. The trail passes between the pylons, beyond and above which we can see the palm grove and houses of the **Contreras** hamlet.

Contreras, junction of trails at Wp.8

Our trail climbs gently along a watercourse, eventually crossing it to follow the opposite bank. Swinging around two solitary palms, our path finally brings us to a junction of trails at **Contreras** (Wp.8 148M), a once prosperous hamlet that flourished in the distant days when these slopes produced abundant cereal crops.

Walk 7 feeds in from the left here, but we continue to the right, passing below the balcony of an impressive two-storey house that could have come straight out of a Wild West film. Crossing minor *barrancos*, we traverse abandoned terraces, soon catching glimpses of the GM-1 road far up on the slope. Passing a big white paint-spattered boulder, we see **Morales** (aka **Seima**), another abandoned farming hamlet. After climbing below several ruins backed by jagged crags, we finally reach the trail junction at **Morales** (Wp.9 185M), where we turn right, taking the path between the ruins (SE).

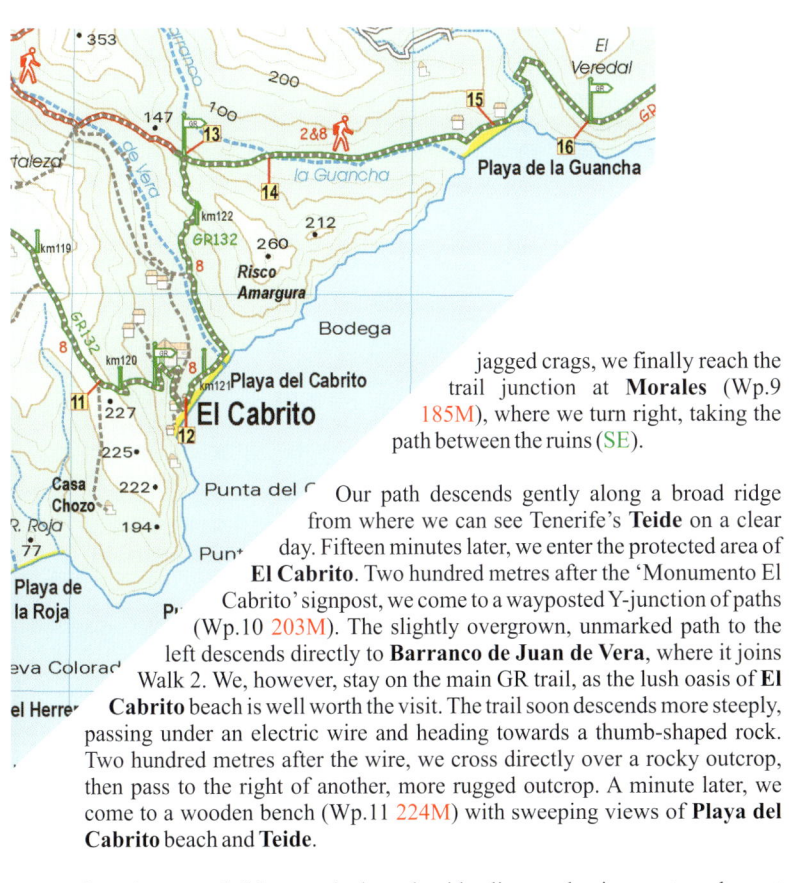

Our path descends gently along a broad ridge from where we can see Tenerife's **Teide** on a clear day. Fifteen minutes later, we enter the protected area of **El Cabrito**. Two hundred metres after the 'Monumento El Cabrito' signpost, we come to a wayposted Y-junction of paths (Wp.10 203M). The slightly overgrown, unmarked path to the left descends directly to **Barranco de Juan de Vera**, where it joins Walk 2. We, however, stay on the main GR trail, as the lush oasis of **El Cabrito** beach is well worth the visit. The trail soon descends more steeply, passing under an electric wire and heading towards a thumb-shaped rock. Two hundred metres after the wire, we cross directly over a rocky outcrop, then pass to the right of another, more rugged outcrop. A minute later, we come to a wooden bench (Wp.11 224M) with sweeping views of **Playa del Cabrito** beach and **Teide**.

Ignoring a much fainter path along the ridge line, we begin our steep descent on a well-maintained trail toward the beach oasis (E), enjoying consistently good views throughout. Well graded switchbacks bring us to the first house, where we turn sharp right before coming to a walkway that frames the shady, verdant maize of **El Cabrito**. Ignoring the confusing 'No pedestrians' sign (this is actually a right of way, though most of the area behind us is private property, so stick to the official trails to avoid disturbing the hotel's guests), we follow the concrete walkway, which is protected from rockfalls by wire netting.

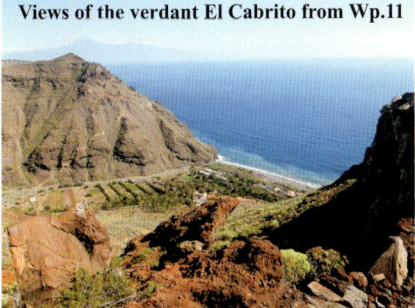

Views of the verdant El Cabrito from Wp.11

Passing a mapboard, we come to the pebbly **Playa del Cabrito** near its southern end, where we bear north-east along the beach to reach the welcoming picnic area (Wp.12 247M). We're in sight of the hotel reception, where we can fill up our water bottles from a tap at the side of a restaurant, or enjoy some basic refreshments.

Walk! La Gomera

From the picnic area, we continue along the beach (NE), passing the km.121 marker of the **GR132**, until the dirt track swings inland, passing vegetable plots. Five minutes after leaving the beach, we bear right on a trail that first crosses a low, sturdy wall marked with a signpost, then an adjacent streambed before skirting below a cliff. Passing a 'Monumento Natural Barranco del Cabrito' signpost, we climb out of the ravine.

After a series of tight switchbacks, the path levels out, passing a fork on the right heading toward a pylon on the ridge. Passing under a telephone wire, we reach a signposted junction at a saddle (Wp.13 277M), where there's a bench and views into the next ravine and **Playa de la Guancha**. This is where we join Walk 2, which we follow from Wp.11 to **San Sebastián**.

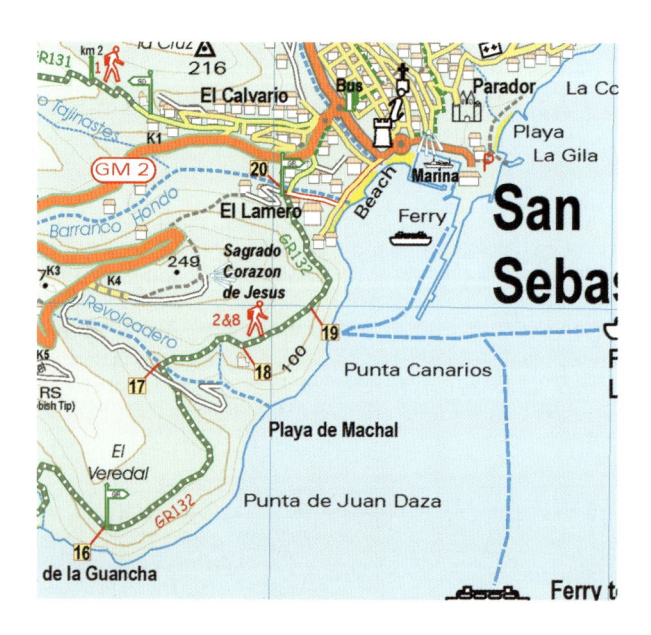

Wp.13, where we join Walk 2

9 LAS TOSCAS - DEGOLLADA DE PERAZA

Like a tour of the entire island in miniature, this walk encompasses the four key features that characterise the La Gomeran landscape: a *barranco*, a hamlet, a *roque* and an *ermita*. It's also a useful linking route for piecing together longer itineraries. See Walks 1, 2, and 11 for possible extensions. Shorter versions on a linear trail are obviously very much at each walker's discretion, but an obvious option would be **Benchijigua** to **Roque Agando**.

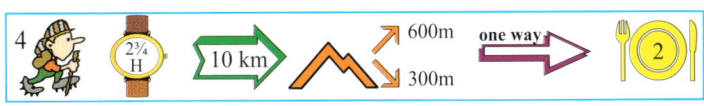

Access by bus: Línea 3 to **Las Toscas**, 1 or 3 from **Degollada de Peraza**.

From **Las Toscas** bus stop, which is situated in a bend of the road, 230 metres west of the southernmost tunnel on the GM2, we take the *pista forestal* signed for 'Benchijigua/Imada' (Wp.1 0M) below a dull orange house faced with decorative stones. The dirt track is driveable, but sufficiently dramatic to be worth walking.

Our start at Las Toscas

After a long steady descent with constantly unfolding views over the **Barranco de Benchijigua,** we pass the tarmac lane down to **Lo del Gato** (Wp.2 45M). Continuing on the dirt track through **Benchijigua**, we bear right at a Y-junction, 150 metres after which we turn sharp right for 'Agando' on a minor track behind a long low yellow building identifiable by a ceramic 'Benchijigua' nameplate (Wp.3 55M). When the track splits in three, we take the right-hand branch, a broad walking trail that swings east after 75 metres, climbing past a small ruin concealing a couple of water tanks.

The trail becomes increasingly rocky as it winds up a wide ridge behind the ruin, rapidly gaining height before skirting to the right of a small, roughly conical peak and heading towards the distinctive bulk of **Roque Agando** (NE).

Fine views of Roque Agando between Wps. 3-4

Walk! La Gomera 53

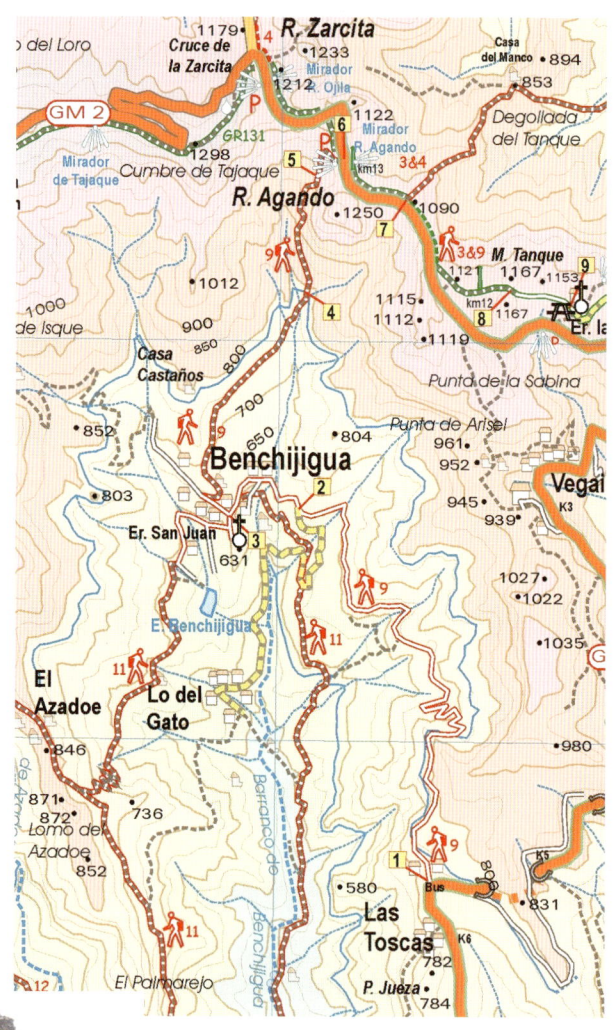

After a steady climb, the trail levels out amid immense agave-scapes before dipping slightly and narrowing to a path as it approaches then climbs to cross the **Canal de Benchijigua** (Wp.4 85M).

After the canal, a clear but narrow path climbs to the left of **Roque Agando**, passing through dense, remarkably varied vegetation. The path gradually broadens, crossing intermittent paving and stone steps, as scruffy heath trees gradually replace the more varied flora.

Mirador de Roque Agando (Wp.6)

54 Walk! La Gomera

Our way then levels out very briefly, crossing a canalized watercourse (Wp.5 110M) just below a pine forest, after which the climb steepens for the final haul up to the **Mirador de Roque Agando** (Wp.6 120M), where there's a memorial to those killed by a forest fire in 1984.

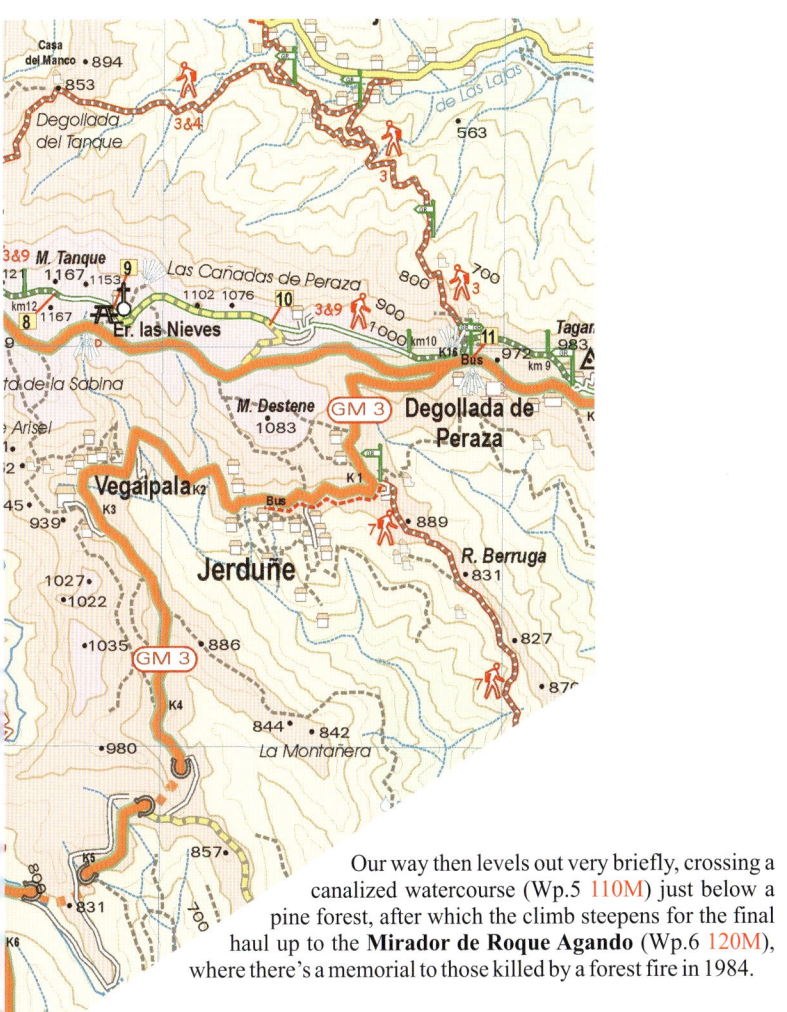

Approaching our junction with Walk 3

Crossing the road and bearing right at a mapboard, we take the path (E) alongside the road beyond the crash barrier, joining Walk 3 at Wp.15 a little over 350 metres later at a junction signposted 'La Laja'.

We follow Walk 3 (Wps.15-16 then Wps.1-3) to the **Degollada de Peraza** bus-stop, beyond which there's a bar/restaurant, the terrace of which has a splendid view.

Walk! La Gomera 55

10 PLAYA SANTIAGO - TARGA

If you're looking for pristine nature, this is not the walk for you. The land adjacent to **Playa Santiago** and the airport is badly degraded and can only disappoint anyone hoping to experience something lush and unspoiled. If, on the other hand, you want a big, uncomplicated climb with good views and a little off-path adventure half way round, then this circuit has a lot to recommend it. Don't even think about it in hot weather though the word 'toast' comes to mind.

Our new version of this itinerary doesn't actually visit **Targa** but merely climbs adjacent to it, since sadly the **Las Palmeras Restaurante** in **Targa** has now closed. However, we are compensated for this loss by a useful little shortcut path cutting some of the climbing involved in the original version of the walk.

| 4 | 4H | 15 km | 670m / 670m | ↻ | 3 |

Our start at Wp.1

Access by bus: Línea 3

Access by car: Park on **Playa Santiago** seafront.

From **Playa Santiago** seafront, we cross the square between **Caja Canarias bank** and **Bodegón del Mar** (Wp.1 0M) to the other side of the podium, where we join a sidewalk on the eastern side of the reinforced river bed.

We follow the sidewalk along the river bed passing the **Centro de Salud**, a football ground and school playgrounds after which the sidewalk ends and we continue along the river bed on a dirt track.

Just before Wp.2; the canalisation channel

After 180 metres, halfway along which we pass a massive road embankment, we turn right to climb along a concrete canalisation channel (which carries a pipe in its upper reaches), onto the **Alajeró** road, within sight of a sign saying 'Aeropuerto 3'.

Just before the 'Aeropuerto 3' sign (Wp.2 15M), which is backed by a rest area, we take a steep track (asphalted for the first zig and zag, after which the tarmac gives way to dirt) signposted 'Targa 7.4km'. This is the old 'road' to **Targa**, which we follow for the outward leg of our itinerary.

There are numerous shortcuts en route, but they're all rough and obscure, so we suggest sticking to the main track. Otherwise the ascent is straightforward; all you really need to know is that the tall red-and-white mast seen on the horizon after twenty-five minutes of climbing, lies shortly beyond the point where we leave this track.

The track climbs past a water tank tucked in a quarry, then winds up the ridge dividing the **Barrancos de la Junta** and **Santiago**, to a point dominating both sides of **Playa Santiago** (Wp.3 35M). The views improve steadily as we climb past a path leading to a ruin on our right (Wp.4 60M), at which point we can see **Antoncojo** (our return route) to the north-west.

We then pass the entrance to a second ruin and climb to a large dry reservoir (Wp.5 80M), after which the track bears west towards **Antoncojo**, passing below an abandoned cabin. Ignoring two tracks and a donkey trail branching left, we approach the head of the **Barranco de la Junta**, shortly before which, our track swings sharp right (E), climbing to pass below a more substantial ruin (Wp.6 100M).

Four more zigzags later, we bear left on a waypointed trail forking NW from a sharp-right bend of the dirt track (Wp.7 120M). Our boulder-lined trail traverses long-neglected terraces, heading towards palm groves and a distinct table-top outcrop in distance. Fifty metres after a 'jubilee' Km100 marker of the **GR132** beside a white house with a garden full of palms, we turn left at a T-junction of trails (Wp.8 130M) for **Antoncojo**. Following roughly paved zigzags, we descend to the **Barranco de los Cocos** watercourse (Wp.9 137M), where we begin a virtually pathless descent to **Antoncojo**.

Crossing sloping rocks on the left bank, we descend into the watercourse itself, below a wall flanking an old reservoir, after which another faint 'path', again on the left bank, descends toward a palm grove in small terraced fields, where we have to squeeze past an overhanging rock. Another short stretch in the bed of the *barranco* is followed by a third left-bank 'path', where we briefly glimpse **Antoncojo**. We then drop back into the watercourse for 150 metres.

Winding between rock pools and picking our way through the rocks (very gingerly if they happen to be wet), we look for a faint 'path' on the right bank (Wp.10 152M) leading to tiny crumbling terraces. These are fairly easily identified as they are backed by a concrete covered canal curving smoothly along the right stroke of the ravine's V-shaped horizon. If you happen to miss the first branch of this 'path' and find yourself above a small waterfall overlooking a mini-reservoir, backtrack 30 metres to find a cairn-marked access onto the terraces.

Following a very faint way, we climb across the terraces, aiming for the point where the canal descends from a low orange crag, where we join a reasonably clear path next to a concrete nameplate commemorating 'Francisco Diaz Barroso' (Wp.11 157M). We follow this path past a more substantial dam into **Antoncojo**.

The 'engine' bus stop (Wp.12)

Sticking to the same path through the village, we join the end of a road leading to a signposted T-junction of roads. Turning right at the T-junction, we follow the road for 75 metres before taking the second branch on the left (S) (Wp.12 167M), a lane branching off at an orange-painted stone bus stop shelter with a decorative old engine tucked in the corner.

200 metres later, just before the branch lane becomes cobbled and climbs back toward the road, we turn left (SE) on a wayposted donkey trail that has been re-paved for the first few metres.

The trail, which soon runs into older, rougher paving, follows two water pipes, one clad in stone, the other exposed with 'Buderus' stencilled on its side. When the trail is swallowed up by a new tarmac lane next to a house with sunflowers painted on its wall, we follow the lane past the **Embalse Cardones** dam wall. 100 metres after the dam, the lane bears right (SW) and we carry straight on (SE) (Wp.13 182M), recovering the old trail that runs alongside the stone-clad water pipe.

We descend along the pipe-path behind two small farmhouses, after which the 'Buderus' pipe resurfaces. Ignoring all paintmarks and cairns indicating apparent ways back into the **Barranco de los Cocos**

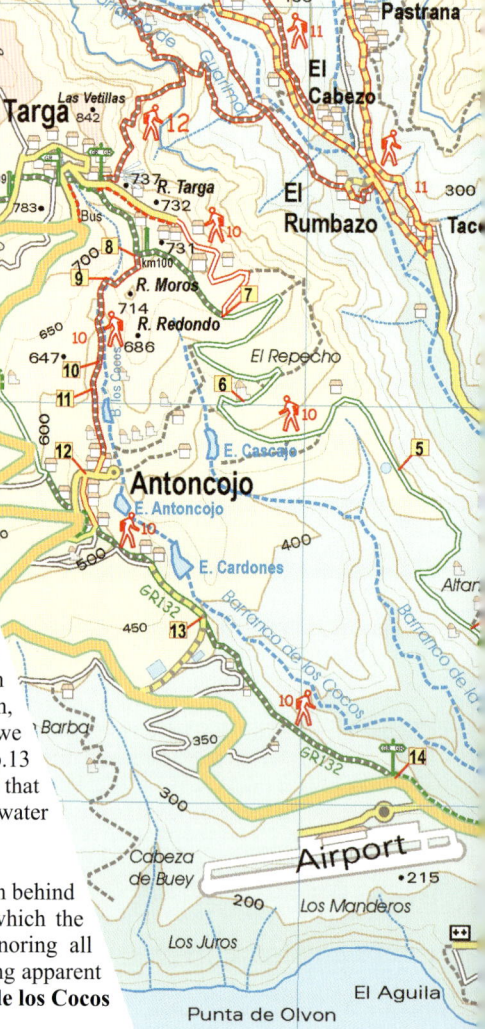

58 *Walk! La Gomera*

(they don't, or at least nothing you'd care to take without feathers or cloven hooves), we follow the pipes to the road (Wp.14 202M) above the airport. Continuing on the road for 600 metres, we pass the airport entrance, 100 metres after which, immediately before the start of green fencing on the left, we slip through the crash barriers to recover the pipe-path, which runs into a dirt track just above **La Trinchera**.

The mirador, after Wp.15

Maintaining direction (SE) we descend to a dangerous bend in the road (Wp.15 217M), which we cross very quickly (think 'Roadrunner'), onto a concrete and stone path leading to the **Mirador de la Trinchera** overlooking **Playa Santiago**.

Continuing along the lane behind the *mirador*, we turn left at a 'retevision' transmitter.

Concrete steps lead to a spectacular path, snaking its way down to join a tarmac lane.

NB while we still have a clear overview of the town, note the wooden pedestrian bridge crossing the riverbed. This bridge will take us back onto the sidewalk on the eastern bank to join our outward route 200 metres from the seafront.

11 BARRANCO DE BENCHIJIGUA

This is one of the classics: hidden idyllic hamlets, gullies quilted with smallholdings, crumbling ruins conjuring DIY dreams, and a landscape that, despite its low altitude, has a real 'high mountain' feel to it.

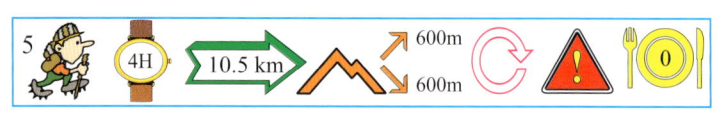

| 5 | 4H | 10.5 km | 600m / 600m | ↻ | ⚠ | 🍴 0 |

Access by car:
To reach the start, take the **Taco/Guarimiar** road behind **Playa Santiago**. At the **Taco/Pastrana** Y-junction, turn left and drive through **Taco**. 450 metres after the junction, we reach the **El Rumbazo** turn-off where there's a mapboard and signposts. Park next to the garages 30 metres to the west.

Non-motorists:
If you don't have a car and are feeling energetic, you can join the present itinerary by taking the bus (Línea 3) to **Imada** and following Walk 6 to the linking path described in that itinerary, or (very energetic) by taking the same bus to **Las Toscas** and following the start of Walk 9.

Our start (Wp.1)

From the **El Rumbazo** turn-off (Wp.1 0M), we follow the **Guarimiar/El Cabezo** road due north, turning left after 150 metres at a T-junction next to a white transformer tower.

After climbing steadily for a little under 10 minutes, we branch right to reach the hamlet of **El Cabezo**, which is perched on the thin ridge of rock at the tip of **Lomo de Azadoe**.

Bearing left at the white transformer tower

Directly opposite the first house, **Casa Maria Angeles** (Wp.2 10M, see photo on next page), we cross a sheet of rock onto concrete and stone steps. Ignoring minor branches to the right, we follow a roughly cobbled path climbing along the western flank of the *lomo*, passing to the left of a small water tower and coming into view of the **Ermita de Guarimiar**.

Wp.2, opposite Casa Maria Angeles

The path winds up to skirt a large outcrop of rock before crossing (roughly parallel with the *ermita*) onto the eastern flank of the *lomo*, bringing us into sight of **Roque Agando** and our return path on the far side of the ravine (Wp.3 40M).

Approaching the large 'bowler hat' bluffs defining the heights of the *lomo*, we briefly cross back onto its western flank, before definitively returning to the eastern flank, where we must take care not to lose the cobbled path when it bears right (N) and a dirt path continues directly ahead (W) (Wp.4 50M).

Rounding the bluffs, our path runs into grubby-golden rock (Wp.5 55M) and the 'bowler-hat' reveals itself as something more akin to a crocodile snout. The path occasionally disappears in the rock, but there's only one way for a sane person to go up here, and we soon pick up its traces again. After a steady climb, we traverse a large, stubby spur (Wp.6 70M) jutting out from the *lomo*. Another steady climb brings us across the back of the next spur, 100 metres after which the gradient eases and we fork left at a Y-junction (Wp.7 80M). We now traverse a hillside dotted with palm and agave, the latter with scapes so tall in soil so dry they frequently topple over.

This last stretch of the climb seems to go on interminably, but eventually, after a little over 15 minutes, we cross a slab of reddish, lightly fissured rock onto a level path from where we can see, way below us, the final stretch of our outward route, snaking along to pass behind the long ridge of rock separating **Benchijigua** from **Lo del Gato**. The level path leads to a junction (Wp.8 100M) with a major, waymarked path climbing from the east and leading up to the pass over **Lomo de Azadoe**.

An old oven, 125 minutes into the route.

Turning right at the junction, we zigzag down the steep slope before a gentler descent leads to a sheet of rock that appears to have been used as a threshing circle. We wind round behind a small ruin (Wp.9 125M), an excellent spot for a picnic, from where it's an easy stroll to the junction (Wp.10 135M) with the dirt track between **Benchijigua** and its dam.

Turning left, we follow the track as it climbs gently round the head of the valley, coming into the hamlet next to a building with a ceramic 'Benchijigua'

Walk! La Gomera 61

nameplate (Wp.11 145M).

75 metres along the main track out of **Benchijigua**, we branch right on a heavily waymarked path that passes below one of the *casas rurales* for which the hamlet is famous.

After crossing a dry watercourse and following a terrace, we descend towards a large ruin where we bear left.

Winding round to cross another watercourse, we pass through a long zigzag, crossing yet another watercourse just above the **Lo del Gato** road, which we join 75 metres later at a small culvert (Wp.12 160M).

Bearing left, we go up the road 50 metres to a U-bend, just before which a large cairn marks the start of our return path, branching off to the right.

Once on this good, broad, partially stepped path, we simply have to follow it all the way to Wp.16, ignoring all branches, so the following is merely for time-keeping.

The path climbs a small rise, bringing us into view of the hamlet of **Lo del Gato** and its neatly terraced fields.

We then descend steadily to cross a canal (Wp.13 170M), after which we wind down alongside a torrent of boulders before bearing left across the broad pleated slope facing **Lo del Gato**.

Ignoring a major branch on the right to **Lo del Gato** (Wp.14 185M), we carry straight on across rusty coloured rocks mottled with seams of ochre and pale yellow. We also ignore another, minor, cairn-marked branch (Wp.15 195M) doubling back to the right, and continue on the main path toward an electricity pylon, shortly before which we pass a very slightly vertiginous stretch.

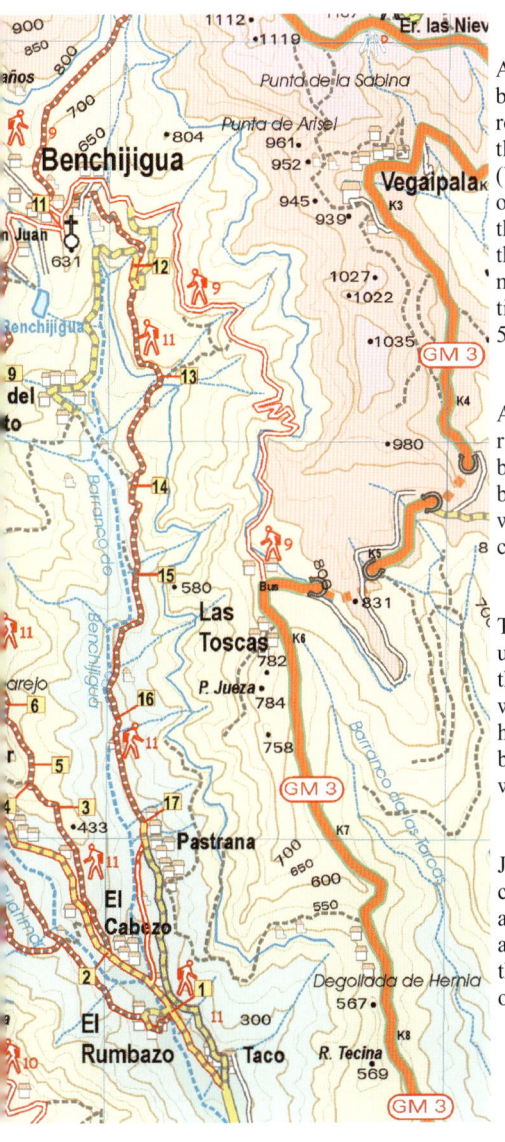

After a second pylon, we pass between a ruin and two reservoirs and descend into the bed of the *barranco* (Wp.16 210M). With the help of occasional blue dashes on the rocks, we pick our way through the boulders in the middle of the watercourse to a tiny cabin on the right bank, 50 metres downstream.

After following a faint path running alongside large brown water pipes on the right bank for another 50 metres, we cross onto a paved trail climbing the left bank.

This runs into a path leading up to **Pastrana** and the end of the road (Wp.17 230M) which we follow for about one hundred metres before bearing right to descend on a wayposted donkey trail.

Just after passing under a clump of water pipes, we meet a concrete track. Bearing left and following the concrete then tarmac track we return to our starting point.

Walk! La Gomera 63

12 BARRANCO DE GUARIMIAR

One sometimes has the impression that in the days before TV, computer games and karaoke, bored but playful Gomerans would studiously pick out apparently impassable cliff faces and make paths up them just to pass the time. To be fair, they didn't have much choice if they wanted to go anywhere, yet you can't help but wonder. In this strenuous circuit, we use two of the most improbable paths you're likely to encounter anywhere, one dropping down we use the phrase advisedly) from the hamlet of **Targa** into the **Barranco de Guarimiar**, the other climbing the same ravine to **Imada**. Not to be missed, unless you suffer from vertigo.

The walk was first researched in 2004. Back then it was, and to some degree remains, very, very airy. If the prospect of lots of empty space below you has your toes curling just at the thought of it, beware. In particular, there is a ten minute stretch prior to Wp.14 that is a wonderful photo opportunity, but which still puts the wind up us when we look at the pictures. That said, it should be stressed that nowadays the vertiginous stretches are all protected by railings. If having some sort of barrier between you and the drop helps your particular version of vertigo, this may still be the itinerary for you.

Access by bus:
Línea 3

Access by car: Park near the town hall (*ayuntamiento*) in **Alajeró**.

Our start at Alajeró town hall (Wp.1)

From the eastern end of the **Ayuntamiento de Alajeró** car-park (Wp.1 0M), we take a cobbled lane beside **Casa Fagundo** down to the principal road through the village, which we follow south, branching off right at the Y-junction (Wp.2 5M).

Descending a minor road parallel to the main road, we pass a transformer tower, 250 metres after which we turn sharp left and climb to the main road (Wp.3 10M) just above the **Bar/Restaurante Las Palmeras** (now closed), opposite which we take a broad, newly paved donkey trail. The trail narrows to a dirt path for 75 metres before broadening on a shelf of rock just before a junction, where we turn left, descending to the horseshoe lane linking **Targa** with the main road.

Fifty metres to the left, we leave the lane, turning right (Wp.4 20M) on a narrow concrete track that soon dwindles to a path. Crossing the horseshoe lane, we climb across a minor ravine to rejoin the lane, where we pass a GR trail junction and a dull orange house with decorative stones set in its walls. 30 metres after the orange house, we take a narrow path to the left, marked with a carved wooden signboard 'Barranco de Santiago' (Wp.5 30M), at which point you may wish to prepare yourself for the inevitable sharp intake of breath.

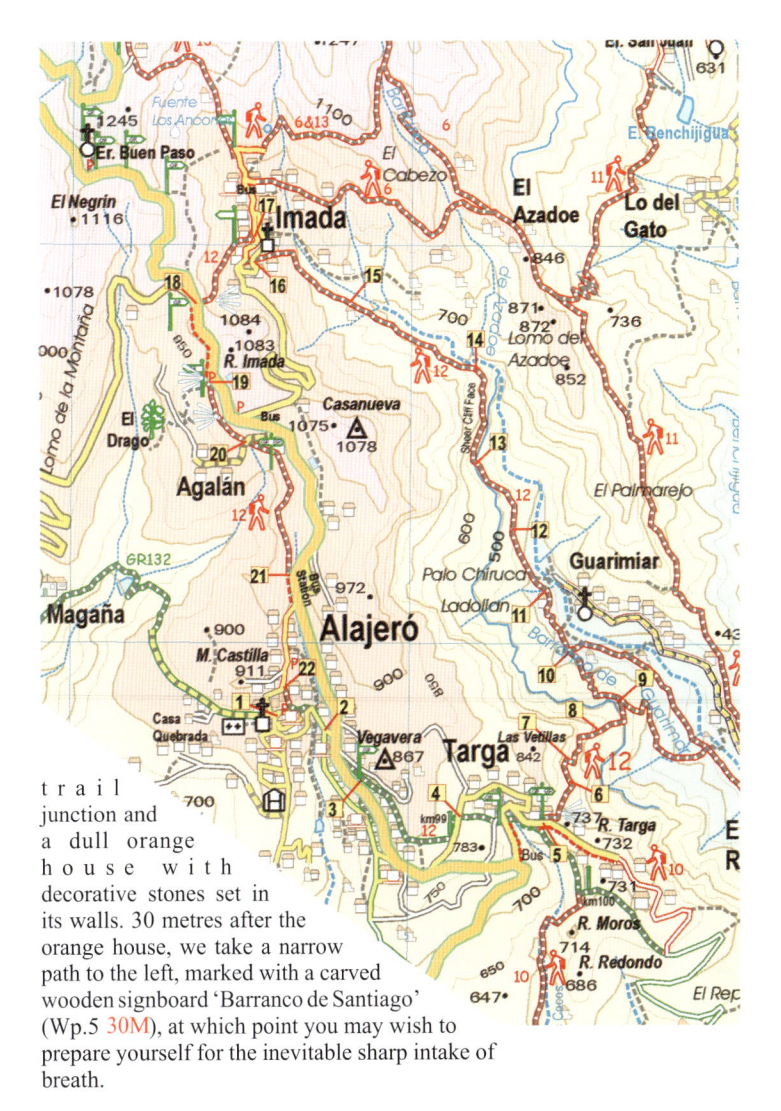

Dull orange house in Targa, just before Wp.5

50 metres from the road, we go through a rock gateway and the view opens out (in every direction, most notably down) across the **Barranco de Guarimiar**, backed by **Teide** and (to our left) **Roque Agando**. Despite the dramatic drop, this is one of the more 'natural' cliff paths, unlike some where you get the impression some stubborn peasant just kept bludgeoning

Walk! La Gomera 65

his way through till something akin to a path appeared in his wake. Heading north-east, we pass under impressive crags, where we come to the first slightly vertiginous stretch before reaching a small cave (Wp.6 35M). The path winds down, passing a solitary palm (Wp.7 40M), the first on the descent, after which another very slightly vertiginous stretch leads north-east to the next series of zigzags. Following a very steep chicane, we pass a line of palms and cross a patch of gritty dirt, where we see **Roque Agando** again (Wp.8 50M). More zigzags pass a shallow sloping cave. Immediately after crossing a canal (visible for much of the descent), we come to **El Rumbazo/Imada** T-junction (Wp.9 60M).

The donkey trail (Wps. 9-10)

Bearing left for **Imada**, we come to a bare rock plateau on a sheer cliff, from where fantastic views of **Barranco de Guarimiar** and the hamlet of the same name open up. The trail swings left and descends along a great example of incredibly steep 'terraces of hunger', a symptom of 'old days' that weren't necessarily good for the people who lived in them. An immaculately maintained donkey trail then descends in zig-zags toward the hamlet of **Guarimiar** in our sight. Passing a small cave on our left, we reach a turn-off for **El Rumbazo** (Wp.10 73M).

We turn left then, two hundred metres later, descend concrete-and-stone steps to the end of a dirt track. Bearing left again, we enter **Guarimiar** beside the access track of a yellow-painted house, in front of which, at a solar panel and a wheelbarrow converted into a flowerpot for aloe vera, we bear right to skirt round the house and its garden.

The yellow house (approaching Wp.11)

Passing alongside a white house, we descend to a gully and cross a broad watercourse (Wp.11 84M). Leaving **Guarimiar,** we cross another watercourse (Wp.12 90M) below cliffs patched with flat planes where fractured rock has yielded to gravity. Continuing our climb, we reach a canal, the same one crossed shortly before Wp.9 (no, a shortcut would not be a clever idea!), below a water-chute so smoothly sculpted it looks like the mould for a concrete pipe. 50 metres later, we cross the canal (Wp.13 100M) and climb alongside a thin metal pipe before bearing right on steps in the rock, signalling the approach of another point where one wonders what on earth possessed anyone to think of making a path up here. Climbing steadily on a broad ledge path, we traverse a sheer cliff face. Though this path, which is undeniably vertiginous, looks appalling in pictures and, from above, frankly terrifying (not recommended as a descent), it's never so narrow as to be seriously

Views back to Guarimiar

dangerous or downright foolhardy, and simply requires a little customary precaution. Picking our way carefully along it and resisting the temptation to peer over the edge, we spend about ten minutes traversing the actual cliff face, after which we wind up very steeply, coming into view of **Imada** (Wp.14 120M).

A clear path climbs to cross a sheet of rock, after which we come to a first Y-junction, the two branches rejoining 10 metres later. After crossing the second of two watercourses, the path is obscured by a long spill of rocks, at the top of which it becomes clearer again as it climbs to a very ruinous ruin (Wp.15 135M) immediately after which there's a second Y-junction. Once again, the two branches soon rejoin, but it's easier to take the left fork. At a third Y-junction a couple of minutes later, we branch left again, crossing rock onto a clear paved trail climbing steadily alongside a final watercourse to the lower branch of the lane into **Imada** (Wp.16 150M).

Bearing right, we follow the lane to a transformer tower, where we turn left, winding between houses and ruins onto a higher lane (Wp.17 155M), emerging in sight of house Nº13, which stands opposite a dull yellow garage with double doors. We climb past the house, just above which we bear left, climbing paved steps to a dirt path and a 'Paisaje Protegido Orone' signpost.

House Nº13, Imada

Climbing steeply, we pass a fine pine and the four-fingered salute of **Roque Imada**, before eventually crossing a canal and the ridge onto the main road (Wp.18 175M) 75 metres south of the **Almacigos** turn-off. We follow the road south for 400 metres to the second bend, where two paved trails branch right (Wp.19 180M). Taking the second trail, we descend to cross the **Agalán** lane (Wp.20 185M), where we join a broad cobbled trail which initially runs alongside a canal, then narrows and gradually bears away from the canal. After passing a warehouse, we emerge next to a bus stop (Wp.21 195M) on the northernmost slip road into **Alajeró**. We follow this road to a zebra crossing 30 metres short of a *mirador* at which point we bear left to descend concrete steps (Wp.22 203M) leading to a cobbled track that takes us back to our starting point (206M).

13 IMADA - GARAJONAY

An interesting and relatively easy alternative approach to **Garajonay** exploring the upper reaches of the **Barranco de Azadoe** and concluding with a spectacular descent. The views are exceptional, so much so that correspondence concerning our updating of this route included a telling phrase. You can get a bit complacent when exposed to fabulous landscapes day after day, but in re-researching this route Jan was bubbling over about how 'dangerously beautiful' it all was. Say no more! Well, two more things. **Bar Arcilia** in **Imada** has a good reputation - something else to look forward to at the end of the walk. Also worth noting that there is one, brief, slightly vertiginous stretch, but it shouldn't pose any challenges for most walkers.

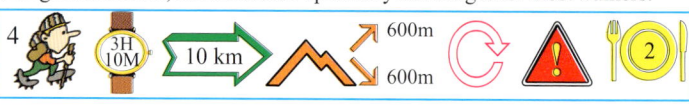

Access by bus: Línea 3 now serves the village of **Imada** itself, stopping in front of **Bar Arcilia**.

Access by car: parking in **Imada** is limited, so it's better to start early if arriving by car. Parking spaces are available 50m south-east of the **Bar-Cafetería Arcilia**. If arriving from **Valle Gran Rey/Vallehermoso**, you can save fuel and be sure of a parking place by starting the walk at the **Pajarito** roundabout (Wp.7) in **Garajonay**.

Starting out at Bar Arcilia (Wp.1)

From **Bar Arcilia** (Wp.1 0M) opposite the bus-stop in **Imada**, we climb very steeply north to the end of the road (Wp.2 5M) where concrete and stone steps lead to a rough path that passes a reservoir and crosses an affluent of the **Barranco de Azadoe**, after which superb views open out to the south.

The steps at Wp.2

Climbing steadily, we cross a succession of minor spurs, each of which looks like it must be the last (but isn't!), until a series of partially paved zigzags brings us onto a ledge with stunning views into the **Barranco de Azadoe** (Wp.3 35M).

From here, a gentle stroll along a level path, with one slightly vertiginous stretch, leads across the **Azadoe** watercourse to a junction (Wp.4 40M), where we turn left to climb alongside the watercourse.

Excellent views!

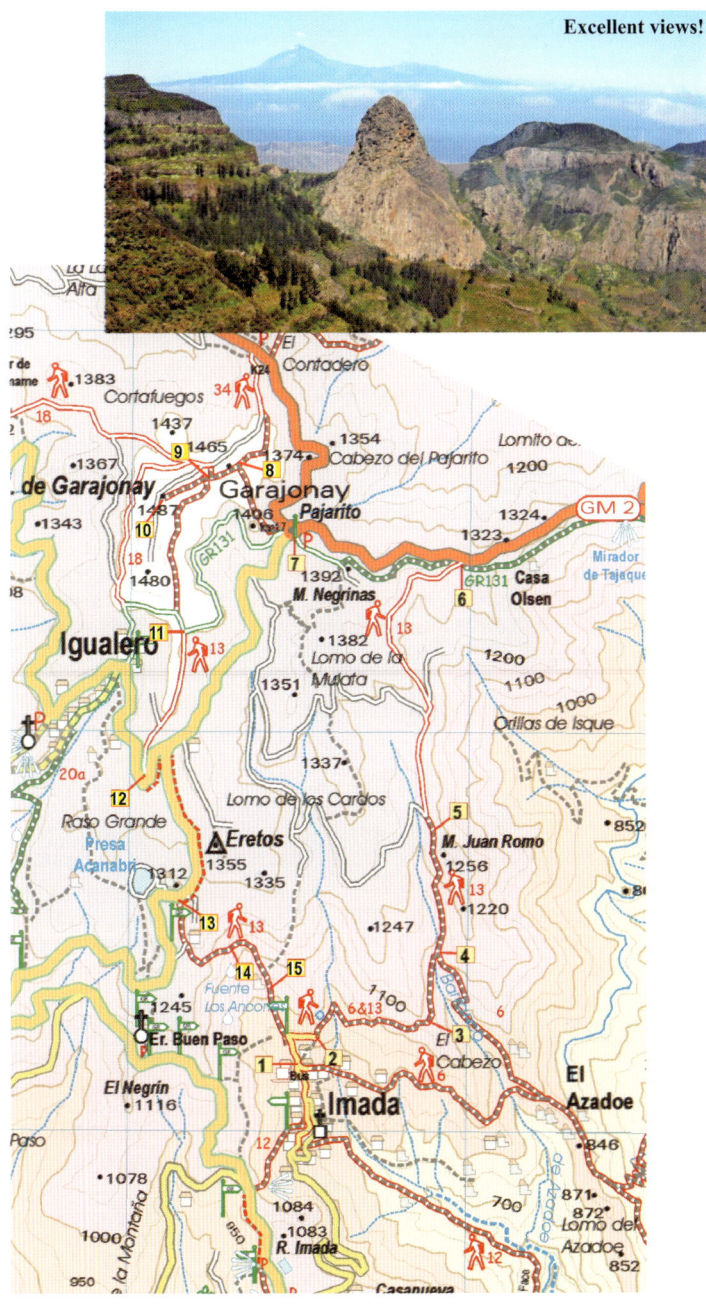

Following a good, partially paved trail, we climb steadily along the left bank of the ravine before bearing right and winding away from the watercourse. After a slightly steeper climb, the path levels off and, 50 metres later, passes a signpost for the 'Reserva Natural de Benchijigua' (Wp.5 60M), from where we have excellent views of **Roque Agando**.

Walk! La Gomera 69

We then enter the *Parque Nacional*, joining a dirt track, which we follow in a northerly direction, ignoring branches to left and right. After a gentle climb, we pass below antenna-topped **Los Noruegos** hut, after which the dirt track swings left just before the GM-2 *carretera dorsal* (Wp.6 85M). In the left bend of the dirt track, we bear right on a red-and-white waymarked trail tucked between the dirt track and the road (W).

The path winds through bracken and *fayal-brezal*, climbing steadily to cross two small tops, after which a second stepped descent brings us onto a dirt track, where we bear right for the **Pajarito** parking area (Wp.7 105M), the alternative starting point for those approaching from **Valle Gran Rey** or **Vallehermoso**.

Garajonay junction (shortly after Wp.7)

Crossing the **Igualero** road, we take the **Alto de Garajonay** dirt track, passing between metal poles, and immediately turn right at a notice board on the 'Alto de Garajonay' log-stepped walking trail. (NB If you don't want to climb to the summit itself, you can stay on the track here, to reach Wp.11 directly.) A steady climb brings us across a small rise, after which we dip down before climbing again to the signposted 'Alto de Garajonay/Contadero' T-junction (Wp.8 120M).

Turning left for 'Alto de Garajonay', we climb onto the island's highest summit, carrying straight on at a crossroads after 150 metres (Wp.9) to the **Alto de Garajonay** *mirador* (Wp.10 130M), from where we have superb views of the neighbouring islands, notably **Tenerife** but also **Gran Canaria** on a clear day.

After enjoying the views, we return to Wp.9 and turn right on a broad trail descending (S) through mixed woodland to rejoin the dirt track circling the summit at a signposted junction of tracks (Wp.11 145M). Carrying straight on (S) on the track signposted for 'Igualero 1.8', we descend to the **Igualero - Chipude** road (Wp.12 155M) 100 metres west of the junction with the **Playa Santiago** road, which we follow (S) for 750 metres. When the **Playa Santiago** road swings sharp right towards a dam seen on our way down, we turn left on a narrow dirt path (Wp.13 165M) defined by low gateway walls and flanked by dirt tracks. After crossing a track leading to a small house on our left, we bear left at an apparent Y-junction (the branch on the right is actually a watercourse), after which we see **Imada**.

Descending steeply between scorched cistus and broom, we reach a rocky spur crossed by a metal water pipe (Wp.14 175M), where we bear left (NE), winding down through increasingly invasive shrubs. The path gradually curves round to the south on a slightly gentler gradient to a canal beside a roofless cabin (Wp.15 185M), from where a straightforward descent on a long, shallow spur brings us into the village 50 metres above our starting point.

THE WEST - REGAL GRANDEUR

From the *mirador* at **Igualero**'s *ermita*, we can glimpse the grand landscapes that lie ahead, but nothing can prepare us for our first descent into **Valle Gran Rey**. After winding along the country road past **Fortaleza** (Walk 19) and through the bucolic, '1,000 metre' villages of **Chipude**, **El Cercado** and **Las Hayas**, we descend to **Arure**, where we take a short detour to the *ermita* to enjoy the stunning views down toward **Taguluche**, a landscape we explore in Walk 25. Now brace yourselves. It's time for a fairground ride.

Beyond the hamlet, the **Barranco de Arure** plunges down beside the road as we head into the first tunnel of the new road leading to **Valle Gran Rey**. Down we go, then down again and down a bit more, freewheeling along a broad carriageway descending steeply past the **Mirador César Manrique** before whipping through a hairpin bend (where there's another *mirador*) into the second tunnel.

Emerging into the light in front of a sheer cliff, we look down on the settlements high up the valley floor, matchbox models that resolve themselves into full size houses as we drop down through successive switchbacks, rounding the church before reaching the first settlements. And still the steep descent continues between towering cliff walls, sweeping through **Retamal**, **Los Granados**, **Casa de la Seda** and **El Guro** before the slope finally levels out at **La Calera**. What a descent! And that is on the 'new' road. Stretches of the old road can be seen and it's no surprise to discover that it was nicknamed the 'screaming route' from the noise made by daytrippers as their driver flung his coach through the tortuous bends.

By comparison, **La Calera** and the seafront developments of **La Playa**, **La Puntilla** and **Vueltas** are havens of tranquility. Once the preserve of hippies and adventurers, including Vietnam draft dodgers, La Gomera's main resort has become relatively up-market in recent years, with new hotels and apartments where camper vans used to prevail. Despite the modern developments, **Vueltas** and **La Calera** still retain plenty of character, ensuring that **Valle Gran Rey** remains a laid-back, charming base for a holiday. And if you want a taste of the old days, you only have to hike north or south of the resort area to the beaches of **Playa del Inglés** and **Las Salinas**, which are still a favoured haunt of the alternative crowd.

Framed by immense cliff walls, **Valle Gran Rey** presents some challenging walking routes, but you can opt for easier alternatives by bussing out of the valley and walking back (see Walk 16 from **Arure** and the second part of Walk 17). While the walking is challenging, you will be well rewarded in the *típicos* en route, and for days when you don't want to be challenged, the island's best beaches are just a stroll away.

WESTERN WALKS LOCATOR MAPS

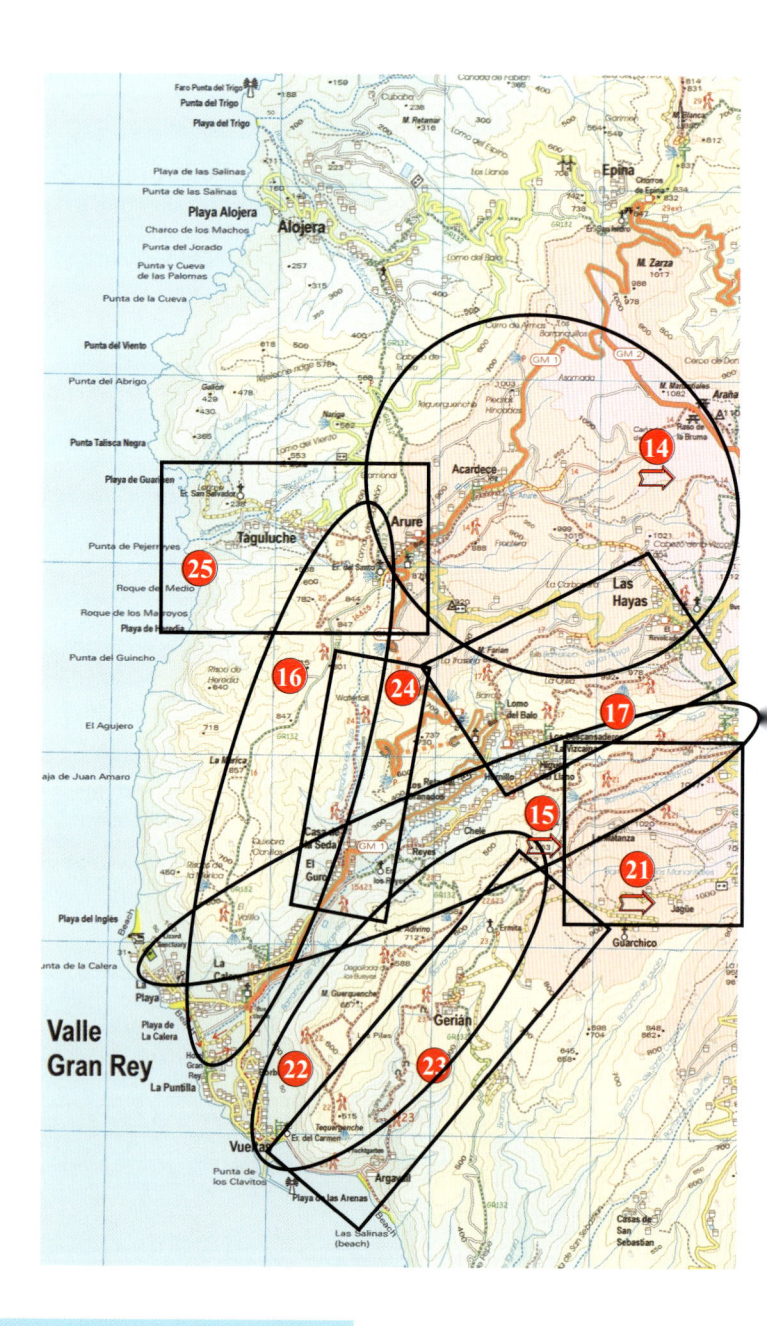

Walk! La Gomera 73

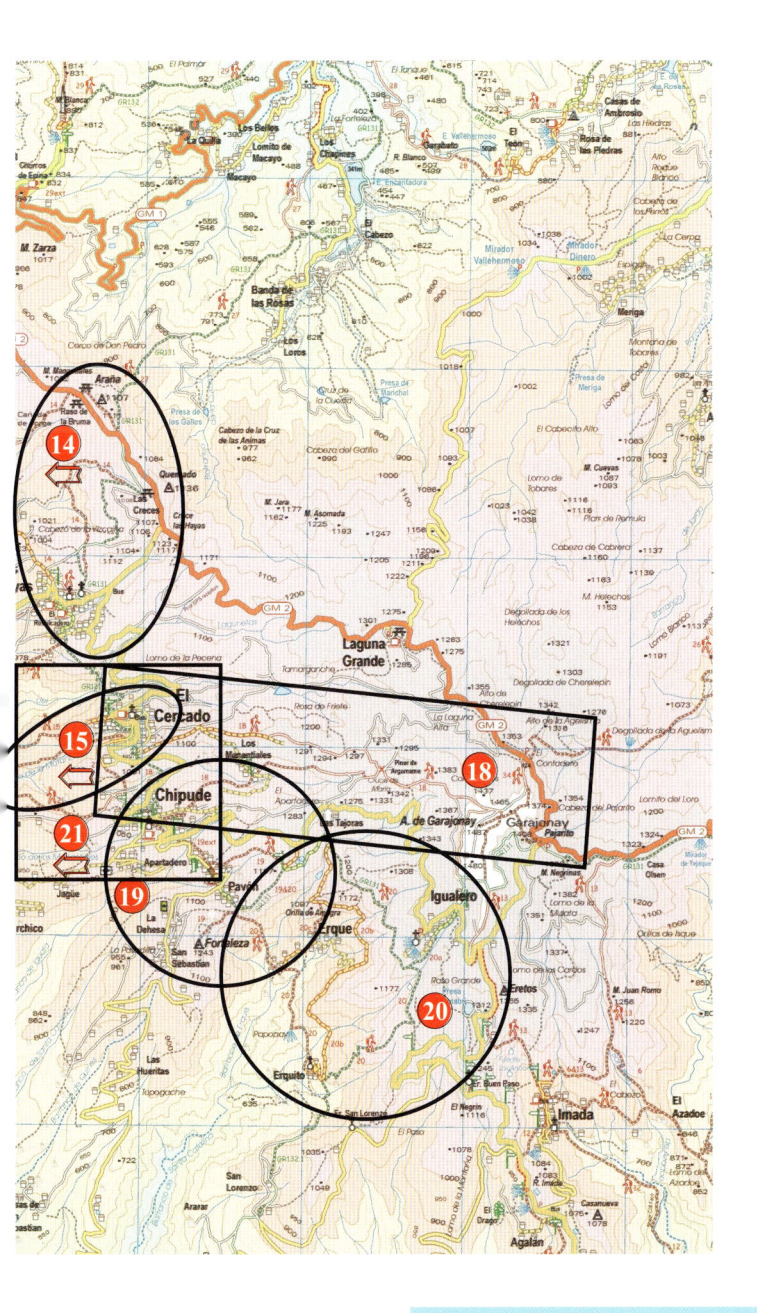

14 ARURE - LAS HAYAS

A perfect introduction to everything good about La Gomera: friendly people, idyllic countryside, fairy tale forests, tiny hamlets and, at the end of it all, a good lunch! Particulary pleasing, since we had feared that fire had blighted the route since the previous edition of this book; however, it all remains most agreeable. Better still, a new path means we can skip a stretch of road walking.

3 | 3¼H | 13 km | 300m / 300m | 4

Casa Conchita (Wp.1)

Access by bus: Línea 1.

Access by car: on-street parking in **Arure**.

Our itinerary starts from **Arure**, 20 metres south-west

The paved trail into the valley

of the **Restaurante Casa Conchita** bus-stop (Wp.1 0M) on a paved trail descending into the valley below the village, signposted 'Las Hayas (por Lo Vasco)'. After crossing a dry watercourse and a rock shelf with carved steps, we bear right to climb past house Nº15 **Casa Marina** then bear left to circle house Nº2, beyond

74 Walk! La Gomera

which we reach the northern end of **Presa de las Hayas** dam wall (Wp.2 10M). Bearing left at the head of the reservoir, we cross bare rock (NE) to pick up another path along the southern flank of the **Arure** valley.

The path joins a dirt track (Wp.3 15M), which we follow to the dam behind **Acardece**. Staying on the track as it passes the **Acardece** reservoir, we cross a small rise and turn right at a T-junction. The track runs into tarmac, and we soon come to a Y-junction (Wp.4 30M), signposted to the left for 'Parque Nacional 1.1km/Raso de la Bruma 1.9km' (our return route).

Bearing right, we ignore three left-hand branches, the third of which (immediately after a line of 3 palms) is another Y-junction (Wp.5 35M), then cross a stream bed and join a donkey trail climbing the **Cabeza de la Vizcaina**. After a steady climb, we turn left to join the end of a tarmac lane (Wp.6 50M), passing a small yellow house and a branch to the left. Still climbing, we see the table-top summit of **Fortaleza** (Walk 19), then **Las Hayas**.

Ermita de las Hayas (Wp.9)

The lane briefly descends, then climbs past a scruffy farmstead toward the village. 20 metres from the main road, we stay on the signposted route, ignoring twin dirt tracks branching left. Joining the main road (Wp.7 65M), we climb to the left, passing in front of **Casa Efigenia** restaurant (Wp.8 67M), 50 metres after which, at house N°20, we leave the road, taking the signposted route for 'Las Creces'. Following the **Camino Coromoto** driveway past an orange garage with white doors, we take a path climbing between houses to a dirt track behind the **Ermita de Las Hayas** (Wp.9 74M).

The track soon dwindles to a narrow path sandwiched between terraces and the edge of the *laurisilva*. Bearing right at a Y-junction 30 metres after a national park limits sign, we enter classic Gomeran woodland, a carpet of sun-dappled leaf mould shrouded by a canopy of contorted lichen-bearded laurel and heath trees. The path descends gently to cross a dirt track (Wp.10 85M). After a steadier, partially stepped descent into a densely wooded gully, we stroll through increasingly lush forest.

Ignoring a branch to the left for **Arure** (Wp.11 95M), we continue on the main path (N), climbing gently to cross another gully (Wp.12 100M). Following the right bank of the gully, we criss-cross an ancient canalisation channel, climbing gently to the *área recreativa* at **Las Creces** (Wp.13 110M).

Approaching Wp.13, Las Creces

Creces are the berries of the *haya*, which means beech on the mainland, but is used here for the Canary wax-myrtle. In the past, the people of **Las Hayas** came here to collect the *creces*, once an important part of the local diet.

Bearing left, we take the *área recreativa* access track up to the main road (Wp.14 115M), which we cross in order to follow the path along the crash barrier to the left (NW) for 130 metres. Leaving the road, we immediately fork left at Y-junction of paths for **Raso de la Bruma**. Passing two benches at a fork leading to the **Mirador Risquillos de Corgo** viewpoints, we bear left at the next Y-junction, 300 metres after which we reach the small **Raso de la Bruma** picnic area next to the main road (Wp.15 125M). Here we cross the road to join a broad trail signposted 'Cañada de Jorge'.

The **Cañada de Jorge** trail descends through dense woodland to join the end of a track leading to the main *pista forestal* (Wp.16 140M) from the road. Bearing left, we follow the *pista* out of the park into scrubby *fayal-brezal*. After briefly dwindling to a walking trail, the *pista* broadens again to a hard-baked dirt track, which we follow (W) towards the large gate of **Finca La Quintana** (house N°5), where we join a tarmac lane (Wp.17 150M). Maintaining direction (W), we follow the lane back to Wp.4 (175M).

Staying on the main track as it circles the **Acardece** reservoir, we turn left 50 metres after the dam wall and descend a metalled track (Wp.18 180M), at the end of which a newly paved path winds through the hamlet before joining the road (Wp.19 185M). 30 metres along the road, another paved trail branches left back into the valley and open countryside.

When this trail switches back sharp left, we continue in a south-westerly direction on a narrow path. Sticking to the main path and ignoring all branches, we come to another newly paved stretch, which rejoins the road 50 metres from our starting point (195M). **Casa Conchita**'s *carne fiesta* (chunks of fried pork marinated in vinegar, lemon juice, cumin and bay leaves) is particularly recommended.

15 EL CERCADO - VALLE GRAN REY

Most people arrive in **Valle Gran Rey** by road, which is dramatic but sufficiently abrupt to be a bit bruising. Arriving on foot by the old donkey trail from **El Cercado** is an infinitely more spacious, gracious and comfortable approach, letting us appreciate just why this was such a haven for hippies in the sixties.

The high exertion rating is all in the knees. There's a slight risk of vertigo between **El Cercado** and **La Vizcaina**, where a number of balcony paths traverse the steeply raked slopes.

NB If time's short and you want to get as much walking in as possible, the present itinerary can be combined with Walk 24, our popular short itinerary visiting a waterfall. Simply carry straight on at Wp.10, climbing to the main road. Bear right, uphill for 200 metres, to reach the start of Walk 24.

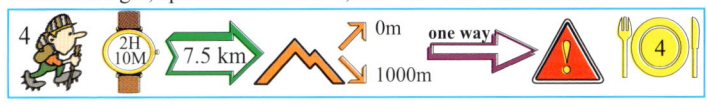

Access by bus: Línea 1 or 4

Directly in front of the **Bar/Restaurante Maria** (Wp.1 0M), we take the dead-end lane (W) along the ridge between the **Barrancos del Agua** and **Matanza**, soon coming into sight of **La Vizcaina**.

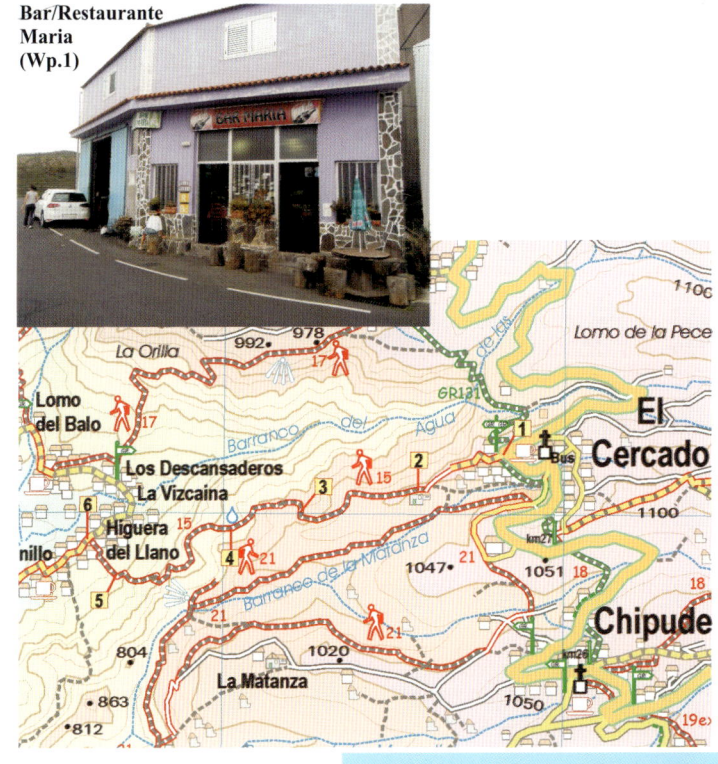

30 metres before an orange farmhouse, we bear right at a 'Parque Rural Valle Gran Rey' signpost on a broad donkey trail marked for 'La Vizcaina' (Wp.2 5M).

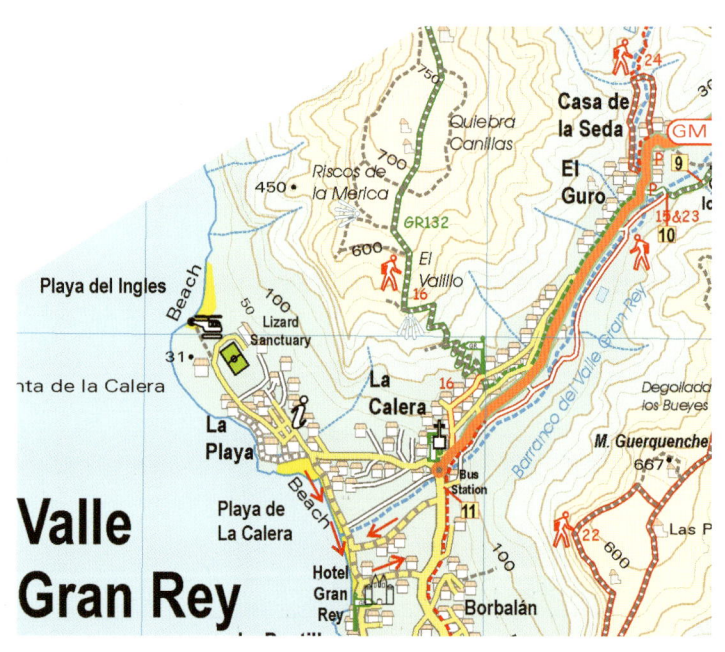

Bearing right on the donkey trail at Wp.2

From here to **La Vizcaina**, we simply follow the donkey trail through successive stretches of zigzagging descent and level 'balcony' paths. There are no major turn-offs, so if you're not interested in pacing progress, close the book for the next hour.

After following the rim of the ravine with spectacular views back towards the dry falls at the confluence of the **Barrancos de las Lagunetas** and **del Agua**, we start our descent, ignoring a minor dirt path branching to the left and staying on the main trail, which is roughly paved and stepped with boulders. Zigzagging down, we pass a painted rock (Wp.3 20M) and traverse the first 'balcony'.

After a second series of zigzags, we pass a plump, solitary palm and come to the second balcony, at the end of which views open out along **Valle Gran Rey**.

We then descend past a small spring (Wp.4 40M) onto the third balcony, after which we cross a rockspill and resume our steady descent onto a fourth balcony.

Descending to La Vizcaina (Wp.6)

Bar La Vizcaina

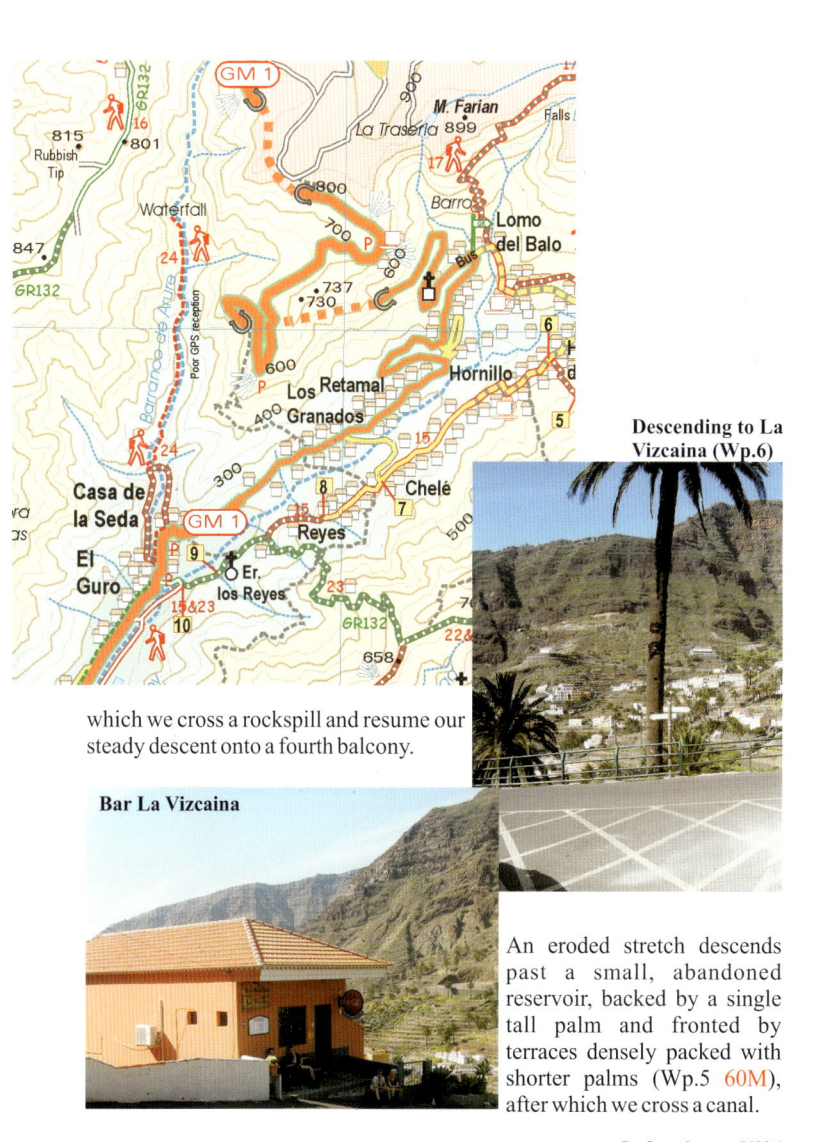

An eroded stretch descends past a small, abandoned reservoir, backed by a single tall palm and fronted by terraces densely packed with shorter palms (Wp.5 60M), after which we cross a canal.

Left at house Nº84

Descending past houses on the periphery of **La Vizcaina**, we emerge next to two mapboards on the lane linking the villages of **Valle Gran Rey** (Wp.6 70M).

Bearing left, we follow the lane down the valley, passing **Bar La Vizcaina**. When the main lane swings sharp right around house Nº84 towards

Wp.9, Ermita los Reyes

Los Granados, we fork left into **Calle Chelé** (Wp.7 85M).

At the end of **Calle Chelé** (Wp.8 90M), we take a surfaced path, **Camino los Reyes**, to the right, passing the **Casa de Chelé**.

The path descends past a semi-troglodytic cabin before passing in front of a larger house, where the modern paving ends, giving way to successive stretches of cobbles and dirt.

After **Casa los Reyes** and **Jardín de Palmeras**, we ignore a branch path down the steps to the right and cross the plaza in front of **Ermita los Reyes** (Wp.9 101M), at the far end of which a newly surfaced trail descends onto the dirt track in the bed of the valley (Wp.10 105M).

Wp.10, descending from the *ermita*

The trail continues up to **El Guro** but we turn left and follow the dirt track down the riverbed, bearing left when the main traces curve up to the road.

At a Y-junction 150 metres before the ravine bed becomes reinforced, we have two options:- either we turn right to climb out of the ravine onto the main road, where a dirt track parallel to the road brings us to earlier refreshments and the Tourism Office in **La Calera**; or alternatively, we continue to the left below a rock face to reach the bus station (Wp.11 130M). Services and taxis can be found to the right in **La Calera**, services and bathing to the left in **Vueltas**.

16 LA MÉRICA

There are many valid reasons for walking; some walk to exercise, some to escape, some to explore, some to see. This long descent is for the last category, taking in some of the most spectacular views on the island. It's a popular walk, often treated as an ascent, apparently premised on the assumption that sweat equals merit. At Discovery Walking Guides we take a more laid back attitude to these things! Though abrupt, the descent is well-graded, hence the low exertion rating.

Views of the Mighty Tejeleche mountains and La Palma en route

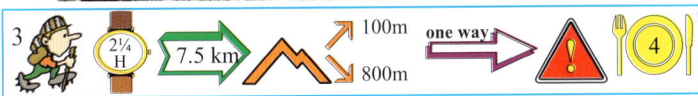

3 | 2¼H | 7.5 km | 100m / 800m | one way | ⚠ | 4

Wp.1, Casa Conchita

Access by bus and car: Línea 1 to **Arure**. If you're arriving by car and can't find room to park in **Arure**, you may find spaces in front of the yellow house at Wp.3.

Starting in **Arure** from the **Restaurante Casa Conchita** bus-stop (Wp.1 0M), we follow the road down towards

Wp.2, turn right towards the *Ermita*

Valle Gran Rey for 500 metres, then turn right at a junction (Wp.2 7M) for the 'Mirador Ermita del Santo'. Following the lane past the *mirador*, already enjoying some fairly toe-curling views, we stick to the tarmac until it ends beside a yellow-painted house (Wp.3 12M), where we continue along a dirt track, passing a short, gated driveway on our left.

Walk! La Gomera 81

On the track towards la Mérica

We then climb past the path (Wp.4 20M) from **Taguluche** (see Walk 25), immediately after which we bear left at a Y-junction marked by a 'Monumento Natural' signpost, bringing into view the **Mérica** ridge.

After passing a neat goat pen, the main track bears right and we maintain our south-westerly direction on a narrower track (Wp.5 30M).

A little over 100 metres later, we leave the track, branching right on a paved trail waymarked 'VGR'.

And that, if you don't like consulting a guidebook when you're walking, is all you need to know. The rest of the trail is broad, easy and obvious, with fabulous views across the *barrancos* and out to sea, and no major turn-offs.

The paving soon gives way to a dirt trail, climbing steadily, to pass above a second, scruffier goat pen, after which it levels out as a ridge path, with superb views of the **Tejeleche Ridge** above **Taguluche** and the distant, cloud tonsured summits of **La Palma**.

Dropping down below a third goat pen, we run into a broad, very slightly vertiginous ledge path, lined with partially walled caves redolent of goats.

Ignoring a minor branch (Wp.6 50M) climbing on the right to the **Mérica** trig point, we begin our first, gentle descent across a plateau that must once have been the bread basket of western La Gomera. We then pass a block of rock, tucked behind which are the ruins of a substantial stone house.

After passing between a second ruin and an immense, starred threshing circle (Wp.7 65M), we come to a Y-junction (Wp.8 75M). The path to the right is a short excursion to the **Riscos**

82 *Walk! La Gomera*

de la Mérica cliffs, but we bear left for our final steep descent.

Although we now descend 600 metres in little over a kilometre, the way is well graded, relatively easy on the knees, and never vertiginous. Our stony, partially stepped trail descends in tight zigzags, down to a comparatively long, easterly traverse, just above which we ignore a branch path (Wp.9 95M) to the right marked with a cairn about 50 metres away.

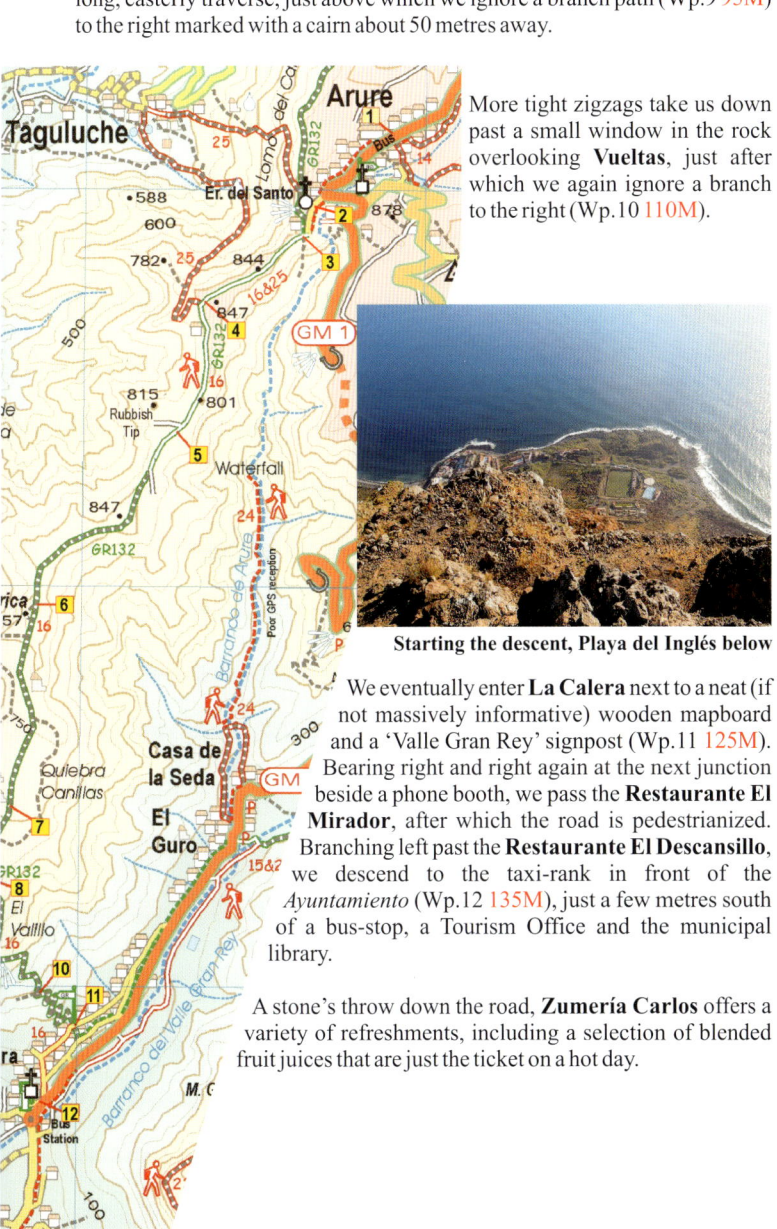

More tight zigzags take us down past a small window in the rock overlooking **Vueltas**, just after which we again ignore a branch to the right (Wp.10 110M).

Starting the descent, Playa del Inglés below

We eventually enter **La Calera** next to a neat (if not massively informative) wooden mapboard and a 'Valle Gran Rey' signpost (Wp.11 125M). Bearing right and right again at the next junction beside a phone booth, we pass the **Restaurante El Mirador**, after which the road is pedestrianized. Branching left past the **Restaurante El Descansillo**, we descend to the taxi-rank in front of the *Ayuntamiento* (Wp.12 135M), just a few metres south of a bus-stop, a Tourism Office and the municipal library.

A stone's throw down the road, **Zumería Carlos** offers a variety of refreshments, including a selection of blended fruit juices that are just the ticket on a hot day.

17 VALLE GRAN REY - LAS HAYAS

Looking at this one from below, it's hard to believe there's a way up the **Barranco de Hayas**. Considerable suspension of disbelief is required en route, too, as we climb incredibly steeply, traversing several vertiginous ledge paths. But there is a way, one strenuous enough to make getting to the top even more of a feel-good moment than usual. You need to be fit, though, and have a good head for heights, not to mention a faintly masochistic taste for the more gruelling side of walking. By contrast, the descent is pure pleasure and within the capacity of any walker with reasonably robust knees. If 'vertiginous' equates to 'impassable' in your vocabulary, it's worth taking the bus to **Las Hayas** and just doing the descent.

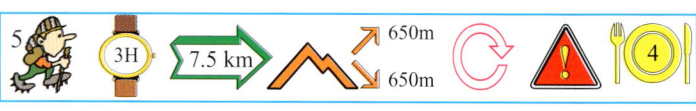

| 5 | 3H | 7.5 km | 650m / 650m | ↻ | ⚠ | 4 |

Access by bus: Línea 1

The bus stop at the start of the route

Access by car: The walk starts from the bus-stop at the **Lomo del Balo/La Vizcaina** turn-off, where there's also a small parking area.

Our left turn after crossing the bridge

Following the **La Vizcaina** road for 100 metres, we turn left immediately after crossing a bridge (Wp.1 2M), on a grassy path wayposted 'Las Hayas 3.1km'.

10 metres later, we ignore a path cutting across wetlands and terraces to the left, and instead climb (over the boulders beside twin palms) directly up the watercourse for 50 metres, before a dirt path bears left, bringing us onto a very steep cobbled path.

Once you've found the path, it's simply a question of keeping on keeping on, climbing and climbing and climbing, and ignoring all apparent branches. If in doubt, look for lines of stones blocking branch 'paths' and cairns indicating the correct way on the mainly stone-laid trail.

After climbing between terraces, we cross a canal, where we ignore an apparent branch to the left up a rockspill, and continue up a steep spur. Toward the top of the spur (Wp.2 20M), the gradient eases briefly and we ignore another apparent branch to the right. Climbing steeply again, we cross the head of the spur, bearing away from the **Barranco de Las Hayas**

84 Walk! La Gomera

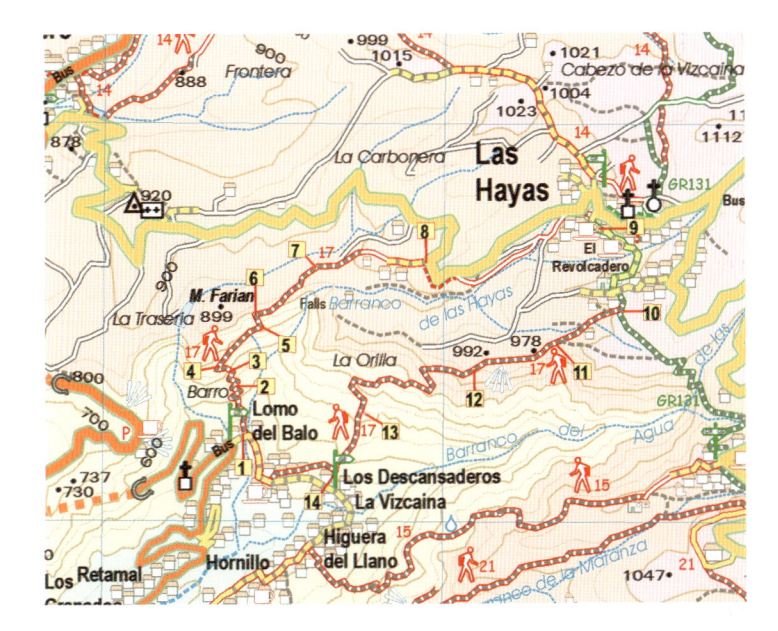

watercourse, before climbing across bare, reddish-brown rock to a T-junction below low crags (Wp.3 30M). Turning left (W) on the main stepped path, we come to our first slightly vertiginous section followed by another steep, winding climb to the top of a watercourse, where we cross five steps carved in the rock (Wp.4 35M).

Bearing right (E), again on a gentler gradient, we climb past a tiny cave, after which the path levels out for 75 metres, in so far as the rough terrain allows, and heads back towards the *barranco* on an occasionally vertiginous ledge. After climbing to cross the head of a second, more precipitous watercourse, our path briefly levels off before resuming its remorseless ascent.

Rounding a bend (Wp.5 50M), we see the falls at the head of the *barranco*, at which point we ignore traces carrying straight on and bear sharp left. Zigzagging up with dizzying rapidity, we cross a stone wall blocking the path (Wp.6 55M), after which we traverse two vertiginous ledges, and come to two more winding ascents interrupted by a long more or less level shelf.

After one last vertiginous stretch, the way broadens, passing shallow caves as it approaches the head of the *barranco*, before finally bearing left (N) on a mixture of bare rock and overgrown path (pathfinding's slightly tricky here - look for the cairns) to join a rough rocky trail (Wp.7 70M) within sight of the **Las Hayas-Arure** road.

Bearing right, we follow the trail east, crossing the end of a dirt track leading to a small house above the falls. Our trail widens to a stony track (later asphalted), which we follow all the way to the road (Wp.8 85M). Turning right, we follow the road round a long bend, after which we branch right on a dirt track.

When the track forks, we continue on the right hand branch, which bears right after 10 metres toward two new houses, at which point we carry straight on, following a narrow path behind the houses.

Wp.9 Restaurante Casa Efigenia

The path leads to a broad trail which in turn joins a dirt track that runs into tarmac shortly before joining the main road. 50 metres along the road, we branch right on a broad path cutting a large bend and re-crossing the road before emerging in front of **Restaurante Casa Efigenia** (Wp.9 100M).

We follow the road for 130 metres to **Bar/Restaurante Amparo**, the starting point for those just doing the linear descent.

Taking the stepped descent beside **Bar Amparo**, we follow **Camino Los Paredones** until two lanes fork off to the left a minute later.

Stepped descent to the right of Bar Amparo

Bearing left on the lane that descends and carrying straight on at the 'El Raso Casa del Ramón' crossroads, we turn left immediately after house Nº 7, taking the wayposted trail below a vineyard. 50 metres later, we take the right hand fork at a Y-junction of walking trails (Wp.10 110M) for 'La Vizcaina/Valle Gran Rey'.

Ignoring all branches, we follow the main trail across a small rise, before bearing right at a T-junction (Wp.11 115M) immediately after which we turn left for 'Los Descansaderos'. Passing a signpost for the 'Parque Rural Valle Gran Rey', we come to one of the finest natural *miradors* overlooking **Valle Gran Rey**, soon after which the trail is paved, marking the start of our descent (Wp.12 120M).

There are several great descents into the 'Valley of the Great King', but for head on impact (we're speaking metaphorically here!), this is probably the greatest. The trail is very steep, but very well made and never vertiginous.

You don't want to be reading a book here. Just walk and enjoy. There's nowhere you can really go wrong unless you actively choose to do so!

The bubble gate before Wp.14

The trail eventually passes under power cables and drops down amid a dense grove of palm onto the head of a long spur (Wp.13 150M), itself considerably steeper than it looks from above.

Descending directly along the back of the spur, we pass a house with a delicately 'bubbled' wrought iron gate and cross a canal, after which we come to a Y-junction (Wp.14 165M).

Approaching our finish

Both ways descend to the road, but since your knees have probably had enough sheer descent for one day, we suggest bearing right to a broad terrace path (clearly visible from above), joining the road 100 metres from the **Bar Macondo**, five minutes from the start of the walk.

The bar has a lovely shady terrace with great views over **Valle Gran Rey**. However, the menu is limited to various pasta dishes, so if you're after a more elaborate culinary experience, turn left on the road and descend to the **Bar-Bodegón La Vizcaina**, a little over ten minutes away.

18 CHIPUDE - GARAJONAY

Another itinerary we feared had been destroyed by the 2012 forest fires, this off-beat approach to the summit of **Garajonay** using the network of tracks and trails behind **Chipude** and **El Cercado**, remains an interesting alternative to better known itineraries. There is more tarmac and concrete than there used to be, but not enough to spoil the adventure, and the views are consistently good. For a shorter excursion, follow the main walk to Wp.10 then turn right and follow the dirt track for 'Chipude', rejoining the main itinerary at Wp.17.

4 | 3H 20M | 14.5 km | 500m / 500m | ↻ | 2

Access by bus: Líneas 1 or 4

Access by car: Park in the centre of **Chipude** (at the *plaza*) or on the road to the cemetery.

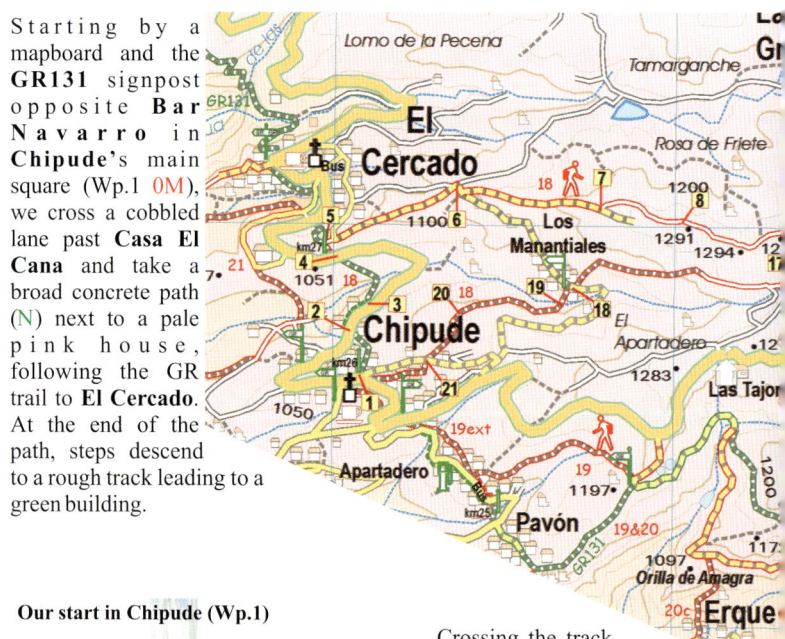

Starting by a mapboard and the **GR131** signpost opposite **Bar Navarro** in **Chipude**'s main square (Wp.1 0M), we cross a cobbled lane past **Casa El Cana** and take a broad concrete path (N) next to a pale pink house, following the GR trail to **El Cercado**. At the end of the path, steps descend to a rough track leading to a green building.

Our start in Chipude (Wp.1)

Crossing the track, we swing left on a dirt path, descending briefly along the left bank of a dry watercourse before turning right at a breeze-block byre. Crossing onto the right bank, we traverse a rock shelf lined with prickly pear and descend to the main road (Wp.2 7M), where we turn right and briefly follow the road. 75

Wp.3, turning left to cross the valley

metres after a breeze-block garage with blue doors, we turn left on a broad trail signposted 'El Cercado' (Wp.3 10M) and cross the valley.

Crossing the road on the far side of the valley (Wp.4 15M), we continue climbing on the donkey trail till we see **El Cercado**.

25 metres after the Km27 marker of the **GR132**, we leave the trail and turn right on a dirt track (Wp.5 20M), joining an asphalted branch from **El Cercado**. Climbing east toward a pylon up on the ridge, we come into view of the antennae at the southern tip of **Garajonay** and, off to our right, the tiny hamlet of **Los Manantiales**.

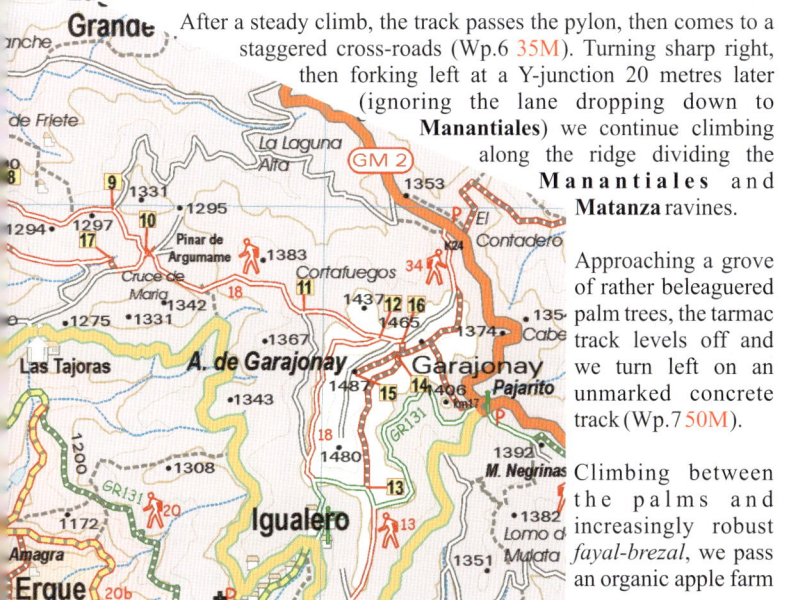

After a steady climb, the track passes the pylon, then comes to a staggered cross-roads (Wp.6 35M). Turning sharp right, then forking left at a Y-junction 20 metres later (ignoring the lane dropping down to **Manantiales**) we continue climbing along the ridge dividing the **Manantiales** and **Matanza** ravines.

Approaching a grove of rather beleaguered palm trees, the tarmac track levels off and we turn left on an unmarked concrete track (Wp.7 50M).

Climbing between the palms and increasingly robust *fayal-brezal*, we pass an organic apple farm

Onto the concrete track at Wp.7

before the concrete gives way to dirt (Wp.8 58M). When we reach a Y-junction, the left-hand branch of which is blocked off to cars by metal posts (Wp.9 65M), we bear right and descend to a signposted junction at the end of a concrete-and-stone track (again with metal posts) in sight of the western flank of a pine forest (Wp.10 70M).

Following the stone-and-concrete paved track (E), we head toward **Garajonay**. The track swings right in front of a stand of tall pine, where there's a signpost for 'Alto de Garajonay 2km', and climbs steadily then steeply. Joining a dirt track at a bend (Wp.11 80M), we bear left and climb to the junction (Wp.12 90M) with the main track round the summit of **Garajonay**.

The quickest way to the top is to turn left then right 100 metres later, but a pleasanter if longer approach is to be had by turning right for 'Pajarito/Igualero'. The track circles the southern side of the summit, passing two branches down to **Igualero**.

We take the first branch on the left (Wp.13 105M), a broad trail climbing through mixed woodland to a cross-roads of paths (Wp.14 115M). Turning left, we climb to the **Alto de Garajonay** *mirador* (Wp.15 120M), from where we have superb views of the neighbouring islands, notably **Tenerife** but also **Gran Canaria** on a clear day.

To continue our itinerary, we descend (S) past the firewatch cabin and take the **Contadero** dirt track; *not* the branch to the antennae. After turning left at the 'Chipude/Pajarito' junction (Wp.16 125M), we rejoin our outward route, which we follow back to the concrete-and-stone turn-off at the western side of **Pinar de Argumame** (Wp.10 145M). Here we take the dirt track signposted 'Chipude'. 200 metres later at a T-junction, we bear right in front of a fenced garden onto a minor dirt track (Signed 'Chipude 1.8km'). After 1 minute, the track swings left in front of another track blocked to traffic and we follow 'Ruta 18' for 'Chipude/El Cercado' (Wp.17 147M).

Approaching Manantiales (Wp.18)

Carrying straight on along the right fork two hundred metres later, we maintain a westerly direction as the increasingly rough track dwindles to a trail. The trail gradually settles into a smooth dirt path descending to **Manantiales** where we cross the tarmac access lane (Wp.18 175M).

Following a concrete walkway, we bear left at a signpost and pass alongside allotments planted with potatoes. Ignoring a narrow branch to the right into the fields, we continue to a white house, where we bear right along a steep cobbled path that descends to cross the **Manantiales** watercourse (Wp.19 180M). A gentle to steady climb brings us onto a ridge (Wp.20 190M) just north-east of **Chipude**, after which we skirt round vineyards and join the cobbled lane (Wp.21 195M) that we crossed at the beginning of the walk. Turning right, we follow this lane past a transformer tower back to the main square.

19 FORTALEZA

The **Fortaleza** or fortress, is the distinctive table-top mountain seen from just about every key vantage point in the south-west. It's usually approached from **Chipude**, but we favour this circuit from the **Erque** turn-off. Though short, the walk involves some strenuous scrambling and a short chimney climb.

There's a slight risk of vertigo, but the difficulty should not be exaggerated. We did it with a forty-kilo Old English Sheepdog in tow and were followed by a man with a baby on his back! The slight risk can be avoided entirely by simply turning left at Wp.7 and cutting out the climb to the summit. The walk starts at the **Erque** turn-off east of **Chipude**, but there are two alternative starting points described in the access details.

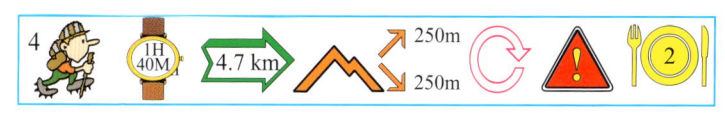

4 | 1H 40M | 4.7 km | 250m / 250m | ↻ | ⚠ | 2

Access by bus: Línea 1 - ask for **Carretera de Erque**, not an official stop, but there's room for the bus to pull over. Alternatively, there is an official bus stop in **Apartadero/Pavón** from where you can pick up the walk at Wp.4. (Línea 4 - limited service; for more frequent service, take the GR trail northwest from Wp.4 to reach the *plaza* in **Chipude** in 700 metres - Línea 1).

The Erque turn-off (Wp.1)

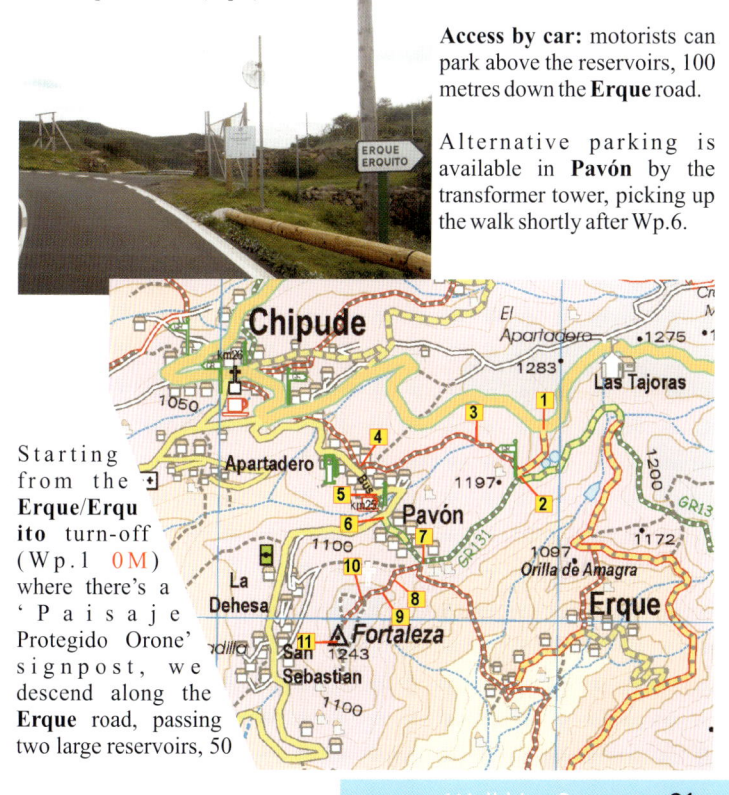

Access by car: motorists can park above the reservoirs, 100 metres down the **Erque** road.

Alternative parking is available in **Pavón** by the transformer tower, picking up the walk shortly after Wp.6.

Starting from the **Erque/Erquito** turn-off (Wp.1 0M) where there's a 'Paisaje Protegido Orone' signpost, we descend along the **Erque** road, passing two large reservoirs, 50

Walk! La Gomera 91

metres after which, at a fenced and covered reservoir, we turn right onto an eroded donkey trail (Wp.2 5M).

Wps.3-4; glimpses of Fortaleza

The trail soon continues as a dirt path and drops down to cross a watercourse (Wp.3 10M) skirting the northern flank of the valley behind the hamlet of **Apartadero**. It's worth pausing here to look up at the **Fortaleza** and orient yourself: the white path through the green tonsure below the summit is our way into the rocks.

Flanked by impressive agave and ignoring all branches, we stick to the main path as it descends into **Apartadero**, passing a small shrine and then joining a tarmac slip road (Wp.4 20M) 100 metres east of the DISA petrol station. Turning left, we descend onto the **La Dama** road near a bus stop.

Following the road toward the head of the **Barranco de Iguala**, we bear right on a donkey trail just after **Bar Los Camioneros** which doubles as a small shop (closed Mondays) (Wp.5 25M).

Bar Los Camioneros; the donkey trail is ahead right (Wp.5)

Our trail cuts across the ravine, rejoining the road in front of a dark grey house (Wp.6 30M), 50 metres west of a cobbled lane.

After bearing left towards a transformer tower, we turn right and take the cobbled lane into the shabbily picturesque hamlet of **Pavón**. After a steady climb, the lane runs into tarmac, then stone-and-concrete, before dwindling to a dirt path.

Tackling the summit - looking back to Wp.7

Climbing past a beautifully restored farmhouse with decorative stones set in its white walls, we bear right at a Y-junction (Wp.7 35M) onto the saddle behind **Fortaleza**, passing a 'Monumento Natural' signpost. After a steady climb on a clear path, we come to the base of the white path (Wp.8 40M) and the climb steepens. 30 metres

Ascending Fortaleza

from two eucalyptus trees, 10 metres from a large red '2' on the rock, the white path swings left, climbing into the rocks defining the summit.

Using partially tailored 'natural' steps, we reach a rough, sloping ledge and bear slightly right to a rock chimney (Wp.9 50M) identifiable by a faint green waymark and two small shelves of rubble, one halfway up, the other at the top. After a very slightly vertiginous five-metre climb during which we have to steady ourselves with our hands, we emerge on a craggy ridge between the chimney and the summit.

Taking care to memorise our route, which is less obvious on the way back, we wind through the rocks onto the sloping rim of the plateau, 50 metres east of a large white metal cross (Wp.10 60M).

Fortaleza's southern tip (south of Wp.11)

We now simply follow the cairns (SW) across the plateau to the trig-point (Wp.11 65M). The summit is a bit of an anticlimax after the chimney ascent, but the views are good, notably of the ravines around **La Dama**.

Retracing our steps to Wp.7 (85M), we have a choice of routes:-

To return to Wp.1, bear right, maintaining direction (ENE) on a broad partially cobbled donkey trail that climbs steadily, to join the **Erque** road 75 metres below the reservoirs (100M).

If you're relying on the bus and don't trust the driver to acknowledge a sweaty rambler at an unscheduled stop, turn left and return to Wp.4 to catch the bus back from the **Apartadero** bus stop, 100m north-west of **Bar Los Camioneros**. Alternatively, continue to **Chipude** from Wp.4 along the *sendero* GR, for more frequent bus service.

20 BARRANCO DE ERQUE

This long tour round one of the island's most spectacular and isolated ravines is probably the toughest walk in the book and is only recommended in its entirety for experienced walkers with excellent pathfinding skills.

For three-quarters of the itinerary, there's not a smooth, straightforward step to be had. We descend on the sort of 'way' that makes you marvel at the intensity of old time neighbourly feeling - you really had to want to get at someone to beat a path down here. And the ascent follows the remains of a donkey trail that's a bit like Dr. Who's Tardis, in that it keeps disappearing at critical junctures of the narrative. In sum, the sort of walk which you end with a faint sense of incredulity, as it doesn't seem wholly feasible to have done all that in a single day.

There's a slight risk of vertigo and a strong risk of dehydration. Take at least 3 litres water per person, plus soft drinks and food. It's worth repeating, given the difficulty of this walk, that timings are 'pure', excluding all breaks and pathfinding pauses. Allow at least eight hours for the full walk. Although the vertigo risk is slight, the walk is already tough enough without adding supplementary anxieties, *so is not recommended for vertigo sufferers.*

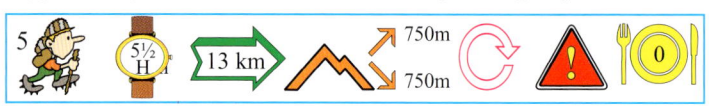

Access by bus: Línea 1. If arriving by bus, ask for **Carretera de Erque**, which is not an official stop, but there's room for the bus to pull over. Alternatively, there is an official bus stop in **Apartadero/Pavón** from where you can pick up the walk at Wp.3 (see the map and Walk 19 for details).

Access by car: motorists park at Wp.2, 300 metres down the **Erque** road or, to avoid a heartbreaking little climb at the end, Wp.28, 1km down the **Erque** road. Alternative parking is available in **Pavón** by the transformer tower, picking up the walk at Wp.3 (see the map and Walk 19 for details).

From the **Erque** turn-off (Wp.1 0M), we follow the road for 300 metres till it swings sharp left (Wp.2 5M) and we continue straight ahead (SW) on a broad trail curving round a bend, from where we can see **Erquito**, the pine forested slopes below **Igualero**, and part of our final, balcony path.

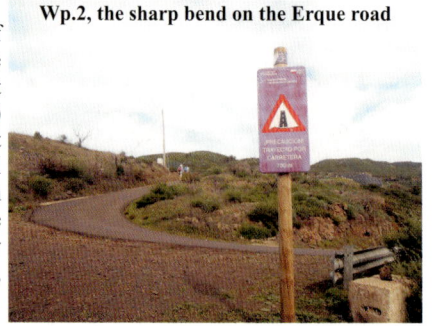

Wp.2, the sharp bend on the Erque road

Our trail descends past a ruin, after which we branch left (Wp.3 15M) just before a neatly restored farm house. We keep left then, off the trail climbing to **Fortaleza** to pass between two stone cabins, where a large cairn indicates the start of a hugely improbable descent (Wp.4 16M). Whether this should be called a path or a 'way' is a moot point, but for the sake of convenience, we'll call it a path.

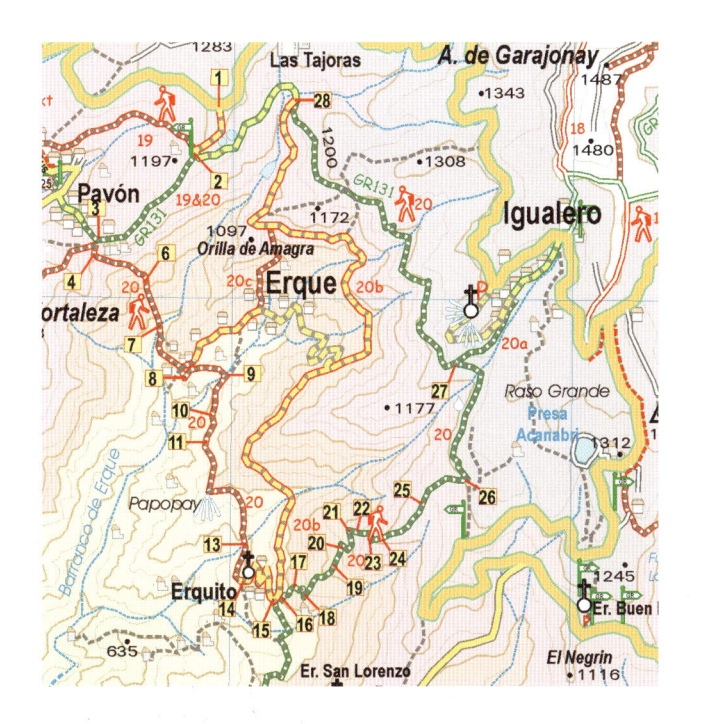

At first, the path is clear, crossing occasional steep rock steps and descending (E) through a great sweep of agave and prickly pear, but after ten minutes, a slightly vertiginous stretch zigzags down a very steep slope onto a ledge where the way becomes unclear (Wp.5 35M).

Bearing right for 20 metres, we pass above a small slightly unnerving drop until we see a curious wall built into the overhang beyond the watercourse ahead of us.

Tackling the shelf descent

On our left, a nub of rock, hopefully marked by a cairn, protrudes from the drop to form a small cleft wedged full of boulders. Edging onto the blocked cleft, we cross the face of the small drop on a naturally stepped shelf, at the bottom of which we recover the path. The rest of the descent is well-marked with cairns.

Bearing left, we follow a natural rock 'terrace' for 150 metres until a cairn indicates the way down onto the next 'terrace', after which the path becomes clearer as it winds down a steep rocky spur toward the great rhino-head ridge extending from the **Orilla de Amagra** - the tallest of the 'horns'.

After traversing a long slab of rock between two dumpy palms (Wp.6 65M), we come to a slightly obscure stretch where sheep have trailblazed dozens of splinter 'paths' through the prickly pear. Bearing right (S), we stick to the cairn-marked way for a very steep descent off the nose of the rocky spur, after which a straightforward but still steep descent brings us to a watercourse feeding the ravine (Wp.7 90M).

After crossing the watercourse, it's worth looking back at the descent: from here what seemed improbable from above is plainly impossible!

Branching right at a Y-junction 50 metres later, we follow a dirt path segmented by outcrops of rock, skirting the southern tip of the rhino-ridge before passing behind a grey bungalow, the **Villagarcia** (Wp.8 100M).

Passing below two small houses directly behind **Villagarcia**, we bear right at a junction, ignoring concrete steps up to the **Erque** track. Descending towards the bed of the main *barranco* on a partially cobbled way, we reach a small spur tipped with a wooden electricity post and 'duck-and-chick' pillars of rock.

'duck and chick' rock pillars

Leaving the main path, which descends to the right of the pillars, we cross the neck of rock behind them and drop down onto a narrow path descending (E) to pass between small terraces and tall, scorched palms. At the end of the lowest terrace, we bear right on an overgrown path descending to cross the stream (Wp.9 110M), beyond which we climb over a terrace wall and scramble onto the **Erque-Erquito** path, the zig-zagging course of which can be seen during our descent.

Bearing right, we climb gently to pass through a tunnel of broom, 20 metres after which we swing left below electricity poles (Wp.10 115M) to cross a rockspill and begin the zigzagging climb seen from above. After crossing a small spur (Wp.11 120M), the path levels out briefly then climbs to cross two more rockspills before emerging on the tip of a ridge from where we can see **Erquito** (Wp.12 135M).

(Looking ESE, we can see a concrete curve in the **Igualero**-**Playa Santiago** road. Between us and the road, there's a knoll of rock on a broad ridge defined by two watercourses. The described route climbs to the left of this ridge and is every bit as arduous as it looks!)

A gentle descent (ESE) brings us onto a rocky spur, at the end of which we bear left, winding down to cross a footbridge (Wp.13 145M) onto a clear path leading to the tiny plaza of **Erquito** chapel (Wp.14 150M), where there's a charmless but functional portico offering shade and under, water.

From the chapel, we follow the track (possibly surfaced by the time you read this) up to the second sharp left-hand bend (Wp.15 160M), just below a stone cabin, which is where the moment of truth comes and we make our choice of return routes.

Sensible people will bear left and follow the track/lane back to the starting point, which takes about ninety minutes. However, there's nothing very sensible about this walk, so if you're up for a VERY GRUELLING but very satisfying ascent, turn right. This is only for the seriously committed. You have been warned!

Climbing behind the cabin, in fact a roofless ruin, we ignore a broad path running SSE, and cut straight up (E) through the rocks for 50 metres to emerge on the remains of an old donkey trail (Wp.16 162M) which we follow for most of the climb. Bearing left, we follow the trail as it climbs (NE) until cairns mark a detour skirting a stretch blocked by fallen rocks and agave. Following the cairns, we cut a corner of the trail and climb towards a small, sturdy palm, after which (Wp.17 170M) we recover the paved trail and zigzag up onto a minor spur directly behind the ruined cabin (Wp.18 175M). Ignoring dirt branches to the east, we bear left (NE). From here, we can see a line of electricity pylons. The highest visible pylon is our general objective.

The trail disappears in a sheet of rock, but maintaining direction (NE), we follow cairns to a seam of yellow rock (Wp.19 185M) and bear left (NNE) on a faint path crossing tiny crumbling terraces, aiming 100 metres to the left of our guiding pylon. 50 metres before the pylon, we climb to the right of a solitary palm to rejoin the donkey trail (Wp.20 190M). Bearing right, away from the pylon, we climb a stretch of extremely rugged trail, until it dwindles to a dirt path leading to our guiding pylon (Wp.21 200M) from where we see the radio masts below **Igualero** *ermita*.

It's worth pausing to catch your breath here. Though the steepest climbing is done, a potentially complicated bit remains. The donkey trail traces a long detour to the north then doubles back above the rocks directly behind the pylon, but last time we were here, the trail was so badly overgrown that it was simpler to climb straight over the rocks, not as difficult as it looks from below. Hands are required, but it's an easy scramble, comparable to the descent at Wp.5. Hopefully though, the donkey trail has been cleared recently and is passable, making the rock scramble unnecessary.

Following the cairn-marked route, we wind up through the lower rocks to a small bluff 30 metres east of the pylon, where we find a shelf similar to the one at Wp.5, but longer and broader. Climbing onto the bluff, we find more cairns leading to a second, much smaller outcrop of rock, behind which we recover the donkey trail (Wp.22 205M), 75 metres from the pylon.

Another very steep, very rugged climb, zigzags up onto a slope below a spine of rock running along the ridge (Wp.23 210M), 150 metres from the pylon. Bearing left (NNE), we follow the trail, which is initially buried by a spill of small rocks, up to a tall cairn on the horizon (Wp.24 215M). Ignoring traces bearing right over bare rock 50 metres after the cairn, we maintain direction

(NNE), on a rough, reddish brown 'way' winding through the rocks and cistus along the north-western flank of the ridge. This way curves round to the right, entering a shallow erosion channel (Wp.25 220M) on the back of the ridge, where all paths disappear!

250 metres above us is a line of wooden electricity poles. One of these poles, directly ahead of us (NE), is lined up with a metal pylon on the horizon. We join a path across the ridge between this wooden pole and its neighbour to the right. Picking our way through low cistus to a wide 'stairway' of rough, grassy terraces, we climb from terrace to terrace (NNE), keeping an eye on the two wooden poles identified from below.

Towards the top, the terraces are again covered in low cistus, but tending towards the pole on the right, we find a final brief stretch of paved trail before joining a good dirt path next to a large boulder cairn (Wp.26 235M). The pathfinding problems are over!

Turning left, we follow this path over a slight rise, passing a small spring and crossing the **Igualero** watercourse. After a gentle climb, we join the waymarked path between **Igualero** and **Chipude** (Wp.27 250M). Bearing left, we follow this superb balcony path as it winds along below the pine trees with great views over the *barranco*. The path finally descends onto the **Erque** road (Wp.28 280M), 700 metres from Wp.2, 1 km from the main road.

21 ERMITA DE NUESTRA SEÑORA DE GUADALUPE

This tiny *ermita*, so diminutive it's little more than an overgrown oratory, is perhaps the most perfectly situated on the island. Perched on a platform overlooking the **Barranco de Argaga** with fine views out to sea across the **Guerquenche** and **Mérica** ridges, it seems utterly isolated and cut off from the world, though the hamlet of **Gerián** is in fact just round the corner. Starting from **El Cercado**, this itinerary is ideal for those wanting tame walking in wild country.

| 3 | 2¾-3H | 10 km | 350m / 350m | ↻ | 4* |

*in **El Cercado**

Stroll
Turn left on the trail just before Wp.4 to climb into **Chipude**, returning via Walk 18 Wps.1-5 carrying straight on at Wp.5.

Extension: Walk 22

Access by bus: Línea 1 or 4.

Access by car: parking spaces are limited in **El Cercado**. If there's no room in the village, drive the start of the walk and park in the lay-by 400 metres from Wp.1.

We leave **El Cercado** a few metres from the bus-stop in a small square, taking a tarmac lane opposite an information board about the region's pottery tradition (Wp.1 0M). Descending gently above the **Barranco de la Matanza**, we follow the lane to the village *colegio* on the ridge between **El Cercado** and **Chipude**,

Wp.1 at the start in El Cercado square

The colegio

where we ignore tracks to the right and maintain direction (SE) on a donkey trail (Wp.2 10M).

The donkey trail descends to cross a dry affluent of the **Matanza** (Wp.3 15M), after which we bear right on a dirt track.

Climbing gently, we look for a blue-waymarked trail branching left, 5 metres after which we turn right on a path (Wp.4 20M) above an immense bank of figs. The path runs along the valley's southern flank, passing overgrown branches to left and right.

Walk! La Gomera 99

After the confluence of the **Matanza** and its affluent, the path loses its defining walls and crosses a grassy terrace then runs along a ledge below low rocks, passing a cairn-marked branch down to our return route (Wp.5 40M). Ignoring faint traces branching left 20 metres later, we stick to the main path as it winds through rocks, crossing two faint X-roads, where we bear left then right, descending to join a dirt track (Wp.6 50M).

We follow the track down towards the junction of the **Matanza** and **Manantiales** ravines, which together form the **Barranco de Argaga**. At the end of the track (Wp.7 55M), we traverse a grassy terrace and, after 15 metres, turn right on a roughly cobbled path partially overgrown with bamboo.

Following the canal

Descending onto vine terraces, where the cobbles give way to dirt, we wind down to pass in front of a small cabin, where we bear left, then right five metres later, crossing the **Manantiales** ravine (Wp.8 65M) 100 metres above the confluence of the two *barrancos*.

We now follow a canal to the *ermita*, sometimes walking in the canal, sometimes on paths running above and below it.

The way is obvious and well-marked with cairns, but if you find yourself more than 10 metres below the canal, check you haven't drifted onto one of the many minor ways descending into the valley, notably at a cairn marked branch (Wp.9 75M), where we carry straight on to rejoin the canal.

100 *Walk! La Gomera*

At the junction with the clear, paved trail from **Valle Gran Rey** (Wp.10 78M), we ignore a branch climbing to the left and continue along the remains of the canal, until a final stretch of path climbs to the *ermita* (Wp.11 85M).

To return, we retrace our steps to Wp.8 (110M). Re-crossing the **Manantiales**, we follow the canal path round to its source at a small silt dam in the **Matanza** (Wp.12 120M), shortly after two small ruins and immediately after a solitary palm tree. At this point the **Matanza** is divided from **Valle Gran Rey** by a narrow rock wall and it's worth crossing the watercourse to enjoy the views.

The *ermita* at Wp.11

Returning to Wp.12, we continue along the left bank of the watercourse for 50 metres. Ignoring a faint path climbing to the right, we cross the watercourse and climb past a cabin built into a cave, bearing left at a Y-junction a few minutes later.

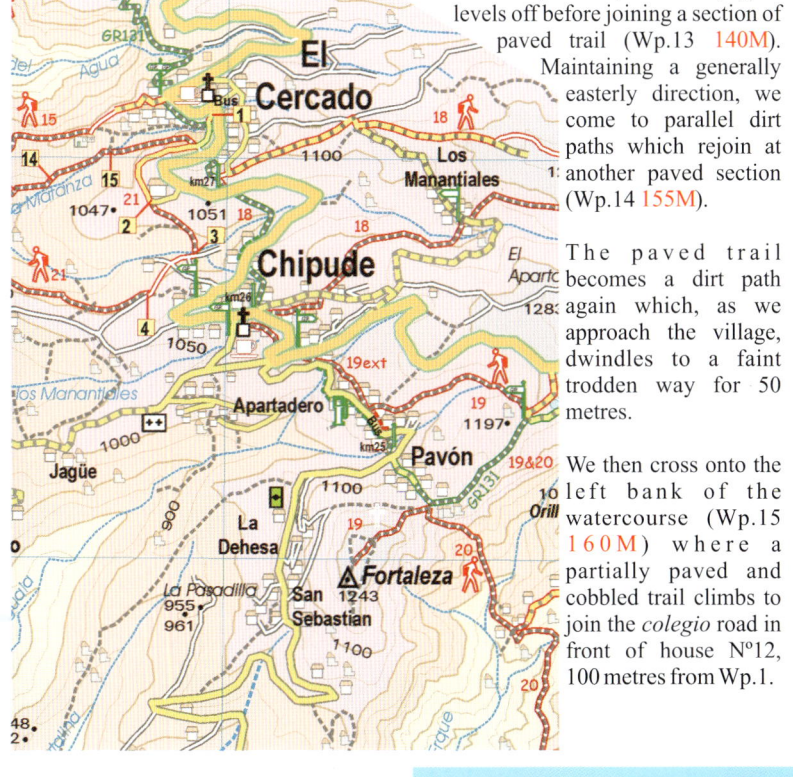

After a steady climb, our stony path levels off before joining a section of paved trail (Wp.13 140M). Maintaining a generally easterly direction, we come to parallel dirt paths which rejoin at another paved section (Wp.14 155M).

The paved trail becomes a dirt path again which, as we approach the village, dwindles to a faint trodden way for 50 metres.

We then cross onto the left bank of the watercourse (Wp.15 160M) where a partially paved and cobbled trail climbs to join the *colegio* road in front of house Nº12, 100 metres from Wp.1.

Walk! La Gomera 101

22 TEQUERGENCHE

This straightforward linear walk (out and back) is a relatively easy way of seeing the **Barranco de Argaga** and also a useful preliminary excursion prior to embarking on Walk 23. The perspective on **Valle Gran Rey** from the **Tequergenche** cliffs is astonishing - perfect for those who are at once fascinated by and fearful of heights! The high exertion rating is due to the rough terrain and the fact that most of the climbing is on the way back. Remember this when you're cheerfully galloping along on the outward leg. Not recommended in hot weather.

4 | 3¼ H | 12 km | 350m / 350m | out & back | 0

Access by car: to reach the **Ermita de Nuestra Señora de Guadalupe**, take the lane to **Chipude** cemetery, which starts at the junction of the **El Cercado** and **La Dama** roads between signs for 'La Dama/La Rajita' and 'Chipude/El Cercado'. Turn right at km 4.3, in sight of **Gerián**. The *ermita* is 500 metres from the turn-off.

Ermita de Nuestra Señora de Guadalupe

Looking in the direction of our route from Wp.1

Just to the right of the *ermita* (Wp.1 0M), at the end of the wall defining its small *plaza*, we take a narrow path heading NE above an abandoned canal.

The path descends to the canal, which we follow for 25 metres before bearing left on a minor path leading down to a broader trail (Wp.2 10M) - you can also join this trail at the top, following the canal for a further 75 metres. Bearing left, we follow the trail into the **Barranco de Argaga**, ignoring a branch to the right about halfway down.

Crossing the watercourse (Wp.3 15M), we bear left through rocks, climbing onto a broad dirt path heading west along the ravine's northern flank. After a long level stretch, the path climbs slightly, passing in rapid succession three branches to the right, the first (a minor path that you may not notice) doubling back north-east, the second running parallel to the main path along a terrace, the third cutting through a wide natural gateway marked by a large, faint white arrow (Wp.4 25M), which is the main trail down to **Valle Gran Rey**.

102 *Walk! La Gomera*

Ignoring all three turnings, we continue along the ridge to the left of two small peaks, the second of which is **Montaña Adivino**. Midway between the two peaks, a path branching right leads to a natural *mirador* overlooking **Valle Gran Rey**. Below **Adivino**, we ignore a minor fork to the left, staying on the higher path, which leads to superb views down the **Barranco de Argaga** and glimpses of the beaches at the mouth of **Valle Gran Rey**. Descending toward the long narrow neck of **Degollada de los Bueyes**, we bear right at a junction with another path (Wp.5 40M) and wind down the ridge, spectacularly poised between **Valle Gran Rey** and the **Barranco de Argaga**.

Skirting to the left of a spine-like necklace of rock, we descend slightly (ignore a cairn indicating a level way along the top) through a rockier, sparser landscape where even the cactus can't get a grip and house-leeks colonise what purchase there is.

We then climb to two distinct, carefully laid steps, where our route is joined by a minor path up from the *barranco*. Approaching the rise of **Montaña Guerguenche**, we pass a gateway of waist-high cairns (Wp.6 55M), where two very minor paths (one vertiginous, the other verging on the suicidal) descend into **Valle Gran Rey**.

Ignoring a fork to the left 30 metres after the gateway, we resume climbing (SW), gently at first then more steadily, with fine views of the **Fortaleza** to the

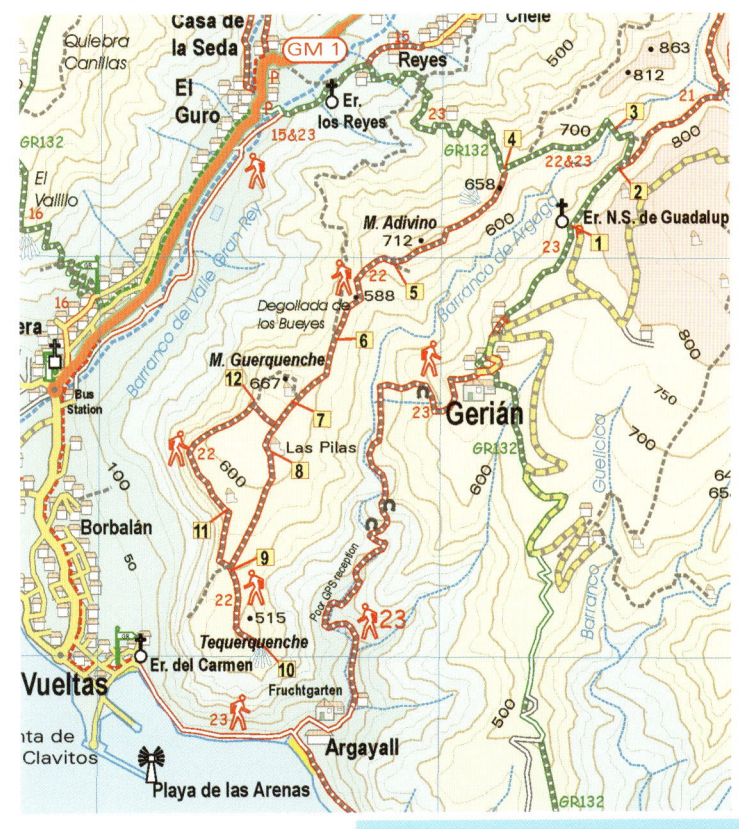

Walk! La Gomera 103

south-east, eventually traversing a forest of snapped agave-scapes to a ruin on top of **Guerguenche** (Wp.7 65M), where we ignore the right fork and carry straight on. Following an increasingly faint path across a stony plateau, we pass a rough threshing circle. Maintaining direction (SW) and ignoring a stone-laid way branching right, we cross rocks topped with a tall cairn, below which we descend to the **Las Pilas** ruins (Wp.8 70M) above an expanse of marginally less stony terraces.

Descending toward the distant mass of **Tequergenche**, we cross the terraces, looking for cairns indicating the way when the path, never better than obscure, virtually disappears altogether. After a steady descent, the terraces crumble into pathless scrub and we drop down to the broad saddle behind **Tequergenche**, where we can see two clear paths heading south. Taking the main, left-hand path (Wp.9 85M), we gradually bear SE to a superb natural *mirador* (Wp.10 90M) overlooking the **Barranco de Argaga**, where we can see the three palms and overhang cave passed in Walk 23.

Once we've had our fill of the views, we retrace our steps to the saddle behind **Tequergenche**, but instead of climbing back to **Las Pilas**, bear left across the reddish dirt slope, picking up a rough, cairn-marked way climbing onto the cliffs overlooking first the port at **Vueltas**, then **La Calera**, and finally the *charcos* and beaches of **Valle Gran Rey**. The views should be sufficiently impressive to discourage going too close to the cliffs.

La Calera seen from the cliffs

Following a faint path, we climb gently between the cliffs and the tips of terraces, eventually coming onto a terrace built along the edge of the cliff and passing a sheet of corrugated iron (Wp.11 105M) weighed down with stones.

Continuing along the cliff path, largely on the level but climbing occasionally, we gradually bear NE then E, coming into view of the entire **Valle Gran Rey** and running alongside a line of young pine clinging to the cliff tops. 100 metres after the first pine, we see a large cairn on our right (Wp.12 120M), the first for some while, at which point we leave the cliff path and turn right, crossing a very broad terrace (SE then E) back to the first ruin, from where we follow our outward route back to the *ermita*.

Note: mountain paths never look the same from different directions. Remember to descend after the ruin, ignoring traces climbing to the crest. Likewise, stick to the main traces skirting **Adivino**. Ignore a fork to the right as you approach the gateway at Wp.4. Look out for silvery white waymarks, most of which are placed for people walking east.

23 BARRANCO DE ARGAGA

This is the best known and most popular 'wild' walk on La Gomera, partly because it's right next door to **Valle Gran Rey**, partly because it really is very wild, most of the climb, though well waymarked with arrows, dots, and cairns, being virtually pathless. Doing the route in reverse is not recommended. Not only are the waymarks placed for people climbing, but descending the *barranco* is potentially dangerous. We do not recommend this route after even the lightest rainfall. The descent into **Valle Gran Rey** is dull, but that's no bad thing after such an exciting climb. Bear in mind that references to left/right banks are the opposite of our direction i.e. the left bank of the watercourse is on our right. Take plenty of water. There's a standpipe at the *ermita*, but if the sun's out, the water will be hot by the time you get there. Only for experienced walkers.

Though far from being the most vertiginous walk in the book, this itinerary is not recommended for anyone without a head for heights. Although the vertigo risk is mild, remoteness and the inadvisability of turning back to descend the *barranco* make the precautionary principle more imperative than ever.

NB Exceptionally for this itinerary, we use the term 'watershed' in the sense of 'a slope or a structure down which water flows' to distinguish ancillary, parallel or affluent watercourses from the principal watercourse. Purists may baulk at this, but it is a valid secondary definition of the term in the dictionary and helps avoid all sorts of confusing verbal gymnastics trying to distinguish between multiple watercourses.

5 | 5¼ H | 11 km | 850m / 850m | ↻ | ⚠ | 2

Access by bus: Línea 1. The described itinerary starts and ends at the bus station opposite the petrol station in **La Calera**, but can easily be adapted if you're staying in **Valle Gran Rey**.

Wp.1, the bus station

Access by car: on street parking anywhere from the bus station, through **Borbalán** to **Vueltas**.

On the track to Argayall from Wp.2

From the bus station (Wp.1 0M), we follow the main road through **Borbalán** for a little over a kilometre, bearing left at the beach-front roundabout to the small port in **Vueltas**. Beyond the port, we take the dirt track (Wp.2 20M) that

Walk! La Gomera 105

runs along the seafront below the intimidating cliffs of **Tequergenche** to the hamlet of **Argayall**, where a signpost marks the mouth of the **Barranco de Argaga** (Wp.3 35M).

Following signs for the 'Fruchtgarten' (where they have planted some 150 varieties of tropical or subtropical fruit), we turn left on a dirt track climbing (NE) alongside the riddled walls of an old banana plantation. Ignoring a ceramic *privado* sign, we stay on the track, crossing the *barranco* watercourse three times, passing the entrance to the Fruit Garden after the second crossing. Immediately after the third crossing, the track is blocked by a wire mesh fence and we drop down into the bed of the *barranco* (Wp.4 45M).

Winding between boulders dotted with cairns, we pick our way upstream to a wooden footbridge where the watercourse narrows between reddish rocks. Bearing left, we climb along the rocks then drop down from a low wall and cross onto the left bank, where a path climbs above a circular reservoir built into the watercourse.

In the mouth of the *barranco*

After crossing or skirting (both routes are waymarked) three long terraces, we traverse the uppermost terrace, at the end of which we climb past three smaller terraces (invisible from below) interleaved with several mini-terraces. Crossing the main watercourse above a silt-dam (Wp.5 60M), we follow the right bank for 75 metres before re-crossing and beginning the real climbing, very steeply, straight up a watershed.

On the ascent (after Wp.5)

From hereon in, the majority of the climb is off-path and principally guided by waymarks. References to 'paths' are very subjective. If you find the climbing (hands required) too much at this stage, turn back, because there's a whole lot more of the same to come.

On the ascent after Wp.7

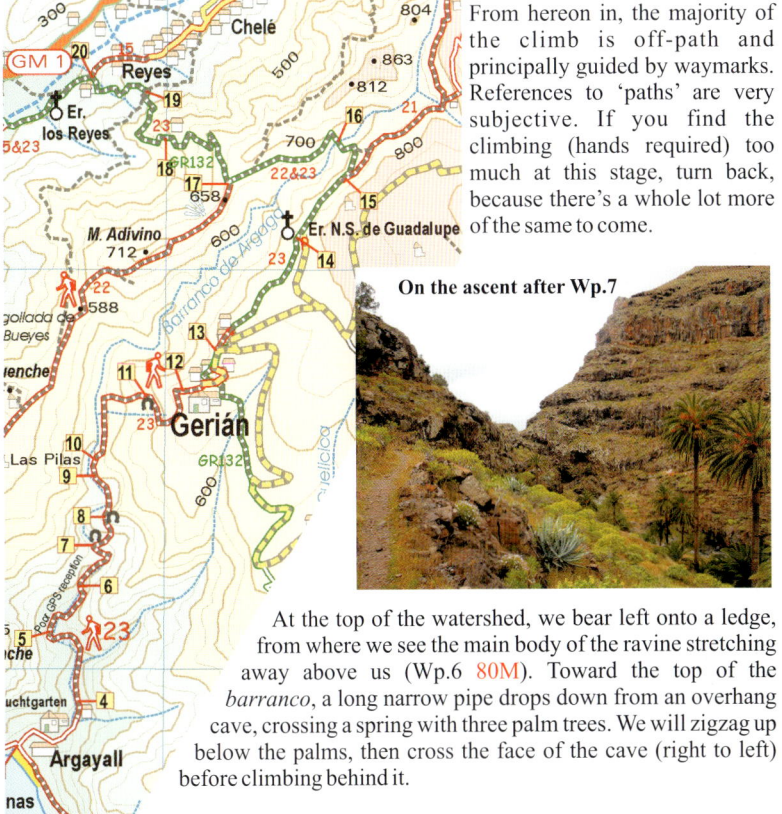

At the top of the watershed, we bear left onto a ledge, from where we see the main body of the ravine stretching away above us (Wp.6 80M). Toward the top of the *barranco*, a long narrow pipe drops down from an overhang cave, crossing a spring with three palm trees. We will zigzag up below the palms, then cross the face of the cave (right to left) before climbing behind it.

At the end of a rough, mildly vertiginous path, a red arrow indicates a roughly stepped descent back into the main watercourse. Ignoring a path bearing left onto terraces, we follow dots and cairns up the watercourse for 50 metres. We then climb onto terraces on the right bank before rejoining the watercourse below a cabin-cave (Wp.7 95M). Climbing back onto the left bank and crossing minute terraces and bare rock, we come to our second and most significant pathless climb. Remember, the waymarks and cairns are your best friends here. When old and new waymarks appear contradictory, follow the new ones.

After following the channel of an ancient canal, we climb onto a ledge below a small overhang cave, passing below the three palms and crossing the pipes seen from Wp.6. We then scramble past a succession of tiny caves, taking advantage of some very approximate but welcome boulder 'stairways'. After a second major boulder stairway, 'handless' walking (not a redundant comment up here) brings us across the face of the large cave seen from below (Wp.8 125M), from where we enjoy superb views back down the *barranco*.

Beyond the cave, we double back on a third major boulder stairway, after which we climb straight across the rocks onto a ridge behind the cave, bringing us into view of the ravine's upper reaches. Still relying on the waymarks, we pick our way across the rocks and follow a rough way along the left bank, passing a precipitous drop and crossing a boulder strewn gully before descending onto a terrace, at the end of which we see a palm and a pipe (Wp.9 140M). We are now in the wildest most isolated corner of the ravine and the silence is total. Skirting a narrow ledge at the end of the terrace, we double back just before the palm on more boulder 'stairs'. After crossing more rocks, we bear right on a very steep but distinct stone path climbing alongside terraces (Wp.10 145M).

After 50 metres, we traverse a terrace to the left before resuming our steep climb on a rough, dirt, gravel, and rock path. The path levels off briefly before climbing on an easier gradient to cross the smooth rocks of a watershed, 50 metres after which we veer right, climbing steadily then steeply up a spur alongside the watershed. Ignoring all branches, we pass a walled-in cave (Wp.11 170M) and cross the head of the watershed.

The hamlet of Gerián

Still climbing, we curve round to the right of and then through rocks speckled with the letter 'M' to a 'Parque Rural Valle Gran Rey' signpost (Wp.12 190M) just below the hamlet of **Gerián**, which is invisible till the last moment. Following the tarmac lane through the hamlet, we pass a small shrine, 30 metres after which, we branch left on a broad path (Wp.13 195M).

Climbing between two houses, we bear north behind the smaller house on the left onto a broad trail from where we can see the tiny **Ermita de Nuestra Señora de Guadalupe**. When the trail bears right, back towards the lane, we branch left on a dirt path running along a terrace to the *ermita* (Wp.14 205M). From the *ermita*, we follow the canal path down to a donkey trail (Wp.15 210M) descending to cross the **Barranco de Argaga** watercourse (Wp.16 215M) before climbing (W) to a wide rock gateway (Wp.17 230M). Leaving the main path as it continues toward **Tequergenche**, we bear right, going through the gateway onto a clear path heading initially NNE, from where we can see the white walls and orange roof of **Ermita los Reyes**, way below us at the bottom of a broad watercourse.

The path gradually bears NW, winding down a narrow rocky ridge to pass a scattered stand of palm below a ramshackle cabin (Wp.18 245M). We then climb very slightly round the nose of the ridge, away from the *ermita* (NEE), after which a series of tight zigzags descend a secondary spur to a junction (Wp.19 255M).

The main trail bears right, but both routes rejoin further down the spur, for a final cobbled descent to two small houses, where we join the path (Wp.20 265M) to **La Calera**, five minutes from the *ermita*, thirty minutes from the bus-station (See Walk 15, Wp.8+ for details).

24 BARRANCO DE ARURE

On the whole, water is altogether too precious a commodity in the Canaries to be allowed to do anything so wasteful as falling and there are only two streams on La Gomera (the **Barrancos del Cedro** and **de Arure**) that aren't siphoned off at source. In this itinerary we follow the **Arure** stream to the prettiest waterfall on the island.

It's a popular walk, largely because it gives a sense of adventure without actually being alarmingly adventurous, so don't be surprised if you meet a large party of elderly German hikers just when you thought you were really getting off the beaten track. For all its popularity though, the deeper we go into the ravine, the more real the adventure seems. Ideal in hot weather. Beware of slippery rocks, especially on the return.

N.B. The only waypoint provided is for the start of the route; the terrain means that GPS signals here are unreliable.

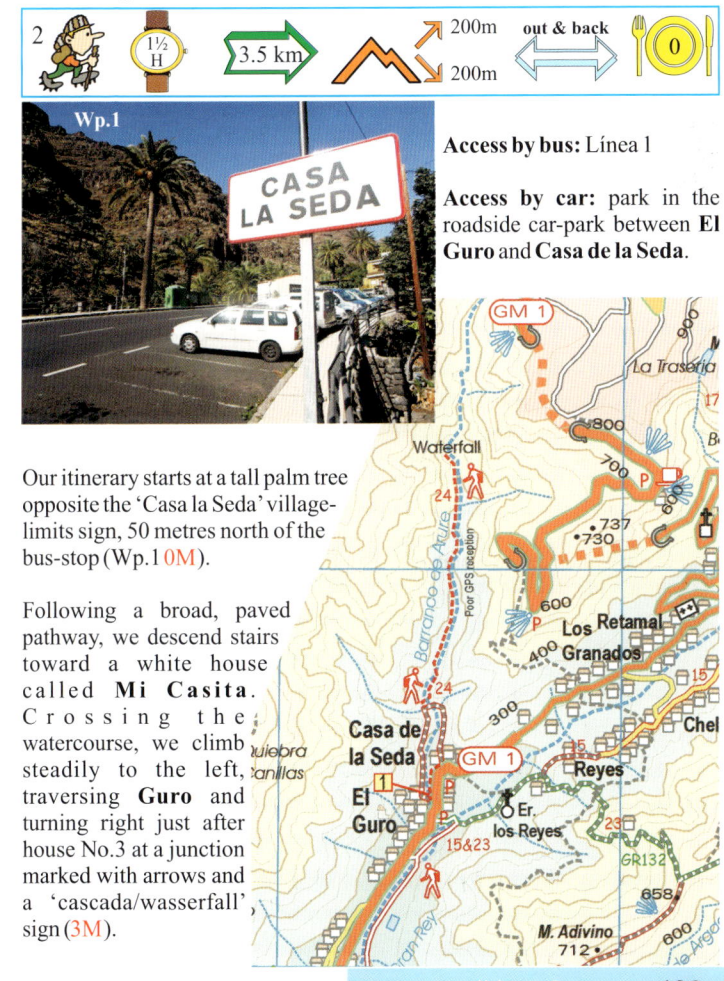

Access by bus: Línea 1

Access by car: park in the roadside car-park between **El Guro** and **Casa de la Seda**.

Our itinerary starts at a tall palm tree opposite the 'Casa la Seda' village-limits sign, 50 metres north of the bus-stop (Wp.1 0M).

Following a broad, paved pathway, we descend stairs toward a white house called **Mi Casita**. Crossing the watercourse, we climb steadily to the left, traversing **Guro** and turning right just after house No.3 at a junction marked with arrows and a 'cascada/wasserfall' sign (3M).

Walk! La Gomera 109

The paved way soon runs into a dirt path and leaves the village, passing the cables at the head of a cargo lift and joining a canal path amid a flurry of waymarks (10M).

We follow the canal for 75 metres till another embarrassment of waymarks indicates where we branch left, climbing across terraces of agave and cactus spurge on a route waymarked to such surreal excess, it's almost decorated. Dropping down to descend a rough gully, we cross the watercourse onto the left bank. Bearing left along a terrace below two tin plaques hanging from a retaining wall, we rejoin the watercourse (now a flowing stream) 75 metres later, next to a length of corroded black pipe (20M).

Either crossing the stream and climbing a small rise or walking directly upstream (both routes rejoin), we weave in and out of the water, following occasional cairns. Emerging from a corridor of bamboo, we climb to the left of the first of four mini-waterfalls. Skirting to the right of a second mini-fall 50 metres later, we climb across a long sheet of rock and, 75 metres after that, bear left (35M), climbing across terraces (hands required) dotted with cairns and waymarks.

Nearing the cascade

A narrow path tunnels through brambles before rejoining the stream, 50 metres along which we ignore a large red arrow (40M) apparently suggesting we take up rock-climbing. Instead, we follow a faint path along the left bank, dipping into, out of, then back into the stream, and passing the figure of a man painted on the rock.

We now simply follow the stream, skirting two more mini-falls before running into, almost literally, the main waterfall (50M).

At the waterfall

Retracing our route to the first crossing of the watercourse (80M), we bear left after the tin plaques and climb behind a small sheepfold onto a canal path. The canal path is overgrown after 25 metres so that we have to drop down beyond the sheepfold before climbing to cross a terrace and rejoin the canal.

After following the canal for another 25 metres, we bear right, descending on a rough path toward orchards, just above which we climb slightly before joining a paved path leading to the road, 100 metres from our starting point.

25 LOMO DEL CARRETÓN

Elsewhere in this book, we talk about paths being 'improbable' or 'impossible', but the two routes between **Taguluche** and the **Mirador Ermita del Santo** simply beggar belief. And why they needed two of them, is anybody's guess! One thing is for certain, you had to be very hungry or very frightened to contemplate beating a path up here. Nowadays all you need is a desire to experience one of the most remarkable walks on the entire island. It doesn't make any more sense than it ever did, but it's tremendous fun *for experienced walkers with a good head for heights*.

Since we first walked it, the route has been improved so that it's all on well established trails or tracks. However, the descent is VERY steep, so if you are uncertain whether it's for you, check the start from the *mirador* to see how you feel about it before you are committed. Although it's probably not the most vertiginous path on the island, it includes features to inspire all varieties of vertigo, notably precipitous slopes and steeply raked natural stairways.

Our original version of this itinerary started in **Taguluche** to do the climbing first. It has been changed to a top-down walk partly to improve access for those without a car, partly because the bottling plant that marked the old start has disappeared, so that the only way of identifying the old start is by GPS or a reliable odometer. That said, there are good reasons for starting a walk with the climb, so for drivers who prefer this option, the old start appears as an 'alternative'.

4 | 2½-3H | 4.5 km | 500m / 500m | | | 3*

* in **Arure**

Access by bus:
Línea 1 to **Arure**. From **Arure**, follow the main road down towards **Valle Gran Rey** for 500 metres, then turn right at the clear, signposted junction to the **Mirador Ermita del Santo**. After a little over hundred metres, join the walk at Wp.2.

Parking and Wp.1 at the yellow house

Access by car:
For the top-down itinerary (recommended, particularly for vertigo sufferers who may need to back out before they're committed), take the clearly signposted turn-off for 'Mirador Ermita del Santo' south-west of **Arure**. Follow the lane past the *mirador* until the tarmac ends (250 metres from the main road) behind a yellow-painted house, where there is sufficient parking. Additional parking is available in **Arure** in front of **Restaurante Casa Conchita**, thereafter following the bus access to Wp.2.

Alternative access and start: if you prefer the bottom-up version of this walk,

Walk! La Gomera 111

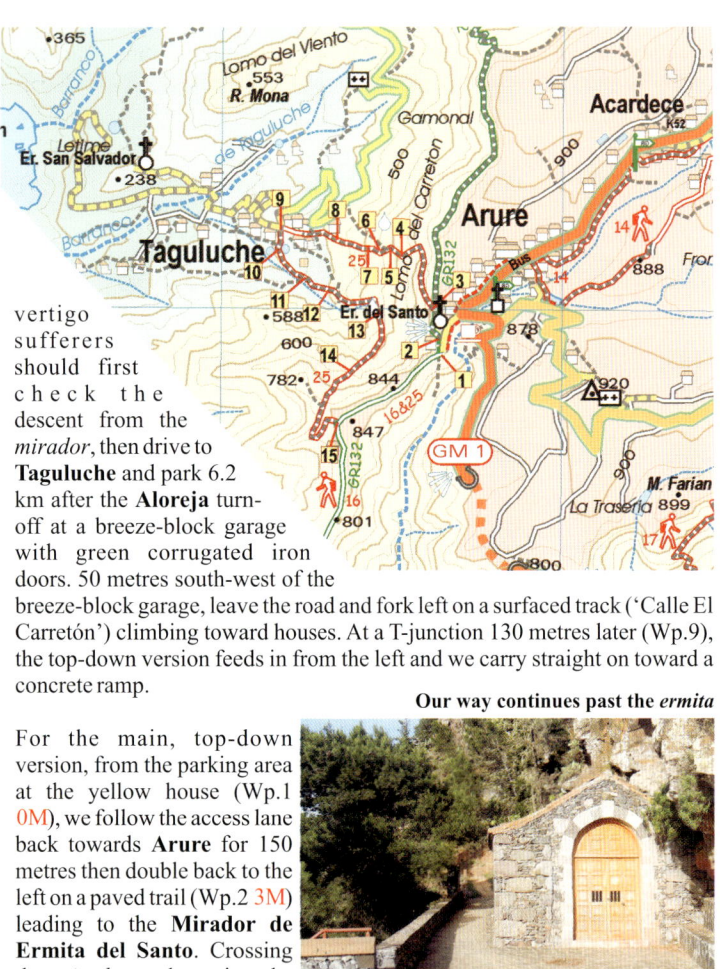

vertigo sufferers should first check the descent from the *mirador*, then drive to **Taguluche** and park 6.2 km after the **Aloreja** turn-off at a breeze-block garage with green corrugated iron doors. 50 metres south-west of the breeze-block garage, leave the road and fork left on a surfaced track ('Calle El Carretón') climbing toward houses. At a T-junction 130 metres later (Wp.9), the top-down version feeds in from the left and we carry straight on toward a concrete ramp.

Our way continues past the *ermita*

For the main, top-down version, from the parking area at the yellow house (Wp.1 0M), we follow the access lane back towards **Arure** for 150 metres then double back to the left on a paved trail (Wp.2 3M) leading to the **Mirador de Ermita del Santo**. Crossing the *mirador* and passing the

Beginning the precipitous descent

Ermita del Santo, we come to a vertiginous path heading north, 70 metres along which we reach a Y-junction (Wp.3 7M).

The main branch straight ahead continues as the **GR132**, but we bear left to begin our precipitous descent.

Given that the descent is a bit delicate, timings are even more subjective than usual. Our path descends a long broad sloping ledge to a small stand of pine, where it narrows as it traverses a low cliff onto the first and most vertiginous of several steeply raked 'stairways'. After picking our way down the steps with considerable circumspection (handholds comforting but not compulsory), we come to a long, more or less level path, below low cliffs - again care required.

After 150 metres, another 'stairway' doubles back onto a painstaking but not manifestly dangerous way zigzagging down across a shallow rocky spur overlooking … well, just about everything (!), at the bottom of which we come to an area of scrub, rock and loose scree next to a wooden electricity post (Wp.4 32M). Two more stairways bring us down to a cement clad, piped spring (Wp.5 37M) next to a small stand of willow clustered round a solitary laurel. Crossing the main pipe and a narrower one just afterwards, we have a short but very steep, very skittery descent on very loose dirt (hands and bottom required!), before passing back under the power cable onto an abandoned terrace (Wp.6 42M).

Bearing right, we follow a very narrow path winding between a small jungle of shrubs, bushes and saplings before crossing another pipe and passing below a tiny ruin (Wp.7 47M), where the path finally clears. Winding down steeply, though nothing compared to what we've done already, we descend a long, narrow spur, following the line of the electricity cable. Joining a more substantial path (Wp. 8 57M), we bear right, passing a new stone house from where we have a straightforward descent on a broad concrete-and-stone walkway to join a tarmac track. At a T-junction 100 metres down this track (Wp.9 67M), we bear left and take a concrete ramp descending in front of two modern houses onto a signposted terrace path above a reservoir (Wp.10 69M).

Bearing left for 'Valle Gran Rey (Camino de las Vueltas) 8.6km', we pass two more reservoirs (ignoring a path descending to the second), 70 metres after which we bear left at a Y-junction on a path climbing from **Taguluche** village (Wp.11 73M). The trail climbs steadily alongside grassy terraces dominated by cactus and *tabaiba* groves before passing a 'Monumento Natural Lomo del Carretón' signpost (Wp.12 83M). Ignoring all branch paths, we climb steadily, coming into view of an orange cliff (SW) below pine trees, the start of our final ascent. Bearing right above a broad watercourse and passing reeds concealing a spring (Wp.13 103M), we head for the orange cliffs on an easier gradient.

After traversing several watercourses and a long, sloping sheet of rock, we pass a line of three pines at the lower end of the hanger (Wp.14 113M) and cross a spill of rubble, from where the retaining walls of the path through the woods are clearly visible. Zigzagging steeply up through the woods, we go through a natural rock gateway before winding round across bare rock to join the **Mérica** dirt track (Wp.15 138M) at a 'Monumento Natural Lomo del Carretón' signpost.

Shortly before joining La Mérica track

Bearing left, we follow the dirt track back to our starting point.

THE NORTH - TRADITIONAL VALUES

Túnel de la Cumbre is **San Sebastián**'s 'gate' to the North. Emerging from the old tunnel, we plunge into the **Hermigua** valley along a road thankfully much improved from the old days, descending into a landscape that is considerably more mountainous than the one experienced during the climb from the capital. Hidden behind the mountains on our left as we sweep down to the first settlements is the delightful valley of **El Cedro**, the locus of some great walking.

Hermigua and **Vallehermoso** were once the power houses of the Gomeran economy, quays being built on the sea-fronts to load the abundant agricultural products directly onto ships. Agriculture is no longer the economic motor it once was, but there are still more terraces in cultivation here than elsewhere on La Gomera, and the quays are still there, along with a gallery of sepia photographs on bar walls that bear witness to a providential past. Old houses line the main road around **Hermigua**'s 16th century church while small settlements flank the valley, all linked by walkways and narrow roads that offer easy strolling when we're taking a day off from more strenuous itineraries.

Leaving the mouth of the valley and heading west, our road returns to a dramatic cliff face setting before crossing the bridge to **Agulo**, one of La Gomera's most photographed settlements due to its picturesque backdrop against **Mount Teide** on **Tenerife**. **Agulo**'s quiet streets provide another opportunity for easy strolling, while across the road, spectacular cliffs climb up to the **Palmita** valley, cliffs that are manifestly impassable, but which in fact we pass (in good weather) on Walk 31.

A tunnel and a cliff-side drive, bring us to **Las Rosas**, where we can turn left to reach the **Centro de Visitantes** information centre, or follow the narrow road out past the *embalse* to the highly regarded **Bodegón Roque Blanco** bar/restaurant, which has great views from its terrace. Passing through **Las Rosas**, the landscape becomes less dramatic until we swing west to overlook the wild northern valleys containing the **Simancas** and **Tamargada** settlements, where even the main road gets quite vertiginous in places. If this isn't dramatic enough, emerging from the next tunnel into the massive **Vallehermoso** valley cannot fail to impress. **Roque Cano** might not be the highest peak on the island, but it dominates the town and valley with its massive presence.

A proliferation of fine old houses give **Vallehermoso** a prestigious air despite the newer developments. Cultivators and trailers (a popular combination of working tool and transport among locals) cluster around the bars alongside modern four wheel drive vehicles, almost everybody seeming to drive something vaguely agricultural in this most traditional of towns. Looking up at the western valley wall, we can see that it is terraced to the very top, though nowadays only the lower terraces are cultivated. From town, the narrow 'main' road climbs past the higher settlements before a tortuous ascent brings us to the spectacularly sited tourist bar/restaurants at **Chorros de Epina**. Yet in the traditional north, even these comparatively modern businesses retain an air of the past about them.

NORTHERN WALKS LOCATOR MAPS

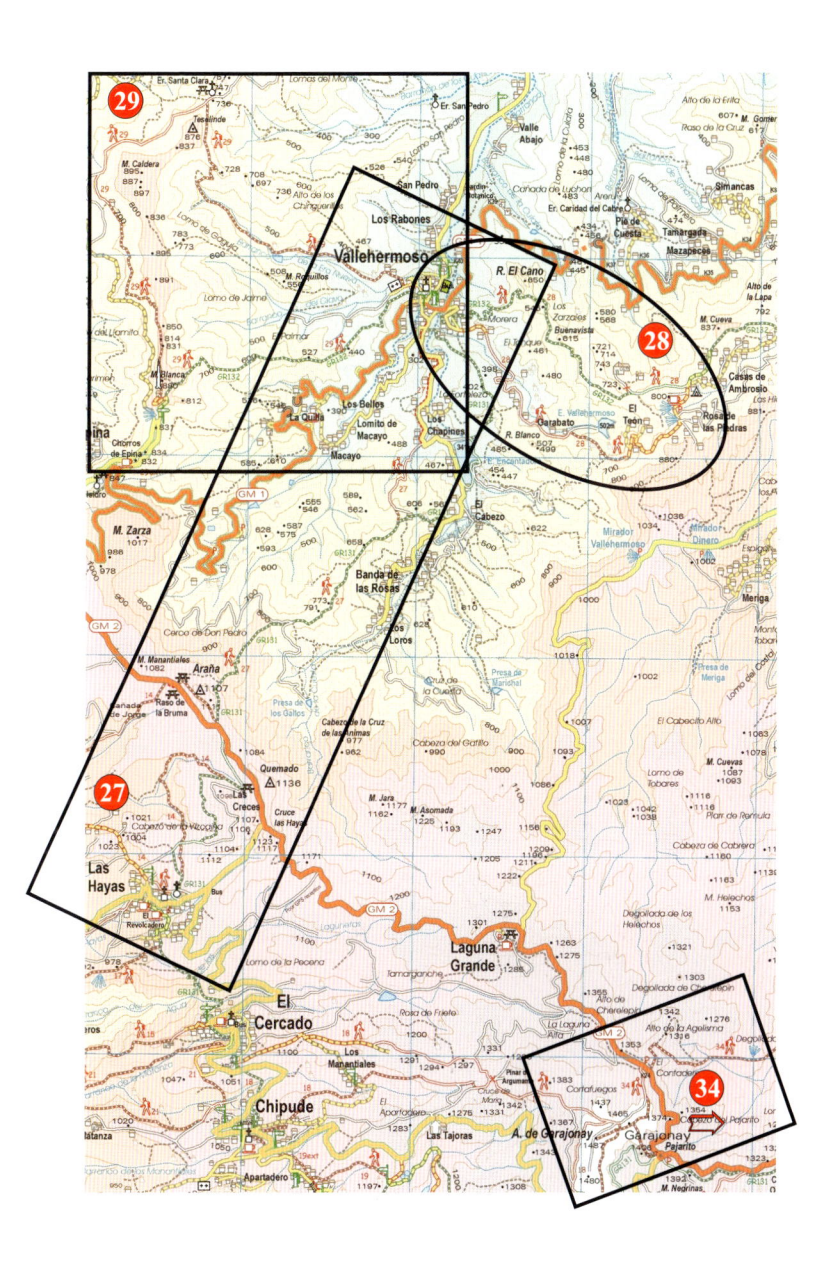

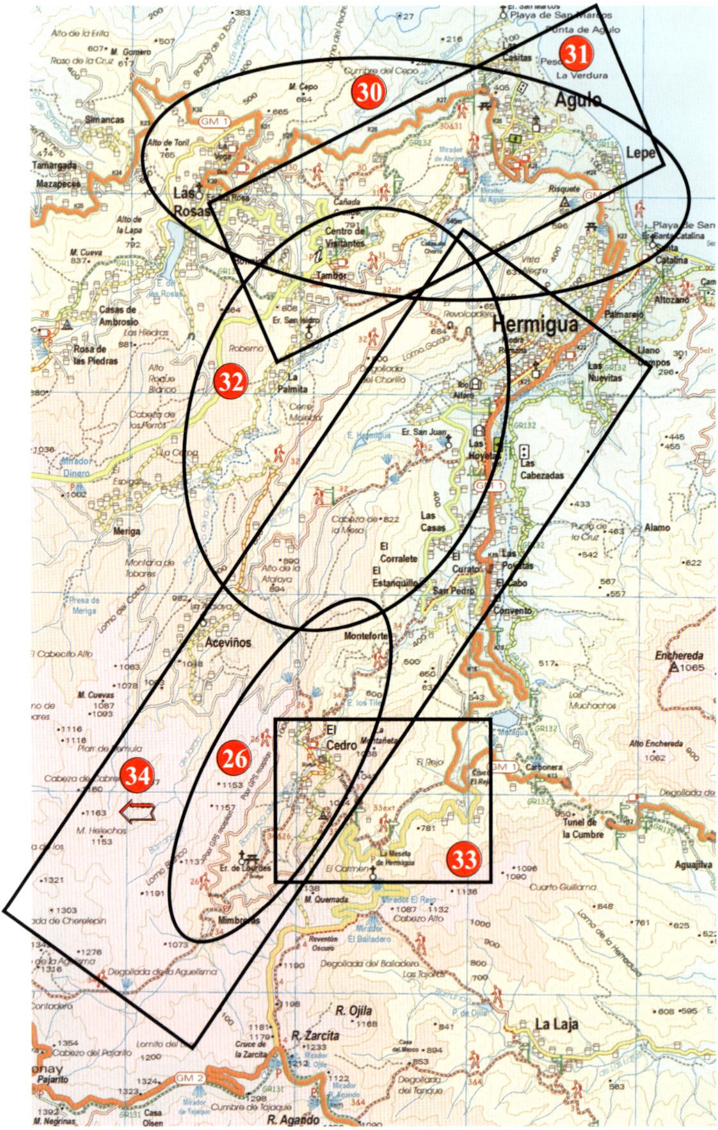
30
31
32
33
34
26
Playa de San Marcos
Punta de Agulo
Las Casitas
La Verdura
Agulo
Lepe
Cumbre del Cepo
M. Cepo
GM 1
Alto de Toril
Las Rosas
Simancas
Tamargada
Mazapeces
Alto de la Erita
Raso de la Cruz
M. Gomero
Alto de la Lapa
M. Cueva
Cañada
Centro de Visitantes
Tambor
Mirador de Abrante
Risquete
Playa de San Catalina
Santa Catalina
Altozano
Palmarejo
Vista Alegre
Hermigua
Llano Campos
Las Nuevitas
Revolcadero
Casas de Ambrosio
Rosa de las Piedras
Roberno
La Palmita
Er. San Isidro
Degollada del Chorillo
Lomo Gordo
Alto Roque Blanco
Cabeza de los Perros
Cerro Molinillo
La Cerpa
Mirador Dinero
Espiga
Meriga
E. Hermigua
Er. San Juan
Las Hoyetas
Las Cabezadas
Cabezo de la Mesa
Las Casas
El Corralete
El Estanquillo
El Curato
San Pedro
Las Poyatas
El Cabo
Convento
Alto de la Atalaya
Montaña de Tobares
Presa de Meriga
Lomo del Cadí
La Palmita
Aceviños
El Cabecito Alto
Monteforte
Alamo
Punta de la Cruz
Enchereda
Los Muchachos
Alto Enchereda
M. Cuevas
El Cedro
La Montañeta
El Rejo
Carbonera
Túnel de la Cumbre
Aguajilva
Degollada de
M. Helechos
Cabeza de Cabrera
Plan de Jamula
Er. de Lourdes
Mimbreras
La Meseta de Hermigua
El Carmen
M. Quemada
Mirador El Rejo
Cabezo Alto
Mirador El Bailadero
Reventón Oscuro
Degollada del Bailadero
Las Tajoras
Cuarto Guillama
Lomo de la Herradura
Degollada de la Aguelisma
Contadera
R. Ojila
R. Zarcita
Cruce de la Zarcita
La Laja
Degollada del Tanque
Cabezo del Pajarito
Lomito del Loro
Pajarito
GM 2
Cumbre de Tajaque
Casa Olsen
M. Negrinas
R. Agando
GR132
GR131

26 LAS MIMBRERAS

For motorists disinclined to tackle the rigorous descent of Walk 34 or the claustrophobia of Walk 33, this short circuit is an ideal ramble through the heart of the **Garajonay**. *Mimbrera* is Spanish for crack willow or osier. In common with other willows, the Canary willow (Salix canariensis) contains salicylic acid and was traditionally used as an analgesic.

3 | 1H 20M | 4.5 km | 200m / 200m | ↻ | 4

Mimbreras car-park (Wp.1)

Access by car: park at the **Mimbreras** parking area at Wp.1. To access it, take the loosely-cobbled track (N) from the **Reventón Oscuro** junction for **El Cedro**. After 1.4 km, the cobble track swings right and we carry straight on along a dirt track, passing a 'No Buses' sign. The dirt car-park is at Km3.1, where there are several map and information boards and a sign for 'Carretera dorsal 3.1'. If you are concerned that the dirt track to **Mimbreras** invalidates your hire car insurance, stay on the cobbled track into **El Cedro** to join the route at Wp.5 where there is a large gravel car-park by the picnic area.

Alternative start, Wp.5

Setting off from the **Mimbreras** parking area (Wp.1 0M), we continue along the dirt track (NNE) for 'Aceviños', immediately passing a series of mini 'caves', in fact barbecue pits once used by forestry workers. After a gentle twenty-minute climb, the track levels out and we glimpse **Hermigua**, the **Barranco del Cedro** and the sea, through trees so heavily rimed with lichen it hangs like hanks of fur.

Shortly before a branch track to the right, we leave the main track, turning right on a path signposted 'Caserío de El Cedro 1.3' (Wp.2 35M). At a Y-junction 30 metres later, our path branches right, but it's worth bearing left for a few metres to a natural *mirador* overlooking the *barrancos* behind **Agulo**. Descending between banks of the colonising 'Cats Ear' creeper (Tradescantia fluminensis), we turn right at a junction next to a minor dirt track and continue through woods so tangled and be-lichened they resemble a fairytale landscape.

A steady zigzagging descent leads to another natural *mirador*, after which we come to a stripped hillside above a military green bungalow. Crossing a tarmac lane leading to the **La Vista Casa Rural** (Wp.3 50M), we bear right on a slithery dirt path descending on log steps and then along a fenced terrace. Towards the end of the terrace, we swing right on a concrete path crossing cultivated terraces then join a tarmac lane (Wp.4 55M) accessing **Bar La Vista**.

Bearing left, we cross the car-park and go through the bar, stopping as long as the stomach stipulates, then take the stepped garden path at the southern end of the terrace down to a paved trail. We follow the paved trail (S) (bearing right once in the ravine) and cross a stream to climb log steps, emerging at a picnic site where there are benches, tables and a car park.

On the far side of the picnic area, we take the access lane across a bridge (Wp.5 60M). Sticking with the lane, we climb to a junction where we turn right. After passing **Casa Rural los Patos** and a transformer tower, we turn left (Wp.6 65M) on a stepped path signposted 'Ermita de Lourdes'. Ignoring all branch paths, we pass two clusters of houses before bearing left at a park-limit sign and returning to the forest.

The Ermita de Lourdes

Climbing gently to steadily between giant fern and towering laurel, we pass in front of the **Ermita de Lourdes** (Wp.7 75M) and cross a picnic area with an extraordinary little *fuente*-in-a-tree (10,000 litres of water pass through this tree every 20 minutes according to one of the park firemen), beyond which a footbridge brings us onto a stepped ascent to a broad dirt trail. Ignoring a branch to the right, we follow the left bank of the stream, re-crossing via another bridge to return to our starting point.

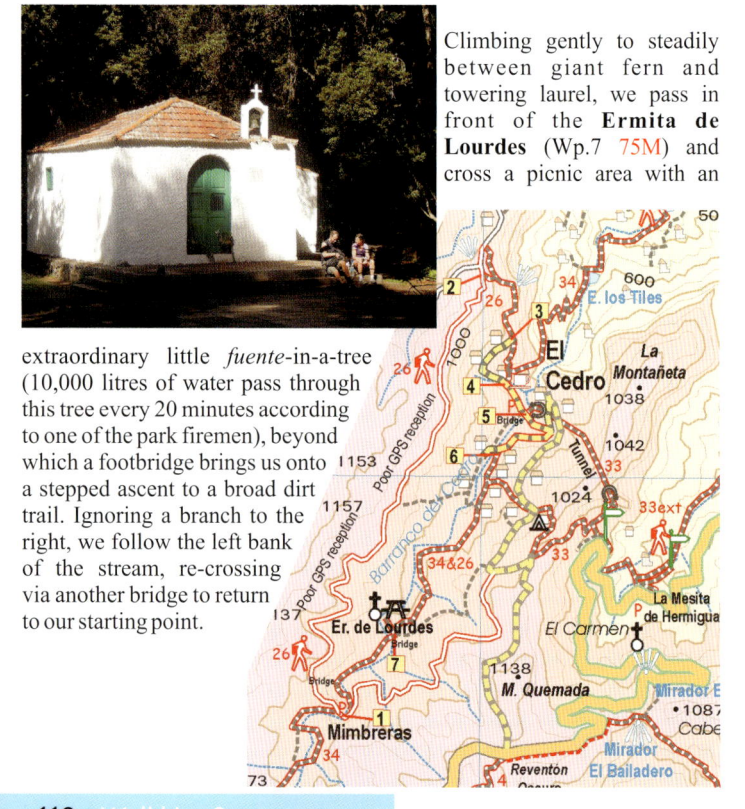

27 LAS CRECES - VALLEHERMOSO

Great views, good paths, lichen-frosted laurel, and a cacophony of birdlife are among the highlights on this lovely commuting trail between two of the island's best walking areas. Given the bus timetables and routes, the itinerary is only practical as a day excursion if you're staying in **San Sebastián**.

However, if you're staying in **Vallehermoso** or arriving from elsewhere by car, there's a taxi service in the town. If you do splash out on a taxi, you may wish to consider making a day of it, extending the route by starting from the **Casa Efigenia** restaurant in **Las Hayas** and using Walk 14 (Wps.8-14) to reach the start of the present itinerary, adding 200 metres to the climb and 3.3km to the distance. At the time of going to press, the number for Taxis Chani in **Vallehermoso** is 679 638 703.

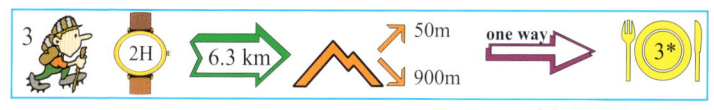

3 | 2H | 6.3 km | 50m / 900m | one way | 3*

* in **Vallehermoso**

Access by bus:
To reach the start, take Línea 1, alighting at **Las Creces**; at the end of the walk, the buses serving **Vallehermoso** are Línea 2 (for **San Sebastián**), Línea 4 (for **La Dama**) and Línea 5 (for **Alojera**), though the last two have a limited service.

Starting at Wp.1

From the bus stop where the **Las Creces** dirt track meets the main road (Wp.1 0M), we follow the path to the northwest along the crash barrier on the northern side of the road. After 130 metres, at the end of the crash barrier, we take the path to the right signposted 'Vallehermoso 5.8' (Wp.2 2M), ignoring a branch immediately on the left for 'Raso de la Bruma'.

Once we're on this path, it's virtually impossible to go wrong, except at the second dirt track at Wp.7. The descent is in two parts, the first dropping off the island's central spine through slightly degraded *laurisilva*, the second running along a narrow ridge cloaked in *fayal-brezal*.

Our signposted path at Wp.2

Vallehermoso comes into view

After strolling along a level path through lichen-frosted laurel with fine views over **Roque Cano** and **Vallehermoso**, we come to the **Risquillo de Corgo** junction (Wp.3 12M).

Bearing right, we zigzag down onto a long north-easterly traverse, after which we wind more tightly through woods alive with the chatter and staccato cries of birds. We then come to a level ridge path (Wp.4 22M) leading across a slight rise.

Gradually emerging from the tree cover, we zigzag down to **Pista de la Meseta** at a 'Sendero Local' signpost (Wp.5 37M).

Crossing the dirt track, we take the path for 'Los Chapines 2.5km', skirting to the east of two small peaks at the head of the ridge we follow down to **Vallehermoso**.

This narrow path would soon be washed away if it wasn't for the bushes and trees underpinning it, but these are a mixed blessing as we duck and weave between hat-snatching, hair-snarling branches. Snaking along the ridge, we descend to a bald chalky dome (Wp.6 52M), where the path continues along a narrow erosion gully.

150 metres before a large outcrop of rock that resembles a recumbent dinosaur, our path drops down onto the eastern side of the ridge before winding round onto the western side

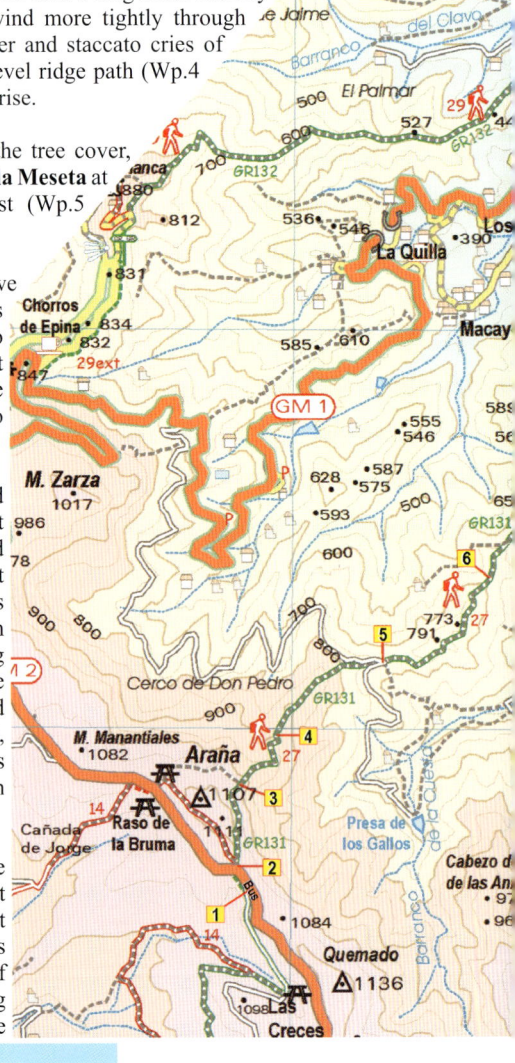

and descending steeply to another 'Sendero Local' signpost just above a dirt track (Wp.7 72M).

The signpost has been misplaced and appears to suggest we bear left on a rough path running parallel to the dirt track, which we can do, but have to rejoin the track 150 metres later.

In either case, it's the track we follow all the way down to the **Barranco de Ingenio** road (Wp.8 97M) emerging opposite the **Artesanía Los Roques**.

Bearing left, we follow the road into **Vallehermoso**, arriving at the end of **Calle Triana** (where the taxi service is based at house Nº33) between the hotel of the same name and the **Kiosco Bar Garajonay** (Wp.9 117M).

Bearing left, we come to the main plaza, next to which there is a bus stop at a roundabout. However, to be sure the bus driver doesn't overlook you, it's best walk another 300 metres to the bus station, which is reached by taking the main road north off the roundabout.

Our finish opposite Hotel de Triana

28 ROQUE CANO

Vallehermoso, or 'Beautiful Valley', suggests one of those anodyne gated communities they're so keen on in southern California, but as this classic circuit shows, in this instance the name is no more than a prosaic statement of fact. Warming up with a pleasant stroll along a *pista forestal*, we continue with a dramatic climb past the hamlet of **El Teón**, after which a well-graded descent brings us back to town via **Roque Cano**, the protean *roque* that dominates the entire valley.

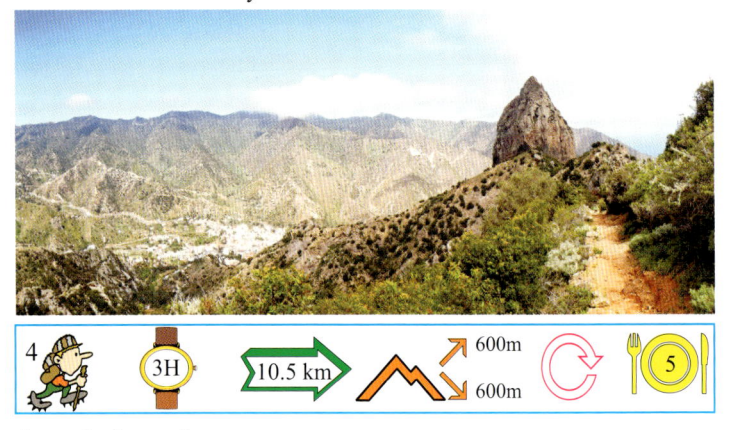

4 | 3H | 10.5 km | 600m / 600m | 5

Access by bus and car:
Vallehermoso can be reached via the regular service of Línea 2 or the more limited services of Línea 4 and 5. There is ample parking in **Vallehermoso**. Our itinerary starts from the **Kiosco Bar Garajonay** in the centre of **Vallehermoso**, which can be reached from the main plaza via **Calle Triana** running south from the Spar shop, past Banco Santander.

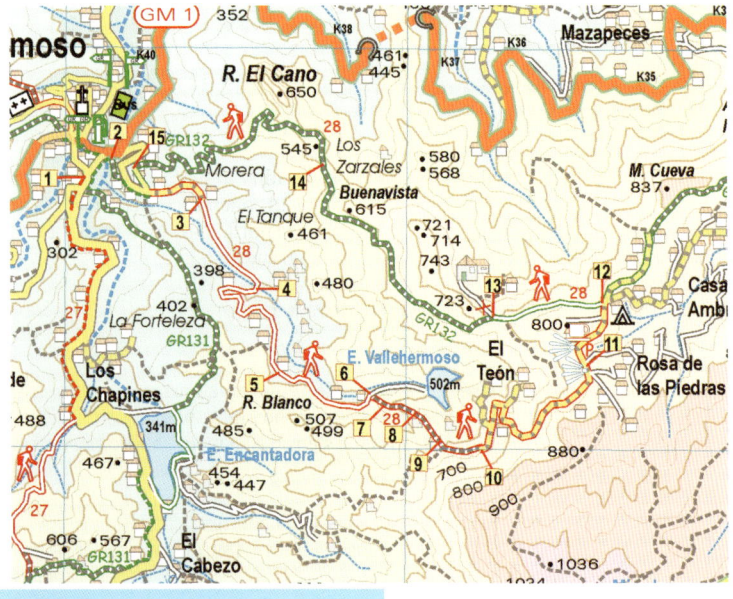

122 Walk! La Gomera

Wp.1 at Kiosco Bar Garajonay

From **Kiosco Bar Garajonay** in the centre of **Vallehermoso** (Wp.1 0M), we descend toward the **Carpinteria Nirgen**, bearing right behind the 'statue' playground, crossing a bridge on the tarmac lane that ascends to **Garabato**. After the first U-bend, we turn right on concrete steps with a green railing (Wp.2 5M), climbing to cut off a long loop in the lane.

Bearing right when we rejoin the lane, we ignore a branch track to the left (our return route) and continue along the lane, which soon becomes a dirt track (Wp.3 15M), climbing gently at first then, after crossing a watercourse (Wp.4 25M), more steadily.

After an attractively restored house with a decorated agave-scape gateway, we see a white cabin and pale green vine terraces at the head of the valley. The 'cabin', in fact a fairly substantial house when you come to it, is the one we reach at Wp.9.

A verdant valley on our ascent

A few minutes after passing a house extended with a second, wooden storey (Wp.5 40M), we see the **Embalse de Vallehermoso** dam wall. 150 metres before the dam, 50 metres after a white water-hut topped with a solar panel, we leave the dirt track, turning sharp right on a broad rock path marked with cairns (Wp.6 50M).

The path, which is partially stepped, climbs steadily to steeply, zigzagging up a rocky spur. Shortly after crossing an abandoned concrete canal (Wp.7 55M), we see the white 'cabin' again and, a little to the north, the largely abandoned hamlet of **El Teón**. After passing a solitary palm and ancient ruin (Wp.8 70M), the spur narrows to a spine with steps cut into the rock leading up to the white 'cabin' (Wp.9 75M), a good spot for a breather, with concrete benches and great views.

Behind the house, we bear left toward **El Teón**, on a narrow terrace path. Ignoring a minor branch doubling back on the right, we take the second turning on the right, climbing steep stone steps past a wooden electricity post to the end of a tarmac lane (Wp.10 80M).

Bearing right at the Y-junction 50 metres later and ignoring all subsequent branches, we climb steeply to the small *mirador* (Wp.11 95M) below the **Restaurante Roque Blanco**.

Walk! La Gomera   123

Following the main lane past the restaurant, we ignore a minor dirt track branching left and, 50 metres later, turn left onto a broader dirt track marked with cairns (Wp.12 100M).

Descending along the dirt track, we get our first glimpse of **Roque Cano**, memorably described by David & Ros Brawn of Discovery Walking Guides as 'Dan Dare's Spaceship', but equally reminiscent of some Gaudiesque experiment in modernist gothic architecture.

At double green gates (Wp.13 110M), we leave the dirt track, bearing left on a broad walking trail, initially running alongside a precipitous drop, happily screened by shrubs.

Splendid views on the descent

A long, gentle descent with superb views up the 'Valley of 1001 Palms', brings us onto the first of several roughly cobbled sections remaining from the days when this was a donkey trail, some of the rocks of which are so heavily burnished they appear to have a worn ceramic surface.

We round a corner for our first really impressive view of **Roque Cano**: spaceship, temple, or simply a very large lump of rock? 150 metres later, our trail broadens to a smooth ridge path, passing a 'Monumento Natural' signpost (Wp.14 130M) and a pockmarked *roque* that would be a celebrated place of pilgrimage itself were it not dwarfed by **Cano**.

Passing below **Roque Cano**, the trail winds down onto a long exposed spur, still high above **Vallehermoso**. Ignoring occasional faint traces branching off the main, paved trail, we zigzag down, criss-crossing and finally veering away from a thick water pipe. Passing between houses on the outskirts of town (Wp.15 160M), our trail runs into a dirt track rejoining the tarmac lane of our outward route, five minutes from **Kiosco Bar Garajonay**.

29 ERMITA DE SANTA CLARA

Ensconced in the domestic beauty of **Vallehermoso** one might suppose the entire north-west of the island is nothing but a charming bucolic. In fact, this area boasts some of the wildest landscapes in the Canaries and climbing up to the **Ermita de Santa Clara** gives us some of the best views to be had of the little visited ravines between **Arguamul** and **Alojera**. Not recommended in hot weather.

| 5 | 4H* | 14 km | 650m / 650m | ↻ | 3* |

* in **Vallehermoso**

Access by bus: Línea 2 (between **San Sebastián** - **Vallehermoso**), Línea 4 (limited service **La Dama** - **Vallehermoso**) or 5 (limited service **Alojera** - **Vallehermoso**).

Access by car: park near **Vallehermoso** cemetery; see the walk description.

To reach the start of the walk from the main plaza in **Vallehermoso**, on foot or by car, take the narrow street to the right of **Bar Central** and past **Zumería Iballa**, up to the **Valle Gran Rey** road. 150 metres up the road, turn right at the *Guardia Civil* barracks for the *cementerio*. Park on the cemetery access lane.

Wps. 1-2, the concrete ramp by the cemetery

(Wp.1) Start on cemetery lane, Guardia Civil Barracks in background

The footbridge

From the junction next to the barracks (Wp.1 0M), signposted 'Ruta 4: Santa Clara/Arguamul' we follow the lane to the cemetery and turn right on a concrete ramp descending to a footbridge over the

Walk! La Gomera 125

Era Nueva ('New Threshing Circle') stream.

Ignoring all branches, we stick to the main trail, climbing to a cluster of houses (Wp.2 10M) where we bear left. Looking up to the left after the last house, we can see the **Montaña Blanca** communications mast where our descent begins. After climbing above the last house, our trail swings left (WNW) and the gradient eases. We follow this trail all the way up **Barranco de la Era Nueva** to the *ermita*. Text-phobes shut the book now!

After a long gentle climb up the valley, dotted with date palm and juniper, (as usual in the Canaries, what Northerners are accustomed to seeing as a bush is a tree) we pass an abandoned house (Wp.3 30M), the second after the cluster at Wp.2, and the gradient steepens on a small rise above a large reservoir, 150 metres after which we reach the 'new' threshing circle (Wp.4 40M).

The trail then winds into the stream bed which it criss-crosses for the next few hundred metres. The watercourse is so densely packed with bamboo and house-leeks, it's a job to know whether you're on the left bank, right bank, or actually in it, but after a long steady climb clearly on the right bank (our left), we pass a terrace wall set with step-ladder stones, immediately after which the watercourse divides (Wp.5 55M) and we branch right, ignoring a minor path to the left.

We soon leave the stream bed, climbing steadily to steeply through *fayal-brezal* and a small stand of eucalyptus, after which we bear left on a ridge below **Teselinde** and the trail levels out alongside wooden railings (Wp.6 80M), from where we have superb views of the coast and Tenerife.

We now stroll alongside **Teselinde** to emerge on a dirt track (Wp.7 90M) 100 metres from the *ermita*.

The track NE to **Chijeré** leads to a dramatic descent: it also leads to some of the driest land on a dry island and a dull slog up the **Playa Vallehermoso** road.

The *ermita*

So, having spent a little while enjoying (weather permitting) the views down toward the coast from the *ermita* and possibly taking advantage of the small *área recreativa* behind it (water available), we retrace our steps to Wp.7 and follow the dirt track (SW) until reaching a signposted Y-junction of tracks (Wp.8 108M).

Bearing left we climb the track for 'Chorros de Epina 4.9km'. After 5 minutes the track ends and we continue on a dirt path lined with wild blackberry bushes, soon passing a fenced garden with a hut on our right hand side.

At the next Y-junction (Wp.9 130M), we ignore the path descending to the right and instead, bear left. Climbing steadily (again within sight of our next objective, the **Montaña Blanca** mast), we ignore a path to the left in a small clearing, after which log steps lead us out of the forest into a clearing where there's a pylon.

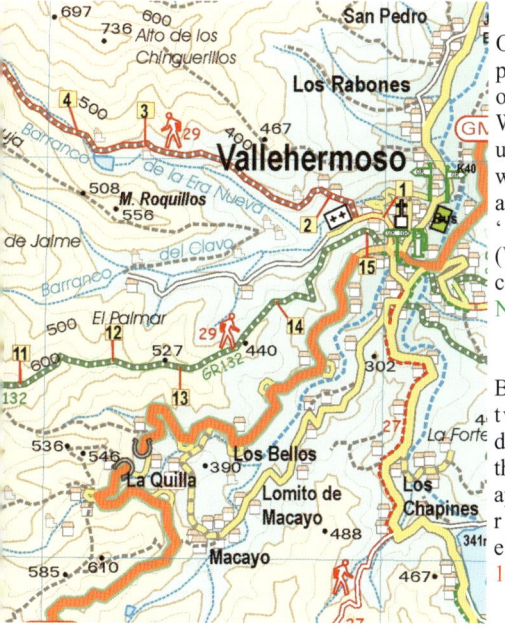

Our trail then joins a lane that passes the fenced compound of the **Montaña Blanca** mast. We follow the lane downhill until it swings sharp right, at which point we bear left onto a broad trail signposted 'Vallehermoso 3.9km' (Wp.10 150M) that follows a contour line (briefly NW, then NE).

Bearing right at a Y-junction two minutes later, we descend, gradually at first and then more steeply, onto what appears to be a gently sloping ridge tipped with an electricity pylon (Wp.11 175M).

In fact, this ridge, which we follow down to **Vallehermoso**, is a sort of giant's stairway, along which we pass a succession of steady descents interrupted by the relatively level 'steps' of the stairway.

Walk! La Gomera 127

There are no branches or path finding problems until very near the end, so the following notes are merely for pacing progress. At the end of 'step' 2 (counting Wp.11 as Step 1) we come to a long paved stretch (Wp.12 190M). On 'Step' 3, the *fayal-brezal* that has dominated for most of the descent so far gives way to prickly pear and agave, and the trail drops down onto the northern side of the ridge next to a large palm (Wp.13 200M), from where we can see the houses at Wp.2.

Down towards Playa Vallehermoso

Running along the last distinct 'step', the trail skirts the southern side of a spine of rough, eroded rock formations before crossing an outcrop of rock and dwindling to a path (Wp.14 210M). The path soon brings us within sight of **Vallehermoso** and, after broadening to an intermittently paved trail again, the cemetery. We then follow the northern side of the ridge and wind down past the top end of a small cargo cable-car to the first house on the outskirts of **Vallehermoso** (Wp.15 225M). Ignoring a branch path to the right, we descend on a concrete walkway, passing a red-painted house Nº128 'Dolores', eventually emerging on the **Valle Gran Rey** road.

To return to the main plaza, we cross straight over onto a stepped descent.

To return to the parking area, we bear left and follow the road round to the start of the walk.

30 LAS ROSAS - HERMIGUA

For anyone wanting to explore the northern coast without the massive climbs that otherwise seem inevitable, this itinerary, using a little-known crossing of the **Barranco de Lepe**, is an almost wholly pleasant introduction to the area. We say 'almost', since the paths out of **Las Rosas** are occasionally invaded by brambles. Long sleeves and trousers are recommended.

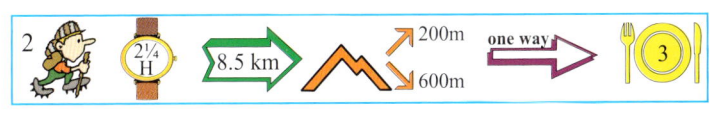

| 2 | 2¼ H | 8.5 km | 200m / 600m | one way | 3 |

Access by bus:
Línea 2. The walk starts at the coach park in front of **Restaurante Las Rosas**, 150 metres north of the **Las Rosas** bus stop.

Immediately north of the **Restaurant Las Rosas** coach-

Restaurante Las Rosas, our start point

park (Wp.1 0M), we take a rough dirt path signed for 'Agulo', that descends alongside the restaurant.

After a steep descent we traverse a sloping sheet of rock, at the bottom of which we turn left along a terrace. Rock-hopping over the **Barranco de las Rosas** stream onto concrete steps, we cross the main road (Wp.2 10M) and come on to a paved track, climbing south-east.

Looking north from Las Rosas

Our route from Wp.2

Ignoring a branch to the north, we stay on the main track as it runs into concrete and then dirt, before ending in front of a private house, where we turn left on a rougher dirt track. The old path to **Agulo** branches off the first U-bend of this track, but is currently (at the time of writing) impassable due to brambles.

If it has been cleared in the interim, follow it down to Wp.6. *Otherwise*, we continue to the end of the dirt track (Wp.3 20M), where we bear left on a faint, partially stepped way passing under an electricity cable and climbing behind a small house. At the top of a pathless slope of bare sandy rock and soil (SE), we join a clear path (Wp.4 25M) and bear left, aiming for wooden posts carrying the same electricity cable passed after Wp.3.

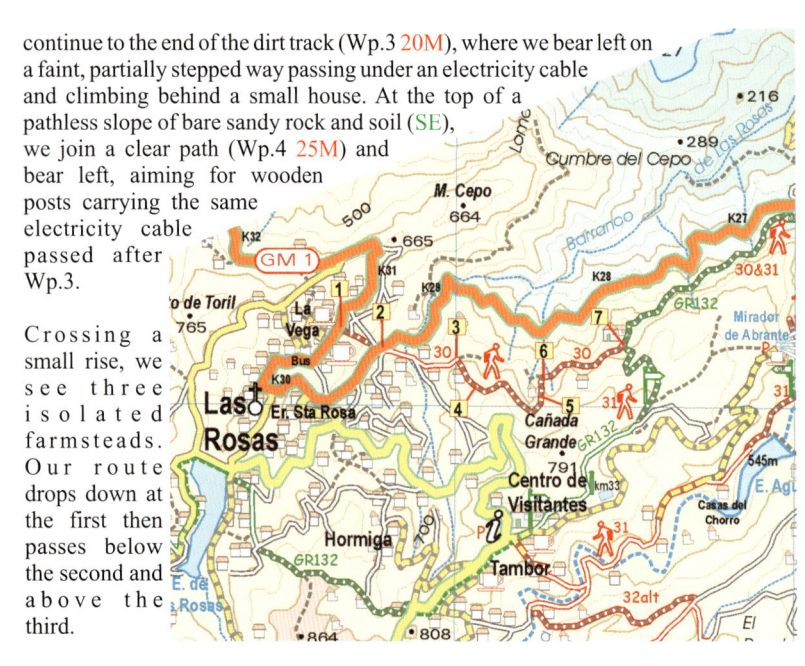

Crossing a small rise, we see three isolated farmsteads. Our route drops down at the first then passes below the second and above the third.

The path narrows amid young heath-trees then crosses a gully, where it suffers a brief but breachable invasion of brambles, before climbing behind the first house, which is a ruin (Wp.5 35M). Bearing left, we pass behind the house and wind down a steep, snaking descent to join the old path from the U-bend in the dirt track (Wp.6 40M).

We then follow a contour line below the second, smallest house, now out of sight. The path gets clearer as it approaches the third farmhouse, which is still maintained, behind which we join Walk 31, at a signpost indicating 'Agulo' straight ahead (Wp.7 50M). From here we follow a good donkey trail down to cross the main road just before the **Agulo** tunnel, where a dirt track runs into a trail to **Agulo** cemetery (Wp.8 80M).

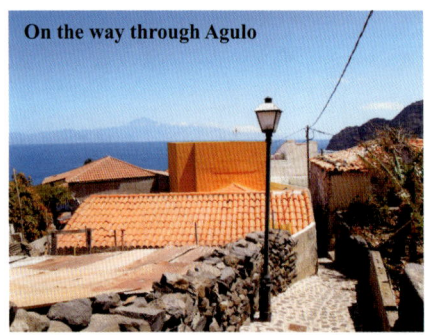

On the way through Agulo

Following the cobbled lane past the cemetery, we bear left at a Y-junction and stroll through the town centre. From the plaza between the church and *ayuntamiento*, we take **Calle del Pintor Aguiar** down towards the **Supermercado Gama**', immediately before which, we bear left on a concrete lane with a dead-end sign.

100 metres after the **Villa Maria Apartamentos**, we turn right on a tarmac lane, at the end of which (Wp.9 100M) a partly paved trail descends to a whitewashed house. Turning right just behind the house, we leave the paved way, crossing a terrace, at the end of which we bear left on a steep concrete

stairway down to another stretch of cobbled trail.

We then pick our way across the bed of the **Barranco de Lepe** via a winding bamboo alley, at the end of which a terrace path leads to a rough stone stairway into **Lepe**.

Turning left into a narrow alley, we pass a house with a ceramic 'BR' nameplate, then bear right at a bright yellow house to reach **Lepe**'s tiny village square (Wp.10 115M).

From here we simply follow the tarmac lane down to **Playa de Santa Catalina / Hermigua** (swimming not recommended - strong undertow!).

From a GR signpost at the beach (Wp.11 125M), we bear right and follow the tarmac lane up to the main road

On the descent into Lepe

At Wp.11

(Wp.12 135M) passing en route the *bar-restaurantes* **El Piloto** and **El Faro**.

The nearest bus stop is 200 metres to the southwest of the roundabout at Wp.12 on the main road toward **Hermigua**. If you're going into the town centre for refreshments, there are several other bus-stops, but bear in mind there is a one-way system in operation, so if you're heading toward **San Sebastián**, make sure you're on a southbound route.

31 PARED DE AGULO

A perfect circuit, provided you're not too susceptible to heights. Going straight up the cliffs behind **Agulo** and strolling along **Barranco de la Palmita**, we visit the **Garajonay Centro de Visitantes** and more pressingly, the **Bar/Restaurante Tambor**, then take a beautifully graded donkey trail for a gentle descent that's the opposite of the ascent in more ways than one. The cliff path should not be attempted in wet or windy conditions and is not recommended for a descent. The old **Mirador de Abrante** featured in previous versions of this itinerary has been superseded by a breathtakingly audacious new *mirador*. It's also worth taking a break at the visitors' centre to discover something of the island's geological and botanical history.

Though some of the vertiginous stretches are railed and most are relatively broad, the fact that this is a cliff path suggests anyone who suffers anything other than the most mild symptoms of vertigo should avoid it.

Access by bus: Línea 2.

Access by car: park on the main road below Wp.1.

Our path, signposted for 'Mirador de Abrante' (the dramatic platform of which we can already glimpse up on the cliff), starts on stone steps climbing away from the main road at the western end of **Agulo** between **Bar La Zula** and a *farmacia* (Wp.1 0M).

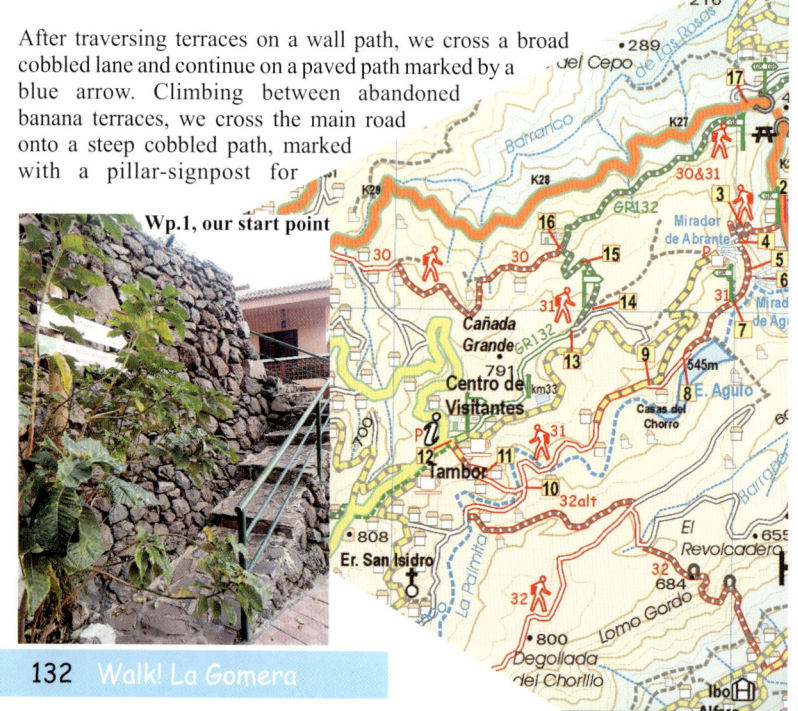

After traversing terraces on a wall path, we cross a broad cobbled lane and continue on a paved path marked by a blue arrow. Climbing between abandoned banana terraces, we cross the main road onto a steep cobbled path, marked with a pillar-signpost for

Wp.1, our start point

132 Walk! La Gomera

The steep cobbled path at Wp.2

'Agulo/La Palmita' (Wp.2 5M). The cliff path is just to the left of the orange crags that come into view as we climb. Climbing steeply between terraces, we cross a large water pipe (Wp.3 15M) below a fluted 'pedestal' at the base of the orange crags. Winding above the pedestal, we cross scrubland and then bear left on our first vertiginous section, passing under stout black plastic water pipes (Wp.4 30M) first seen draped over the pedestal. Zigzagging steeply up the cliffs, we reach a broad ledge beside a shallow cave (35M) roofed with fractured rock.

The wooden handrail (Wp.7)

After traversing another broad, slightly vertiginous ledge, the path swings right, muddied by a meagre spring, then re-crosses the black pipes (Wp.5 40M). After a second shallow cave, we traverse another broad ledge and join an old canal.

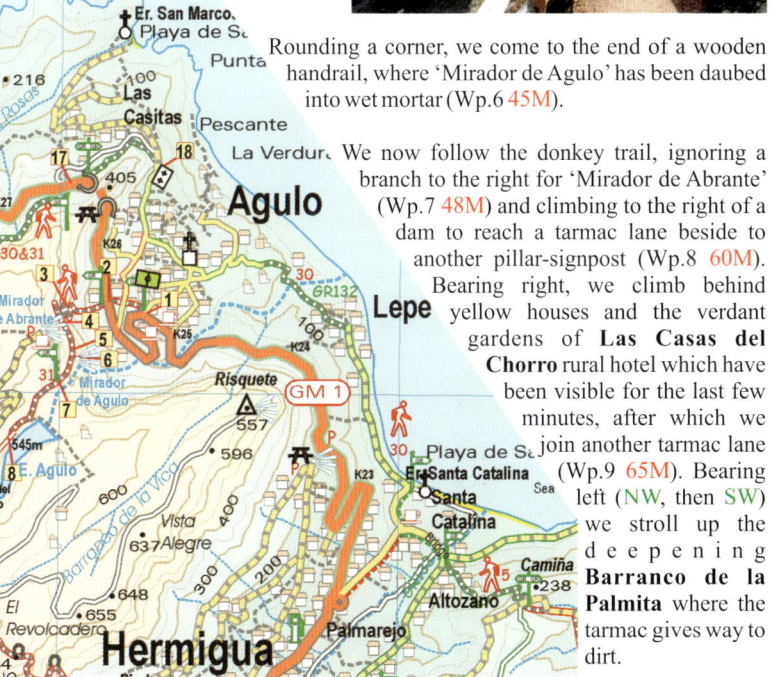

Rounding a corner, we come to the end of a wooden handrail, where 'Mirador de Agulo' has been daubed into wet mortar (Wp.6 45M).

We now follow the donkey trail, ignoring a branch to the right for 'Mirador de Abrante' (Wp.7 48M) and climbing to the right of a dam to reach a tarmac lane beside to another pillar-signpost (Wp.8 60M). Bearing right, we climb behind yellow houses and the verdant gardens of **Las Casas del Chorro** rural hotel which have been visible for the last few minutes, after which we join another tarmac lane (Wp.9 65M). Bearing left (NW, then SW) we stroll up the deepening **Barranco de la Palmita** where the tarmac gives way to dirt.

Five minutes after passing between two gateway palms, just as the tarmac resumes, we turn right on another surfaced lane (Wp.10 80M), marked by a faint signpost on the bridge railing for 'C.Visitantes'. Crossing the bridge and climbing steeply, we ignore all branches, and simply follow the lane till it ends at a yellow house (Wp.11 85M), alongside which we pick up a partially cobbled path. We now embark on a steep, gruelling climb, in the course of which the path joins a lane and we pass the white **Casa Tambor**, after which we come to a junction between the **Centro de Visitantes Juego de Bolas** (well worth a look around) and **Bar/Restaurante Tambor** (Wp.12 100M).

Bearing right, we follow the lane between the restaurant and visitors' centre, then branch left 50 metres later, taking a dirt track (NE) that climbs away from the lane and runs along the eastern flank of the **Cañada Grande** ridge. Ignoring a branch climbing to the left, we stick to the main track which soon dwindles to a partially cobbled donkey trail, leading to a small stand of a pine and a Y-junction (Wp.13 110M) where we bear left. 100 metres later, we come to a clump of signposts at another Y-junction (Wp.14 111M). For a unique if slightly unnerving experience, turn right here for a 700 metre diversion to visit the sky-walk and restaurant of the new **Mirador de Abrante**. To continue the main walk, bear left to follow a red dirt path between erosion gullies, enjoying superb views over **Barranco de las Rosas**, where we join the head of a cobbled donkey trail (Wp.15 115M).

'branch left 50 metres later'

Mirador de Abrante

After a steady, easy descent, we turn right above a large farmhouse at a T-junction marked with tree trunk signs for 'Las Rosas' and 'Agulo' (Wp.16 125M). Descending past the farmhouse and a modern petroglyph of a naked torso, we see our broad trail winding down to the road. After a steady descent, the trail levels out, curving round a contour below a sickly looking palm tree, where the final easy descent to the road begins - easy that is, apart from one very short vertiginous section and a distressingly big boulder that's fallen onto the path 75 metres from the road. Crossing the road (Wp.17 155M), we ignore steps down to a shack and bear right for 30 metres to a dirt track that descends to a reservoir where it dwindles to a path. Skirting round the ridge housing the **Agulo** road tunnel, we cross another spill of massive boulders and descend onto a cobbled lane behind the cemetery (Wp.18 165M), within sight of **Agulo** church. We follow the cobbled lane to the village, turning right at a major junction to rejoin our outward route behind **Bar La Zula**.

32 THE HEAD OF THE TABLE AND THE FAT BACK

Superb views on the descent

If you've ever looked up at some towering summit and said to yourself, "I'm going to do that, I'm going to go up there", largely because it's bigger than you and you want to be on top of it, then this is the walk for you! Climbing via the **Ermita de San Juan** to the **Cabeza de la Mesa** or 'Head of the Table', we trace a large loop round the **Barranco de Liria** then descend the **Lomo Gordo** (literally 'Fat Back') by what is probably the most spectacular path on the island. It also happens to be one of the least well known, unheard of by most people, even locals, though it does now feature on the *ayuntamiento* website.

Don't bother trying to trace it out from below: it's completely invisible and manifestly impossible. *Only for experienced walkers able to master their vertigo.* Unless otherwise described, all ascents and descents are steep! As always with long, difficult walks, remember, the timing excludes all breaks. Since the entire descent is vertiginous, this itinerary is only recommended for walkers with a good head for heights.

5 | 4½-5H* | 14 km | 750m / 750m | ↻ | ⚠ | 3**

* see <u>warning</u> above and on P.138   **in Hermigua

Access by bus: Línea 2; descend at the **Museo Etnográfico** in **Hermigua**.

The church and signpost at Wp.1

Access by car: motorists start from the long parking area south of the church in central **Hermigua**.

From the twin fingerposts twenty metres south-west of **Hermigua** church (Wp.1 0M), we follow the main road uphill (SW), passing on our left **Panadería Dulcería Caprichito Gomero**, then on our right the *correos*. 250

Walk! La Gomera 135

Wp.2, climbing west

metres further (or 30 metres north of the **Museo Etnográfico** if arriving by bus), we leave the road, climbing west on concrete steps (Wp.2 15M), signposted for 'Ermita San Juan / Los Aceviños'.

After passing several houses, the concrete gives way to dirt, then resumes just before reaching the lower of the two back-roads linking the higher hamlets of **Hermigua** (Wp.3 20M). Ten metres to the right, we continue climbing on concrete steps, apparently onto a private porch, before bearing right alongside the house.

Crossing the second back-road (Wp.4 30M), we take another stepped ascent, signposted 'Ayuntamiento de Hermigua, Rutas Senderos, San Juan, Aceviños', onto a path that climbs above the last houses before emerging at the end of the lane (Wp.5 45M) to the *ermita*, 50 metres to our right and well worth a visit.

Either retracing our steps to Wp.5 or taking the cinder path past the *ermita* barbecue wall, we climb the narrow ridge behind the *ermita* on a clear trail that sometimes follows rough cobbles or paving, sometimes bare rock and later, dirt, but is always evident.

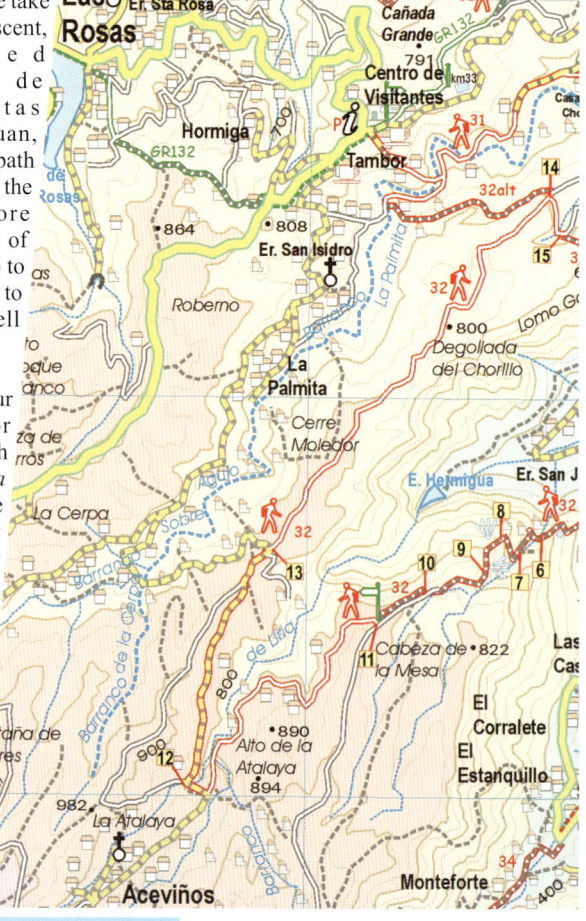

Details are for timekeeping rather than pathfinding, though rest-stops are virtually compulsory. Passing a reservoir, we cross the **Cabeza de la Mesa** watercourse (Wp.6 60M) to a ruin.

Zigzagging up to pass between two more ruins, we reach the first of four stretches of metal railing, at the end of which (Wp.7 70M) we ignore a faint branch to the left. Climbing past another small ruin, we come to a broader cobbled stretch.

Ignoring all apparent branch paths, we stick to the main trail, passing a small *mirador* (Wp.8 80M) and bearing away from the **Cabeza de la Mesa** watercourse towards the **Barranco de Liria**. At the fourth stretch of railing, we ignore an overgrown cutting to our right and follow the railings back towards the **Cabeza de la Mesa** watercourse. We then repeat the same pattern, bearing right towards the **Barranco de Liria** before swinging left back to the **Cabeza de la Mesa** watercourse, passing a small *mirador* (Wp.9 95M), after which the gradient eases and our trail gradually broadens to a dirt track.

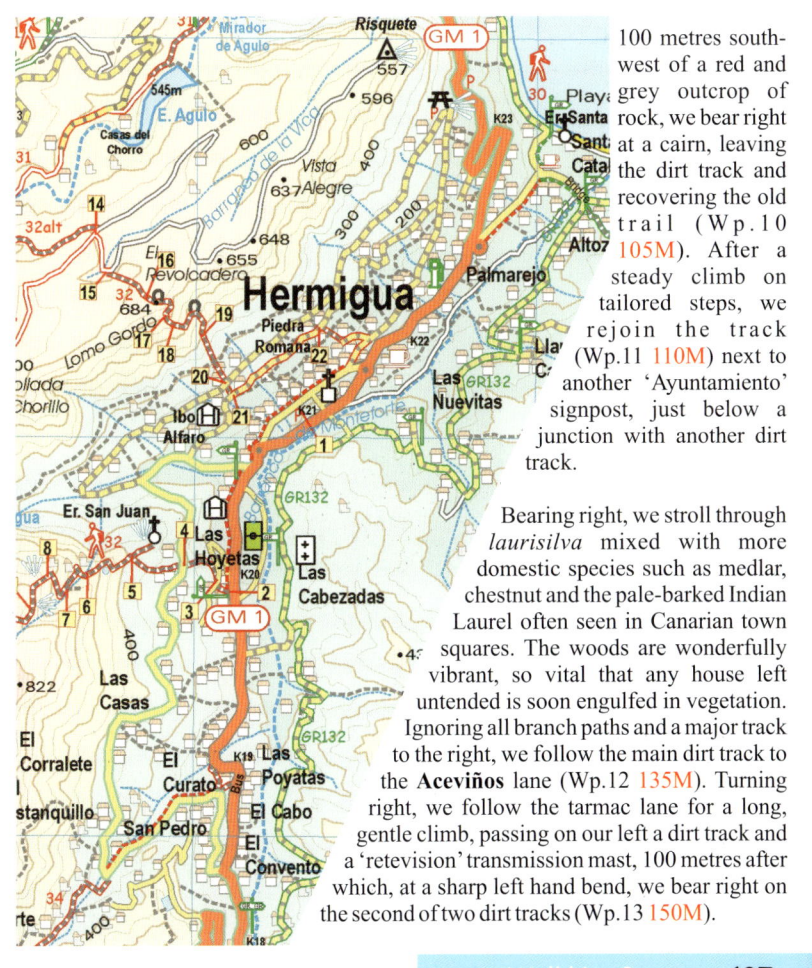

100 metres south-west of a red and grey outcrop of rock, we bear right at a cairn, leaving the dirt track and recovering the old trail (Wp.10 105M). After a steady climb on tailored steps, we rejoin the track (Wp.11 110M) next to another 'Ayuntamiento' signpost, just below a junction with another dirt track.

Bearing right, we stroll through *laurisilva* mixed with more domestic species such as medlar, chestnut and the pale-barked Indian Laurel often seen in Canarian town squares. The woods are wonderfully vibrant, so vital that any house left untended is soon engulfed in vegetation. Ignoring all branch paths and a major track to the right, we follow the main dirt track to the **Aceviños** lane (Wp.12 135M). Turning right, we follow the tarmac lane for a long, gentle climb, passing on our left a dirt track and a 'retevision' transmission mast, 100 metres after which, at a sharp left hand bend, we bear right on the second of two dirt tracks (Wp.13 150M).

Walk! La Gomera 137

The track winds along a ridge, gradually descending into the shallow **Barranco de la Vica**, where it doubles back to the south and a minor branch continues to the north-west (Wp.14 179M). Immediately before the junction of dirt tracks, a narrow path marked with a cairn heads west below a stand of eucalyptus (the second on the ridge). This path is your escape route if you don't like the look of the descent to **Hermigua**. Bearing right at the junction, we follow the main track down to the first sharp left bend (Wp.15 180M) where we branch right on a stepped ascent, marked by a cairn and a signboard.

From the top of the steps a broad trail, delineated by large stones, traverses a sandy ridge to the **Lomo Gordo** cliffs (Wp.16 185M) from where we can see the model village of **Hermigua** and its tiny toy church way below us. If at this stage you prefer not to tackle this descent, which is daunting but not dramatically dangerous, retrace your steps to Wp.14 and take the path into the **Barranco La Palmita** to pick up Walk 31 at the **Garajonay Centro de Visitantes**.

Warning!
The descent is very steep, rough and vertiginous, but never suicidally dangerous (not always the case with Canarian paths!) and well within the capacity of experienced walkers. As a guideline, if you managed either the **Pared de Agulo** climb or **Barranco de Erque** descent, then you can do this descent, which is more impressive due to the greater height, but not so vertiginous. It is all walking and hands, though helpful, are never essential. There's only one way to go, so don't worry about getting lost. However, a few ground rules:

Wonderful views on the descent

1. Go Slow This may sound fatuous, but take it one step at a time. Everyone must go at their own pace, which, according to your own lights, should be slow. Hence the 'cleft' walking times, which in this instance are even more subjective than usual.

2. No Leaning Don't rely on the handrails; they only give a false sense of security.

3. Stop To Look Don't walk and watch at the same time. Stop to admire the view.

Descending over rocks with rough steps cemented into them, we pass a small cave and come to a declivity with a rope 'banister' (the first of several) set in the rock (Wp.17 190M-200M). We then climb to cross a slightly vertiginous ledge, at the end of which we pass a tap (probably dry).

A second slightly vertiginous stretch is followed by a second cave (Wp.18 205M-225M), beyond which we get the distinct impression we're heading for an abyss. In fact, an easy chicane with another rope 'banister', brings us through a declivity on an increasingly clear trail. We then reach a long level northerly traverse, again slightly vertiginous as the trail narrows to a dirt path.

The path broadens again as it resumes its descent, before yet another slightly vertiginous chicane brings us past a partial cave formed by an overhang and shallow recess. After a second tap (Wp.19 220M-250M), we descend through a small stand of pine and cross two abandoned canals, the second immediately above a large reservoir. Passing between the reservoir and several houses, we follow concrete steps down to the upper of the **Hermigua** back-roads (Wp.20 245M-275M). Remaining times are calculated from the minimum descent time.

Twenty metres to the left, we take the driveway down to an orange roofed house, from the gateway of which a faint path leads down to a dirt track and the lower back-road (Wp.21 250M). Following the road north, we ignore two tempting cobbled paths apparently descending to the village but in fact going nowhere, only turning right 10 metres before a wooden sign for 'Finca La Era' and a ceramic sign for 'Casa Ico Piedra Romana' (Wp.22 260M). Stairs wind down between houses to the end of a tarmac lane, which we follow to the start of the back-road. Turning right, we descend into the village, doubtless glancing back with a 'been-there-done-that' smugness.

33 EL CEDRO TUNNEL

Short does not necessarily mean dull, at least not in the emotional sense, though things do get pretty obscure visually on this exciting circuit pioneered (with some help from the waterboard engineers!) by Ros and David Brawn of Discovery Walking Guides.

The depth of water in the tunnel can vary from a few scattered puddles at the end of summer to knee deep at the end of winter. It's worth noting that if there is water at the point where we enter the tunnel, there will probably be more at the other end, in which case it's best to take your boots and socks off before venturing into the dark. *A torch is highly recommended*. There is a slight risk of claustrophobia.

| 3 | 1½ H | 5.5 km | ↗ 340m / ↘ 340m | ↻ | 4 |

Access by car: our walk starts from the **La Meseta de Hermigua** parking area (identified by two mapboards), 2km south of the **Cruce El Rejo** junction with the GM1, or if approaching from the south, 5.2km north of **Cruce de la Zarcita** junction with the GM2.

Non-motorists: take a taxi to Wp.1 (ask for **Aparcamiento La Meseta de Hermigua**), then use Walk 34 (see Wp.8 below) to return to **Hermigua**, bearing in mind that Walk 34 does have a vertigo warning.

Starting between the mapboards (Wp.1)

From the **Meseta de Hermigua** car-park (Wp.1 0M), we take the cobbled track heading north between two mapboards, descending gently to a Y-junction at a small shrine (Wp.2 4M).

It's worth making a short detour along the right branch here, turning right after 130 metres to reach a forked wooden walkway overlooking two waterfalls.

Otherwise, we bear left at Wp.2 for **El Cedro**, passing a ruin backed by a beautiful sentinel finger of rock. The track narrows down to a trail and passes a white hut as we climb between terraces and brambles, fine views alleviating the steady slog

Wp.2, the small shrine

until we eventually emerge in a lay-by near a hairpin bend on the road (Wp.3 11M).

Ruin and 'finger' rock between Wps.2&3

Bearing right, we walk up to the bend and take a broad trail, signposted 'Caserío del Cedro 0.7'. Branching left ('por el monte') after 50 metres, we climb onto a covered canal, which we follow for a few metres before bearing right on a narrow path.

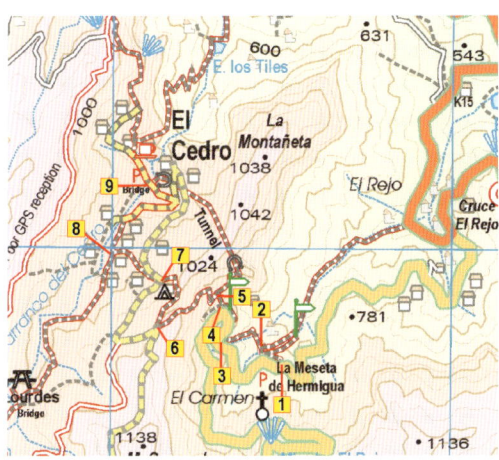

Immediately after a large, solitary palm tree, we swing right (Wp.4 21M) ignoring a branch to the south. Climbing steadily to steeply on a path partially stepped and paved with boulders, we curve round below a low white cliff, where more regular, tailored steps climb to a 'Parque Nacional' sign (Wp.5 31M).

After a cutting flanked by tall trees, we climb more steeply through a series of tight zigzags to emerge at a bend of the **El Cedro/Mimbreras** track/lane (Wp.6 41M). Bearing slightly right for 'Aula de la Naturaleza/Caserío del Cedro', we follow a lovely shady path down to the nature centre car-park (Wp.7 46M).

The T-junction at Wp.8

Taking the paved trail to the right, we descend between the buildings, bearing right after solar panels and left after a row of washbasins. Following a dirt path, we cross the **El Cedro** track/lane and descend through woods to a red house and a white ruin to join Walks 26 and 34 at a T-junction (Wp.8 51M).

Walk! La Gomera   141

Picnic area near the tunnel entrance

Turning right, we maintain direction (N) when the stone-paved path runs into a tarmac lane that, after passing a transformer tower and **Casa Rural los Patos**, in turn joins the **El Cedro/Bar La Vista** lane. Descending to the left, we cross a bridge (Wp.9 61M), just a few minutes (not counted in the global timing) short of **Bar La Vista**.

The bar is accessible via the tarmac lane or by crossing the picnic area on the right and descending to the stream, to take a paved trail climbing sharply to the left, up to the bar's terrace.

Returning to Wp.9, we head north from the bridge to reach the tunnel entrance, within sight of the picnic area. Turning on our torches, we duck into the tunnel and set off into the darkness – claustrophobes and lumbago sufferers beware: as water tunnels go, this one is relatively high, but we still have to walk like Groucho Marx to avoid braining ourselves on the roof.

The tunnel curves round, so that for a while, there is no light at either end, but we soon see a distant beam of sunlight as we splash through shallow puddles where the concrete has started to break up.

The southern entrance

In a little under ten minutes, we emerge at the far end and bear right, blinking in the bright sunlight, to cross an eroded gully and rejoin our outward route, 50 metres from the road.

34 CLASSIC GARAJONAY

Perhaps La Gomera's most famous path, and with some justification, including as it does the island's highest summit and longest waterfall, the beautiful **Barranco del Cedro**, and a forest so dense and dark it elicits a lively sympathy with gingerbread men.

It's usually approached as an ascent, though why anyone would climb a thousand very steep metres to a bus-stop on a main road is beyond us. Far better hop off the bus at **Pajarito**, stroll across the **Alto de Garajonay** and let gravity do the rest. Even then it's quite energetic enough. There's a slight risk of vertigo between Wps.13&14. Although not overtly dramatic, this vertiginous section is prolonged and should not be undertaken unless you have experienced some of the other vertiginous walks in the book and have an idea of what to expect from La Gomeran paths.

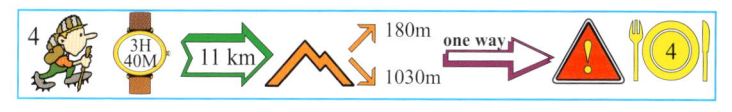

4 | 3H 40M | 11 km | 180m / 1030m | one way | ⚠ | 4

Access by bus: Línea 1, alight at **Pajarito** (AKA **Los Pajaritos**).

Access by car: If you're arriving by car and prefer to catch the bus at the end of the walk, you can park at Wp.1 or Wp.6.

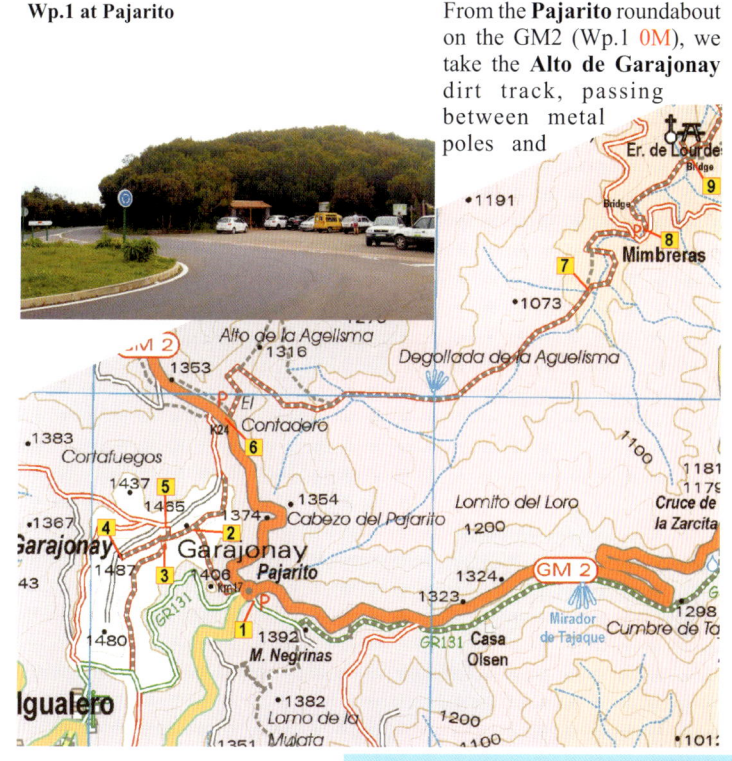

Wp.1 at Pajarito

From the **Pajarito** roundabout on the GM2 (Wp.1 0M), we take the **Alto de Garajonay** dirt track, passing between metal poles and

Walk! La Gomera 143

immediately turn right at a notice board on the log-stepped walking trail. A steady climb brings us across a small rise, after which we dip down before climbing again to the signposted 'Alto de Garajonay/El Contadero' T-junction (Wp.2 15M). To skip the detour to the summit, bear right to join the paved track between Wps.5&6 (there are two neatly situated viewpoints along this short stretch).

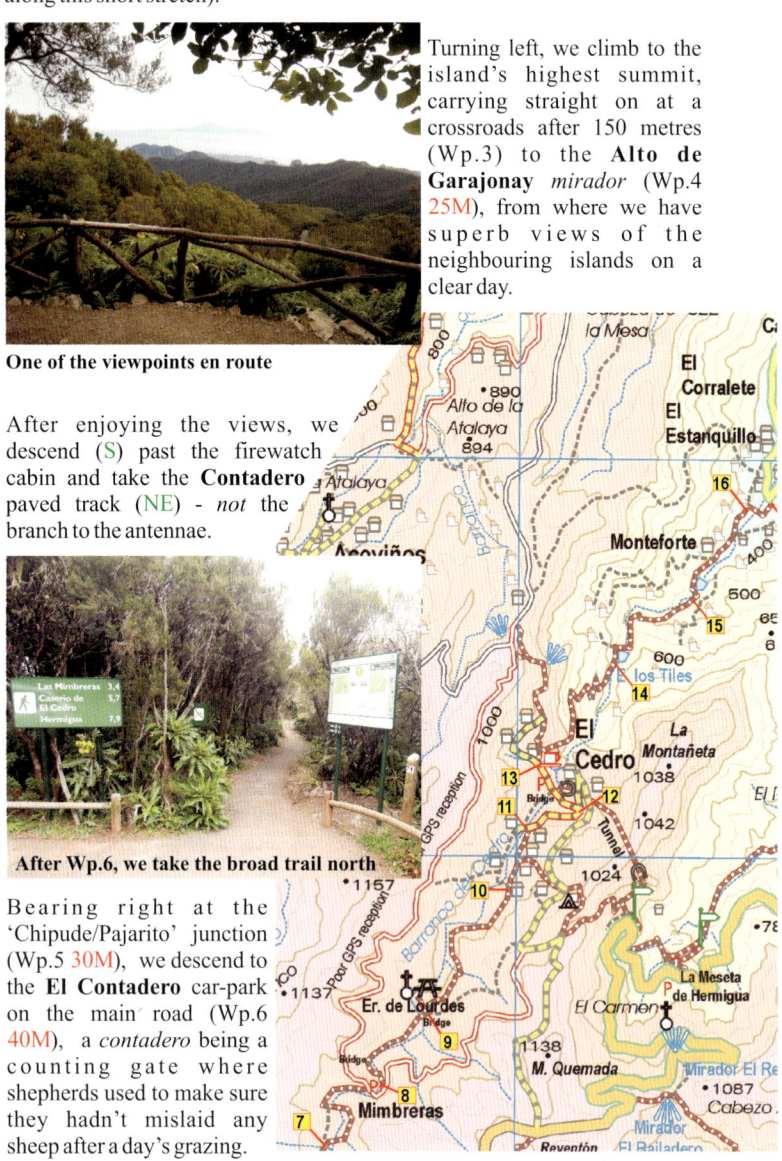

Turning left, we climb to the island's highest summit, carrying straight on at a crossroads after 150 metres (Wp.3) to the **Alto de Garajonay** *mirador* (Wp.4 25M), from where we have superb views of the neighbouring islands on a clear day.

One of the viewpoints en route

After enjoying the views, we descend (S) past the firewatch cabin and take the **Contadero** paved track (NE) - *not* the branch to the antennae.

After Wp.6, we take the broad trail north

Bearing right at the 'Chipude/Pajarito' junction (Wp.5 30M), we descend to the **El Contadero** car-park on the main road (Wp.6 40M), a *contadero* being a counting gate where shepherds used to make sure they hadn't mislaid any sheep after a day's grazing.

Crossing the road, we take the broad walking trail to the north between a mapboard and 'Las Mimbreras 3.4' sign.

144 *Walk! La Gomera*

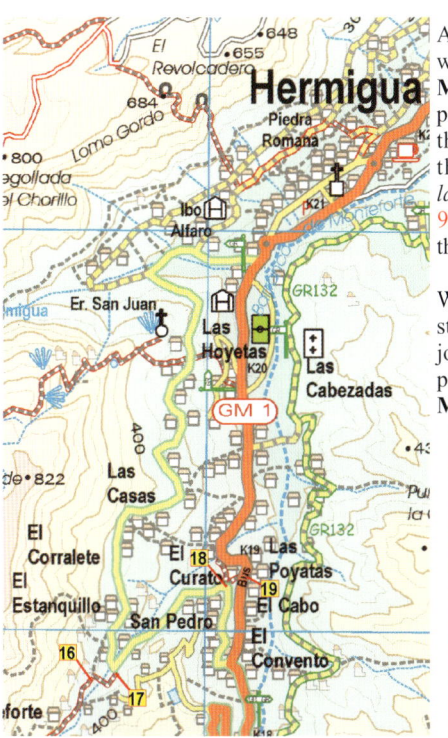

Apart from Wp.7, there's no going wrong between here and **Las Mimbreras** as there's only the one path. All you really need to know is that the path descends steeply through successive grades of *laurisilva* to a Y-junction (Wp.7 90M), where we bear right to cross the **Arroyo del Cedro** stream.

We then follow the right bank of the stream, crossing it once again, before joining a broader trail leading to the parking area and dirt track at **Las Mimbreras** (Wp.8 105M).

Ermita de Lourdes (Wp.9)

The *fuente*-in-a-tree

Bearing right, we take the 'Ermita/Caserío de El Cedro' path, crossing the stream and following its left bank until a second bridge brings us to the picnic area and *fuente*-in-a-tree at **Ermita de Lourdes** (Wp.9 111M).

Passing in front of the *ermita*, we ignore a path to the right and bear left, descending for 'Caserío de El Cedro'. Sticking to the main trail above the stream, we stroll through disorderly ranks of immensely tall laurel frosted with moss and lichen.

Emerging from the woods, we ignore a branch doubling back to the left, and climb slightly to pass between the first of the **El Cedro** houses. Ignoring another branch to the left (Wp.10 125M), we pass more houses, carrying straight on at a junction by a red house and a white ruin (where the present itinerary intersects with Walk 33), after which a paved, stepped section leads to a tarmac lane (Wp.11 130M).

Bearing right, we follow the lane past a transformer tower to the junction with the main **El Cedro** access lane (Wp.12 135M), where we turn left for **Bar/Restaurant La Vista** (Wp.13 140M), a walkers' institution, famous for its cress broth.

Taking the concrete path between the restaurant and camping area, we descend to the bottom terrace of the campsite and turn left on a cobbled path. Ignoring a branch on the right down to the river, we climb briefly toward an electricity pylon, where **Hermigua** comes into view and we start our steep, vertiginous descent into the *barranco*.

The *Salto de Agua*

Zigzagging down the cliff, we come into view of the celebrated *Salto de Agua* - Spanish water 'leaping' where English water only 'falls'!

After what seem like interminable zigzags, we emerge at the apex of a reservoir (Wp.14 170M), the **Embalse de los Tiles**.

Embalse de los Tiles

Bearing left, we descend via a staircase in front of the dam wall, after which we follow the canalisation pipes nearly all the way to the road, though not slavishly, since the pipes occasionally drop into places ramblers aren't fitted for dropping into.

The path is obvious, except above a concrete reservoir, where we ignore a branch to the right and bear left, crossing the watercourse behind the reservoir (Wp.15 185M). With superb views throughout, notably of the westernmost pinnacle of **Los Enamorados** (**The Lovers**), we continue alongside the pipes. 100 metres after the trail narrows to a canal path, the old canal visible under the pipes, we reach a shack roofed with corrugated iron, where we turn right (Wp.16 200M), leaving the pipes and crossing the stream for the penultimate time before a footbridge leads to the road below **The Lovers** (Wp.17 205M).

Turning right, we head into **El Convento**, from where we see the **El Curato** bus stop, just north of a bridge spanning the lower reaches of the **Cedro**. As the road swings south at a line of stone benches (Wp.18 215M), we branch left on a concrete and stone path, which we follow to the main road, where we emerge opposite **Plaza de Santo Domingo**, forty metres north-west of the main bus stop (Wp.19 220M).

GLOSSARY

This glossary contains Spanish and Canarian words found in the text (shown in *italics*) plus other local words that you may encounter.

abandonado	abandoned, in poor repair	*colegio*	college, school
abierto	open	*comida*	food
acequia	water channel	*cordillera*	mountain range
aeropuerto	airport	*correos*	post office
agua	water	*cortijo*	farmstead
agua no potable	water (not drinkable)	*costa*	coast
		coto privado de caza	private hunting area
agua potable	drinking water	*Cruz Roja*	Red Cross (medical aid)
alto/a	high		
aparcamiento	parking	*cuesta*	slope
área recreativa	official picnic spot, usually with barbecues, toilets, water taps	*cueva*	cave
		cumbre	summit
		degollada	pass
		derecha	right (direction)
arroyo	stream	*desprendimiento*	landslide
ayuntamiento	town hall	*drago*	'Dragon' Tree
bajo/a	low	*embalse*	reservoir
barranco	ravine	*ermita*	chapel
bocadillo	bread roll, snack	*Espacio Natural Protegido*	protected area of natural beauty
bodegón	inn		
bosque	wood		
cabezo	peak, summit	*estación de autobus/ guagua*	bus station
cabra	goat		
cabrera	goatherd		
calle	street	*farmacia*	chemist
camí	path or way	*faro*	lighthouse
camino	trail, path, track	*fiesta*	holiday, celebration
camino particular	private road		
		finca	farm, country house
camino real	old donkey trail (lit. royal road)		
		fuente	spring or source
campamento	camping	*gasolinera*	petrol station
carretera	main road	*guagua*	bus
casa	house	*guanche*	original Canary Islands inhabitants
casa forestal	forestry house		
casa rural	country house, accommodation to let		
		Guardia Civil	police
		guía	guide
cascada	waterfall	*hostal*	hostel, accommodation
caserío	hamlet, village		
cementerio	cemetery	*hoya/o*	depression (geological)
centro salud	health centre		
cerrado	closed	*iglesia*	church
cerveza	beer	*información*	information
choza	shack, hut	*isla*	island
clínica	clinic, hospital	*izquierda*	left (direction)

laurisilva	ancient laurel forest	*pozo*	well
lavadero	laundry area (usually communal)	*prohibido el paso*	no entry
		puente	bridge
librería	bookshop	*puerto*	port, mountain pass
llano	plain		
lluvioso	rainy	*refugio*	refuge, shelter
lomo	broad-backed ridge or spur dividing two valleys or ravines	*río*	river, stream
		risco	crag or cliff
		roque	(a) lava fill exposed by erosion to form a broad, blunt pinnacle (b) rock
malpaís	'bad lands' wild, barren countryside		
		ruta	route
mapa	map	*salida*	exit
mercado	market	*senda*	path, track
mirador	lookout/viewing point	*sendero*	foot path
		sierra	mountain range
montaña	mountain	*sin salida*	no through road/route
nublado	cloudy		
nueva/o	new	*sirocco*	hot, dust-laden wind from Africa
oficina de turismo	tourist office		
		tapas	bar snacks
peligroso	dangerous	*tienda*	shop
pensión	guesthouse	*típico*	traditional bar/eating place
pescado	fish		
pico	peak		
picón	black volcanic rock/sand	*tormentoso*	stormy
		torre	tower
piscina	swimming pool	*torrente*	stream
pista	dirt road/track	*tubería*	water pipe
pista (forestal)	forest road/track	*valle*	valley
		vega	meadow
playa	beach	*ventoso*	windy
plaza	square	*vieja/o*	old
policía	police	*zona recreativa*	recreation area

APPENDIX A

USEFUL ADDRESSES & TELEPHONE NUMBERS

TOURIST INFORMATION

A number of travel companies both large and small offer package holidays to La Gomera.

For official tourist information, including exhaustive lists of **accommodation** in hotels, pensions, guest houses and *casas rurales* try the following websites:-

www.lagomera.travel/canary-islands/la-gomera/en

www.spain.info/en/que-quieres/ciudades-pueblos/provincias/la_gomera.html

Official Tourist Offices

San Sebastián
Calle Real, 32 (Casa Bencomo)
38800 San Sebastián de La Gomera
Phone +34 922 141 512
Fax +34 922 870 281   sansebastian@lagomera.travel

Monday to Saturday: 09:00 - 13:30, 15:30 - 18:00 Sundays: 10:00 - 13:00

Valle Gran Rey
Calle La Noria, 2 La Playa
38870 Valle Gran Rey
Phone +34 922 805 458
Fax +34 922 805 458   vallegranrey@lagomera.travel

Monday to Saturday: 09:00 -13:30, 15:30 - 18:00 Sundays: 10:00 - 13:00

Playa de Santiago
Edificio Las Vistas, local 8
Avda. Marítima, s/n
38812 Playa de Santiago (Alajeró)
Phone +34 922 895 650
Fax +34 922 895 651   playasantiago@lagomera.travel

Monday and Tuesday: 09:00 - 13:30, 16:00 - 18:00
Wednesday, Thursday and Friday: 09:00 - 14:45 Saturdays: 09:00 - 13:00

CAR & BIKE HIRE

Car rentals are plentiful and easily arranged on arrival. For bicycle hire:-
www.gomeralive.com/gomera-marketplace/activities/cycling/bike-station-gomera.html

www.gomera-bikes.com/en/verleih.htm

TAXIS

Valle Gran Rey	699 261 297 & 629 689 080
San Sebastián	922 870 524
Tecina - Playa de Santiago	922 895 300
Airport - Alajeró	922 895 022 & 922 697 029
Agulo	922 801 074
Vallehermoso	922 800 000
Hermigua	922 880 047 & 922 805 058
Plaza de Playa de Santiago -	
Airport - Alajeró	922 895 022

EMERGENCIES

General Emergencies/Medical Emergencies	Tel: 112
Guardia Civil emergency number	Tel: 062

APPENDIX B

BUS TIMETABLES

This information is for guidance only. Ask in Tourist Offices or the bus station in **San Sebastián** for up-to-date information on all lines and for approximate journey times to individual destinations.

www.guaguagomera.com/lineas-y-horarios/

Line 1: Valle Gran Rey - San Sebastián

Valle Gran Rey bus station - La Playa - La Puntilla - Vueltas - La Calera - Guadá - Las Hayas - El Cercado - Chipude - Igualero - Pajaritos - Degollada de Peraza - San Sebastián

Starting from **San Sebastián**:   Starting from **Valle Gran Rey**:

Monday-Friday: **Monday-Friday:**
- 10.30 h   05.00 h
- 12.00 h   08.00 h
- 15.30 h   13.00 h
- 18.30 h   14.30 h
- 20.30 h   18.00 h

Saturdays: **Saturdays:**
- 10.30 h   05.00 h
- 12.00 h   08.00 h
- 15.30 h   13.00 h
- 18.30 h   14.30 h
- 21.30 h   18.00 h

Sundays and bank holidays: **Sundays and bank holidays:**
- 10.30 h   08.00 h
- 21.45 h   16.30 h

Line 2: Vallehermoso - San Sebastián
Vallehermoso - Tamargada - Las Rosas - Agulo - Hermigua - San Sebastián

Starting from **San Sebastián**:
Monday-Friday:
  10.30 h
  12.00 h
  15.30 h
  18.30 h
  20.30 h
Saturdays:
  10.30 h
  12.00 h
  15.30 h
  18.30 h
  21.30 h
Sundays and bank holidays:
  10.30 h
  21.45 h

Starting from **Vallehermoso**:
Monday-Friday:
  05.30 h
  07.30 h
  13.30 h
  15.30 h
  18.00 h
Saturdays:
  05.30 h
  08.00 h
  13.30 h
  15.30 h
  18.00 h
Sundays and bank holidays:
  08.00 h
  17.00 h

Line 3: Alajeró - San Sebastián
Imada - Alajeró - Antoncojo - Airport - Santa Ana - Playa de Santiago - Tecina - Las Toscas - Vegaipala - Jerduñe - Degollada de Peraza - San Sebastián

Starting from **San Sebastián**:
Monday-Friday:
  07.00 h
  10.30 h
  12.00 h
  15.30 h
  17.45 h
  20.30 h
Saturdays:
  07.00 h
  10.30 h
  12.00 h
  15.30 h
  17.45 h
  21.30 h
Sundays and bank holidays:
  10.30 h
  21.45 h

Starting from **Alajeró**:
Monday-Friday:
  05.30 h
  07.00 h
  13.30 h
  15.30 h
  19.00 h
Saturdays:
  05.30 h
  07.00 h
  13.30 h
  15.30 h
  19.00 h
Sundays and bank holidays:
  07.00 h
  17.30 h

Line 4: Vallehermoso - La Dama
Vallehermoso - Macayo - La Quilla - Epina - Las Hayas - El Cercado - Chipude - La Dama

Starting from **Vallehermoso**:
Monday-Friday:
  06.30 h
  12.00 h

Starting from **La Dama**:
Monday-Friday:
  08.00 h
  13.30 h

Walk! La Gomera

Line 5: Vallehermoso - Alojera (from Monday to Friday)
Vallehermoso - Macayo - La Quilla - Epina - Alojera

Starting from **Vallehermoso**:
05.30 h
13.30 h

Starting from **Alojera**:
06.30 h
14.30 h

Line 6: Valle Gran Rey - airport Gomera
Valle Gran Rey bus station - La Playa - La Puntilla - Vueltas - La Calera - Guadá - Arure - Las Hayas - El Cercado - Chipude - Igualero - Alajeró - Airport

Starting from **Valle Gran Rey**:
Daily -
2 hours prior to flight departure

Starting from the **airport**:
Daily -
waits for aircraft arrival

Line 7: San Sebastián - airport Gomera
Airport - Santa Ana - Playa Santiago - Tecina - Las Toscas - Vegaipala - Jerduñe - Degollada de Peraza - San Sebastián

Starting from **San Sebastián**:
(Departures from the **bus station**)
Daily - 1 hour 45 min prior to flight departure

Starting at the **airport**:
Daily -
waits for aircraft arrival

FERRY TIMETABLES

This information is for guidance only. Ask in Tourist Offices or ferry port offices for up-to-date ferry information.

FERRY TIMETABLE Benchijigua Express (Compañía Fred.Olsen)
www.fredolsen.es/en

Fast ferry for foot passengers and vehicles with passengers. Daily service from **Los Cristianos/Tenerife** to **San Sebastián de la Gomera**, sailing time 50 min.

From Tenerife (Los Cristianos) to La Gomera (San Sebastián)

MON	TUE	WED	THU	FRI	SAT	SUN
09:00	09:00	09:00	09:00	09:00	09:00	08:30
14:00	14:00	14:00	14:00	16:00	14:00	11:30
19:00	19:00	19:00	19:00	19:00	19:00	19:00

From La Gomera (San Sebastián) to Tenerife (Los Cristianos)

07:30	07:30	07:30	07:30	07:30	07:30	07:00
12:00	12:00	12:00	12:00	14:00	12:00	10:00
17:30	17:30	17:30	17:30	17:30	17:30	17:30

FERRY TIMETABLES

This information is for guidance only. Ask in Tourist Offices or ferry port offices for up-to-date ferry information.

FERRY TIMETABLE Naviera Armas
www.navieraarmas.com/en/

Ferry for foot passengers and vehicles with passengers. Daily service from **Los Cristianos/Tenerife** to **San Sebastián de la Gomera**, sailing time 60 min.

From Tenerife (Los Cristianos) to La Gomera (San Sebastián)

MON	TUE	WED	THU	FRI	SAT	SUN
08:45	08:45	08:45	08:45	08:45	08:45	08:45
13:30	13:30	13:30	13:30	14:30		17:45
18:30	18:30	18:30	18:30	18:30	19:00	21:00

From La Gomera (San Sebastián) to Tenerife (Los Cristianos)

07:00	07:00	07:00	07:00	07:00	07:00	07:00
11:00	11:00	11:00	11:00	11:00		
16:30	16:30	16:30	16:30	16:30	17:00	19:30

INTER-ISLAND FLIGHT TIMETABLES

This information is for guidance only. Ask in Tourist Offices or airport offices for up-to-date flight information.

INTER-ISLAND FLIGHTS SERVING LA GOMERA

INTER-ISLAND FLIGHTS

BinterCanarias flies seven days a week between **Tenerife North Los Rodeos** airport and **La Gomera** airport (flight time 30 minutes).
www.bintercanarias.com/eng/
Booking hotline: +34 902 391 392

Tenerife North (TFN) - La Gomera (GMZ) (every day)
Departure   Arrival
09.30   10.00
17.00   17.30

La Gomera (GMZ) - Tenerife North (TFN) (every day)
Departure   Arrival
10.30   11.00
17.50   18.20

APPENDIX C

CYCLE HIRE   www.bike-station-gomera.com
www.gomera-bikes.com/en/
www.gomeracycling.com/

USEFUL PUBLICATIONS

Maps

La Gomera Tour & Trail Super-Durable Map
Published by Discovery Walking Guides; see www.dwgwalking.co.uk for details of the latest edition and how to buy

Bird Watching

A Field Guide to the Birds of the Atlantic Islands: Canary Islands, Madeira, Azores, Cape Verde
by Tony Clarke, Chris Orgill, Tony Disley
£31.50 ISBN: 9780713660234
Publisher: Helm Field Guides 30 June 20016

A Birdwatchers' Guide to the Canary Islands
by David Collins, Tony Clarke
£15.99 ISBN: 9781871104066
Publisher: Prion Ltd; 1st Edition edition (Jan. 1996)

Checklist of the Birds of the Canary Islands
by Eduardo Garcia del Rey
£7.50 ISBN: 9788495412140
Publisher: Publicaciones Turquesa (Jan. 2001)

Birds on the Canary Islands
by Ulrike Strecke, Horst Wilkens
£5.33 ISBN: 9783942999076
Publisher: by Naturalanza (1 Jan. 2016)

Finding Birds in the Canaries
by Dave Gosney
£7.95 ISBN: 9781907316449
Publisher: Easybirder (1 Dec. 2013)

Rare birds in the Canary Islands - Aves raras de las Islas Canarias
(Spanish)
by Eduardo García Rey, Francisco Javier García Vargas
£34.00 ISBN: 9788496553910
Publisher: Lynx Edicions (Jun. 2013)

History

The History of the Discovery and Conquest of the Canary Islands
by Juan de Abreu Galindo, George Glas
£8.99 ISBN: 9781402172694
Publisher: Adamant Media Corporation 2005

Plant Life

Tenerife Nature Walks
by Sally Lamdin-Whymark
ISBN: 9780957548602 £14.99
Publisher: Flintwork Publications (Mar. 2013)

Geology

The Geology of the Canary Islands
by Valentin R. Troll, Juan Carlos Carracedo
£49.49 ISBN: 9780128096635
Publisher: Elsevier (15 Jun. 2016)

MUSEUMS

Arqueological Museum and **Los Telares Handicraft Centre**
C/ Torres Padilla, Nº8 (Plaza Inglesia Ntra. Sra. de la Asunción) Hermigua

Ethnographic Museum of La Gomera
Crta. General de Las Hoyetas, Nº89
Hermigua
Tel: 922 881960

El Conde Tower (Torre del Conde)
C/Ruiz Padrón 19, San Sebastián de La Gomera.

Casa de Colón (Columbus House)
Calle Real 56
38800 San Sebastián de La Gomera

PLACE NAMES INDEX

A

Acardece	75, 76
Aceviños	117, 136, 137
Aeropuerto	56, 147
Agalán	67
Agulo	5, 114, 117, 129, 130, 132-134, 138, 150, 151
Alajeró	39, 56, 64, 67, 149-152
Almacigos	67
Alojera	13, 119, 125, 152
Aloreja	112
Alto de Garajonay	31, 70, 90, 143, 144
Alto de Tacalcuse	45
Altos de Utera	36
Altozano	38
Antoncojo	57, 151
Apartadero	91-94
Apartamentos Playa	38
Arcilia Bar-Cafetería	42, 68
Argayall	105, 106
Arguamul	125
Arroyo del Cedro	145
Artesanía Los Roques	121
Arure	2, 4, 5, 71, 74-76, 81, 85, 109, 111, 112, 152
Avenida de las Galanas	22
Ayamosna	21-23
Ayuntamiento de Alajeró	64
Azadoe	3, 42, 43, 60, 61, 68

B

Balcón de Santa Ana	39
Bar Amparo	86
Bar Arcilia	42, 68
Bar Central	125
Bar Conchita	74, 76, 81, 111
Bar La Vista	118, 142, 146
Bar La Zula	132, 134
Bar Los Camioneros	92, 93
Bar Macondo	87
Bar Navarro	88
Bar Peraza	20, 39
Bar/Restaurante Amparo	86, 1
Bar/Restaurante Chorros de Epina	114
Bar/Restaurante El Piloto	38, 131
Bar/Restaurante Maria	77
Bar/Restaurante Tambor	134
Baranco de Hayas	84
Bar-Bodegon Vizcaina	79, 87
Bar-Cafetería Arcilia	42, 68
Barranco Biquillo	47
Barranco de Argaga	5, 99, 100, 102-106, 108
Barranco de Arure	2, 5, 71, 109
Barranco de Azadoe	3, 42, 43, 60, 68
Barranco de Benchijigua	4, 42, 53, 60
Barranco de Chinguarime	45, 46
Barranco de Erque	4, 94, 138
Barranco de Gallon	36
Barranco de Guarimiar	4, 43, 64-66
Barranco de Iguala	92
Barranco de Ingenio	121
Barranco de Juan de Vera	24, 25, 51
Barranco de Juel	37
Barranco de la Barraca	38
Barranco de la Era Nueva	126
Barranco de la Guancha	24, 25
Barranco de la Junta	57
Barranco de la Matanza	99
Barranco de la Palmita	132, 133, 138
Barranco de la Vasa	46
Barranco de la Vica	138
Barranco de la Villa	19
Barranco de Las Hayas	84
Barranco de las Lagunetas	78
Barranco de las Lajas	29
Barranco de las Rosas	129, 134
Barranco de Lepe	129, 131
Barranco de Liria	135, 137
Barranco de los Cocos	57, 58
Barranco de los Manantiales	89, 90, 100

156 Walk! La Gomera

Barranco de Palopique	36	Casa Tambor	134
Barranco de Santiago	65	Caserío de El Cedro	117, 141, 145
Barranco de Tapahuga	47	Centro de Visitantes	11, 114, 132, 134, 138
Barranco del Agua	77, 78	Chijeré	126
Barranco del Cedro	109, 117, 143	Chipude	4, 70, 71, 88, 90, 91, 98, 99, 102, 144, 150-152
Barranco del Matanza	77, 89, 99, 100	Chorros de Epina	12, 114, 125, 127
Barranco Hondo	19	Contadero	70, 90,144
Barranco Juan de Vera	24, 25, 51	Contreras	39, 45, 46, 50
Benchijigua	4, 12, 39, 42, 53, 60, 61, 62, 69, 152	Costado de la Guancha	26
Bodegón del Mar	56	Cruce de la Zarcita	30, 140

C / D

Bodegón Roque Blanco	114, 123	Degollada de los Bueyes	103
Borbalán	105	Degollada de Peraza	3, 4, 20, 23, 27-29, 39, 44, 53, 55, 150-152
C		Drago tree	147
Cabeza de la Mesa	135, 137	**E**	
Cabeza de la Vizcaina	75	El Bailadero	30, 32, 34
Calle Cañada del Herrero	22	El Cabezo	60
Calle Chelé	80	El Cabrito	24-26, 44, 45, 48, 51, 52
Calle del Pintor Aguiar	130	El Casa del Ramón	86
Calle Triana	121, 122	El Cedro	5, 30, 34, 114, 117, 140, 141, 145, 146
Calvario	39	El Cercado	4, 71, 77, 88-90, 99, 102, 150-152
Camino Coromoto	75	El Contadero	144
Camino Forestal de Majona	3, 35	El Convento	146
Camino Los Paredones	86	El Curato	146
Cañada de Jorge	76	El Faro	38, 131
Cañada Grande	134	El Guro	71, 80
Canal de Benchijigua	54	El Palmar	2, 37
Casa de Chelé	80	El Piloto Bar/Restaurante	38, 131
Casa de Chelé	80	El Rumbazo	60, 66
Casa de la Seda	71, 109	El Teón	122, 123
Casa del Leon y Graciana	32	Embalse de Cardones	58
Casa del Manco	29	Embalse de los Tiles	146
Casa Efigenia	75, 86, 119	Embalse de Vallehermoso	123
Casa El Cana	88	Enchereda	35, 36
Casa El Lomito	27	Epina	151, 152
Casa Fagundo	64	Ermita de Guarimiar	60
Casa Ico Piedra Romana	139	Ermita de las Hayas	75
Casa Jasmin	32	Ermita de las Nieves	12, 27-29
Casa los Reyes	80	Ermita de Lourdes	12, 118, 145
Casa Maria Angeles	60, 61		
Casa Marina	74		
Casa Rural los Patos	118, 142		

Walk! La Gomera 157

Ermita de Nuestra Señora de Guadalupe	4, 102	Jerduñe	3, 44, 151, 152
		Joradillo	47, 49
Ermita de San Isidor	12, 39		
Ermita de San Juan	12, 135, 136	**K**	
Ermita de San Salvador	12	Kiosco Bar Garajonay	121-124
Ermita de Santa Clara	5, 12, 125	**L**	
		La Calera	71, 80, 83, 104, 105, 108, 150, 152
Ermita del Santo	81, 111, 112	La Caleta	3, 35, 37, 38
Ermita Los Reyes	80, 108	La Dama	92, 93, 102, 119, 125, 151
Erque	91, 93, 94, 96, 98, 99	La Laja	20, 21, 27-32, 55
Erquito	91, 94, 96, 97	La Matanza	99
		La Mérica	4, 81-83, 113
F		La Meseta de Hermigua	140
Finca la Era	139	La Palmita	132, 133, 138
Finca La Quintana	76	La Playa	71, 149, 150, 152
Fortaleza	4, 71, 75, 91-94, 103	La Puntilla	71, 150, 152
		La Quilla	151, 152
Fruchtgarten	106	La Trinchera	39, 59
Fuente de la Berraca	37	La Vista Casa Rural	118
		Laguna de Santiago	39
G		Las Casas del Chorro	133
Garabato	123	Las Creces	5, 75, 76, 119
Garajonay	3-5, 7-9, 11, 30, 31, 68, 70, 88-90, 117, 121-124, 132, 138, 143, 144	Las Hayas	4, 71, 74-76, 84, 85, 119, 150-152
		Las Mimbreras	5, 117, 144, 145
Gerián	12, 99, 102, 108	Las Pilas	104
GR131	10, 20, 31, 88	Las Rosas	5, 11, 114, 129, 134, 151
GR132	10, 50, 52, 57, 89, 112	Las Salinas	13, 71
Guadá	150, 152	Las Toscas	4, 53, 60, 151, 152
Guarimiar	4, 39, 43, 60, 64-67	Lepe	131
Guerquenche	99	Llano de la Cruz	45
		Lo del Gato	53, 61, 62
H		Lomada del Camello	22
Hermigua	5, 9, 30, 35, 37, 38, 114, 117, 129, 131, 135, 136, 138-140, 146, 150, 151, 155	Lomo de Azadoe	3, 42, 43, 60
		Lomo del Balo	84
		Lomo del Carretón	5, 111, 113
		Lomo Gordo	135, 138
Hotel de Triana	121	Los Chapines	120
Hotel Jardin Tecina	3, 39, 43, 44, 47, 48, 150, 151, 152	Los Cristianos	18, 152, 153
		Los Enamorados (The Lovers)	146
I		Los Granados	71, 80
Igualero	70, 71, 90, 94, 96-98, 150	Los Manantiales	89, 90, 100, 101
		Los Noruegos	70
Imada	4, 42, 43, 53, 60, 64, 66-68, 70, 151	Los Órganos	13
		Los Revolcaderos	26
		Los Roques	3, 27, 30, 31, 121
J			
Jardin Tecína	3, 39, 43, 44, 47, 48, 150, 151, 152	**M**	
		Macayo	151, 152

Magro	23, 24
Majona	3, 35
Manantiales	89, 90, 100, 101
Mirador César Manrique	71
Mirador de Abrante	132, 133, 134
Mirador de Agulo	133
Mirador de La Laja	28
Mirador de la Tortuga	21
Mirador de la Trinchera	59
Mirador de Los Roques	31
Mirador de Peraza	39
MIrador del Bailadero	34
Mirador Ermita del Santo	81, 111, 112
Mirador Risquillos de Corgo	76
Mirador Roque de Agando	31, 54, 55
Montaña Adivino	103
Montaña Blanca	126, 127
Montaña Guergeguenche	103
Monteforte	38
Morales	50, 51
Museo Etnográfico	135, 136

O

Orilla de Amagra	96

P

Pajarito	68, 70, 90, 143, 144, 150
Parador	19
Pared de Agulo	5, 132, 138
Pared de Agulo	5, 132, 138
Pastrana	60, 63
Pavón	91, 92, 94
Peraza	20, 39
Pico Gomera	21
Pinar de Argumame	90
Pista de la Meseta	120
Pista Forestal de Majona	3, 35
Playa Alojera	13
Playa Chinguarime	13, 50
Playa de la Caleta	3, 35, 37
Playa de la Guancha	3, 19, 23, 25, 26, 52
Playa de Santa Catalina	131
Playa de Santiago	3, 4, 8, 9, 13, 18, 28, 39, 44-48, 56, 57, 59, 60, 70, 96, 149, 150-152
Playa de Tapahuga	47, 48
Playa de Vallehermoso	13, 126, 128
Playa del Cabrito	2, 51
Playa del Inglés	71, 83
Playa del Medio	13, 47-49
Plaza de Santo Domingo	146
Plaza Fuerteventura	22
Plaza las Galanas	22
Presa de las Hayas	75
Presa de Ojila	32

R

Raso de la Bruma	75, 76, 119
Restaurante Casa Conchita	74, 76, 81, 111
Restaurante Casa Efigenia	75, 86, 119
Restaurante El Descansillo	83
Restaurante El Mirador	83
Restaurante Las Palmeras	56, 64
Restaurante Las Rosas	129
Restaurante Roque Blanco	123
Restaurante Tagoror	47
Retamal	71
Reventón Oscuro	34
Revolcadero	26
Riscos de Juel	37
Riscos de la Mérica	83
Risquillo de Corgo	76, 120
Roque Agando	27, 29, 31, 36, 42, 53-55, 61, 65, 66
Roque Cano	5, 114, 122, 124
Roque Carmen	27
Roque García	25
Roque Imada	67
Roque Magro	23, 24
Roque Ojila	27, 33, 34
Roque Sombrero	3, 21, 23, 24
Roque Zarcita	27

S

San Sebastián	3, 8, 10, 18-23, 26, 27, 30, 35, 39, 44, 46, 48, 52, 114, 119, 125, 131, 149-152

Seima	25, 50	**V**	
Simancas	114	Valle Gran Rey	4, 8, 9, 13, 18, 30, 68, 71, 77-79, 81, 83, 84, 86, 87, 101-105, 108, 111, 113, 125, 128, 149-150, 152
T			
Tacalcuse	44, 45		
Taco	60, 99, 101		
Tagamiche	21, 29		
Taguluche	37, 38, 71, 82, 111-113	Vallehermoso	5, 9, 10, 13, 68, 70, 152
Tamargada	114, 151	Vegaipala	151, 152
Targa	4, 56, 64, 65	Villa Maria	
Teide	51, 65, 114	(apartments)	130
Tejeleche	81, 82	Villagarcia	96
Tejiade	47, 49	Vizcaina	75, 77-79, 84, 86, 87
Tequergenche	4, 102, 104, 106, 108		
		Vueltas	71, 80, 83, 104, 105, 113, 150, 152
Teselinde	126		
The Lovers (Los Enamorados)	146	**Z**	
Túnel de la Cumbre	114	Zumería Carlos	83
		Zumería Iballa	125
U			
Utera	36		

160 Walk! La Gomera